Ed Slott's RETIREMENT ROAD MAP

From Forever taxed to NEVER taxed!

By **ED SLOTT**

Copyright © 2016

Program Guide

Table of Contents

Ed Slott's Retirement Road Map

... From Forever Taxed to Never Taxed!

By Ed Slott, Copyright © 2016

Program Guide
The Program

Part 1

▶ **Big Message:**

Higher taxes are coming and you need to plan for them now.

There is a big difference between tax-deferred and tax free.

Tax-deferred means you won't pay taxes on that money, yet… but you will, and probably at a higher rate. Tax-free means you'll never pay tax on that money.

Move your money from accounts that are ***forever taxed*** to accounts that are ***never taxed*** and do it now, before tax increases make this move more expensive.

At some point, taxes will have to increase. It's plain math. Now is the time to get rid of Uncle Sam as a partner on your retirement savings.

The first half is over, but too many of you are still overly focused on investments. From here on in, that is no longer your priority.

My number one retirement rule:
You cannot lose money going into retirement, or in retirement.

Now it's all about managing the taxes.

"You need to manage your investments on the way in, and manage your taxes on the way out."
—Ed Slott

Spend your time now on the tax strategies and you'll have plenty more later on and it will last longer.

5

Part One

Welcome to retirement road map.

Your trip from **_forever taxed to never taxed!_**

We'll be taking a trip to tax-free territory, but just like any other trip there will be bumps in the road, tolls, detours and potholes. But that's the price of admission, so don't let that stop you.

Here's the big master plan:

Move your money from accounts that are **_forever taxed_** to accounts that are **_never taxed_**, and do it now, or else your retirement savings will be devoured by future taxes.

Higher taxes mean you have less to spend in retirement and you're more likely to run out of money feeding Uncle Sam.

First, you should know the difference between tax-deferred and tax free. It's the difference between you having more or you having less. Does anyone want less? Tax-deferred means you won't pay taxes on that money, Yet… but you will, and probably at a higher rate. Tax free means you'll never pay tax on that money.

Unfortunately most of us have our retirement savings in tax-deferred accounts like IRAs, 401(k)s and 403(b) plans, because these were the only options offered when we began saving for retirement.

This money has not yet been taxed, but it will be. And taxes are going to increase for all of us. No one knows the future, but based on our current situation, taxes have got to up, and soon.

Our country is broke and any Congressman who tells you he can cut your taxes is really just saying "I'm bad at math. Please help me".

It's math. Not only are we broke, but we are losing hundreds of billions in tax money in two big ways.

From big corporations who don't pay taxes and the Wall Street Banks who will soon need another bailout when they crash the economy again. Yep. They're back to their old tricks, and now they even have Congress behind them who let them write their own rules.

In addition to this, the biggest companies in America also have a scam. They pay no US taxes, gaming the system doing these so called offshore corporate "inversions" to escape hundreds of billions in taxes by claiming they don't do business in the US even though they still do.

Who do you think makes up the shortfall? That's right. Us!

The worst part is that these schemes are legal because these companies and the big banks wrote the laws. They have powerful lobbyists.

We don't have a retirees lobby, so we're on our own.

But let's just fantasize for a moment. Let's make believe that we did have our own retirees lobby.

What tax laws would we write?

How about no taxes ever in retirement?
How does that sound?
Like a land of make believe right?
Where retirement is a tax-free, happy place. Think about it.

Well guess what? That place actually does exist, and I'm going to take you there.

We're going from ***forever taxed to never taxed!***

The sooner you move your money to tax-free territory, the longer it will last.
Life is short, but retirement can be long, and you don't want to run out of money.

Do you know that people are more afraid of running out of money than dying?

Normally, you buy insurance to protect you when something bad happens, like an accident, a storm, a fire, an illness.

But what if something good happens? Like you live a long, healthy life.

Is there insurance for that?

Actually, yes.

It's having a plan or what I call your own retirement "road map" structured to keep more of your retirement savings protected from taxes so that your money can last as long as you do.

All that time, while you were working, you thought you were building your retirement savings in your 401(k) or your IRA, and you were.

But guess what? It's not all yours – you know that right?

A good chunk of that is owed right back to Uncle Sam. In fact, if taxes go up higher, Uncle Sam becomes your Senior Partner. That means he gets more than you. Sorry to say, you have a partner.

Every time you make money, so does he. Every time your IRA balance increases, so does Uncle Sam's share.

So isn't it obvious what we have to do? Get rid of your partner!

How do you do it? The same way you get rid of any partner... you buy him out.

Your savings are being suffocated with a mortgage. A tax mortgage.

And just like your home, your retirement account isn't all yours until you pay off the mortgage.

Actually the mortgage on your retirement savings is way worse than a home mortgage. With a home mortgage, you know exactly how much you owe the bank at any given time. You just look on the statement each month and it tells you the balance you owe.

IRAs don't work that way. The mortgage on your IRA is owed to the IRS, not the bank. That is a huge difference.

What is the mortgage on your IRA or 401(k)? How much will you owe Uncle Sam? You can't look that up anywhere because it's based on two factors that are both unknown – The future balance of your IRA and the future tax rate.

A higher tax rate on a higher balance multiplies to a big loss for you, just when you need the money most.

For example, let's say you bought your home years ago for only $100,000 and now it's worth $1 million dollars. Let's also assume you still have a small mortgage balance of $5,000 left. If you want to sell it, how much do you owe the bank? The $5,000 left on the mortgage. Right? That's easy. The bank doesn't get one dime more than the $5,000 you owe them.

But what would you say if instead the bank said, wow, you're selling for $1 million dollars. That's a great profit. Instead of paying us the $5,000 you owe us, let's raise it to $500,000, so we can share in your profit. What would you say to that?

That would be outrageous wouldn't it? That would be like stealing from you. Is that how you might feel? Well, that's exactly how it works with your IRA. The difference is, with the bank it's a loan. You pay back what you owe them and they don't share in your appreciation, because they are not your partner.

But when it comes to your IRA, Uncle Sam *is your partner.*

That's why the faster you pay off your IRA mortgage, the sooner you can get rid of your partner, and the sooner you'll know exactly how much is yours to keep.

You'll no longer have to share your earnings with Uncle Sam.

"I'm proud to be an American paying taxes. The only thing is that I could be just as proud for half the money."
Arthur Godfrey said that – and I agree with him.

Always be moving your money away from Uncle Sam and back to your very own tax-free safety zone – your destination.

Imagine a cage here. Your own tax-free safety zone.

Every dollar you pile up here is tax free. Now also imagine there's a gate here on this cage, with a big lock on it and you are the only one with the key.

It's untouchable by Uncle Sam. No one can get in here, except for you. Every dollar you take from here, will be 100% spendable, because it's tax free.

It's all yours. No partners and no taxes. All spendable money.

That's what I mean by moving from **forever taxed to never taxed!**
Tax free is always better.

Keeping that in mind, remember that there are two halves in the retirement game.

The first half of the game is working, building and investing your savings and the second half is taking your money out and enjoying it – but that's where all the tax rules come in and that's why you need a road map to navigate all the dangerous twists and turns on your retirement journey.

The first half is over, but too many of you are still overly focused on investments. From here on in, that is no longer your priority. That train has left the station.

Here's why. To be clear, I'm not an investment advisor, I'm a tax advisor, but when it comes to your retirement money, it's the managing of the taxes that will have the biggest impact, not the investments.

"You need to manage your investments on the way in, and manage your taxes on the way out."
– Ed Slott

It's all about the taxes.

You've already invested and you have that money. Don't lose it, listening to the wrong people with their "strategic", "magic", "secret", "can't lose" investment ideas.

I'm not only talking about financial advisors. I'm more worried about your friends, neighbors and – the worst – family!

Once I hear the words "son-in-law" – I know it's over. And you know what I mean, right?

Here's my number one retirement rule:

You cannot lose money going into retirement, or in retirement.

This is not the time to chase the next hot stock or hot fund, or talk to relatives.

You also need to avoid what I call "restaurant advisors" on TV with their daily investing specials. What are you supposed to do? Change your investments every day? That's like a restaurant. What's today's specials? Which stocks are best today? Are they really even today's specials or yesterday's leftovers?

Ignore all of them. Investing has become a race to the bottom. You're not going to beat out the big Wall Street companies who are getting bigger and faster computers every day.

I have a much better plan. Spend your time now on the tax strategies and you'll have plenty more later on and it will last longer.

If you're worried about stock market exposure, maybe because you don't have a long time horizon to recover from a crash, you may want to look into protecting your retirement savings with annuities and even life insurance – both of which provide guarantees – an essential part of any retirement plan.

That's up to you, but the point is to not get bogged down with investment advice in the second half of the game. You're past that point. We're on the back nine now.

You need to be working with the money you already have. Once again, follow my golden rule: Don't lose that money!

When we come back I'll show you how to follow my road map and start stockpiling your money in your tax-free safety zone.

I'll show you what to do, how to do it and when to do it

We're going from ***forever taxed to never taxed!***

Part 2

▶ Big Message:

Your "exit strategy" – How to turn your taxable IRA funds into tax-free retirement money

Now that you know there is a tax problem, you need a plan, or what I call an "exit strategy" for your retirement savings.

Focus on minimizing taxes in retirement by making plans now.

There will be a cost to this, but the cost to ignore this will be much greater.

You should be converting your IRAs to Roth IRAs to eliminate the risk of what future taxes could do to your retirement savings.

I mention this – and life insurance – in every program because these are the two best roads to move the largest amounts of money to tax-free territory.

With Roth conversions, you get a second chance to undo it. It's called a Roth recharacterization and that is the key to your Roth conversion planning strategy.

It's not how much you convert; it's how much of the Roth IRA conversion you keep.

You can also use your IRA for building a tax-free life insurance fund. That's powerful leverage. You are using one IRA dollar to do the work of many.

Key Points from Part Two:

The absolute best time to do this with your IRAs is in your 60s. This is the sweet spot for tax planning. Specifically, I mean between ages 59½ and 70½, when there are no IRA distribution penalties to worry about.

If you do nothing, and leave those funds in your IRA, as the balance increases, so does the amount you'll eventually have to share with Uncle Sam.

Life insurance can also be invaluable if you have a large IRA and you're worried that your children might squander it when they inherit it.

Your child could be one divorce away from losing your IRA to an ex-spouse.

You could leave your IRA to a trust to protect against this, but using life insurance is an effective alternative to setting up an IRA trust. Life insurance can eliminate the taxes and when the life insurance is left to a trust, and it can provide creditor protection for your heirs.

Use taxable IRAs and your other taxable investments to build up tax-free money for your retirement.

Using only tax-free money retirement will lower your current taxes and lower your future taxes. Your retirement money will last longer.

Part Two

Welcome back.

Now you know there's a problem. It's the taxes in our retirement savings.

"You can complain about taxes, or you can do something about them." – *Ed Slott*

You need a plan, or what I call an "exit strategy" for your retirement savings.

You put the money in, you put the money in, but do you have a plan to take it out? Because it's the way you take it out that will determine how much you keep and how much goes to the government.

Everyone thinks they have a plan, but they don't. You may have a nice retirement account, but that's only half the game. If that's all you have, you don't have a plan.

Let's start our journey from **forever taxed to never taxed!**

You should be converting your IRAs to Roth IRAs to eliminate the risk of what future taxes could do to your retirement savings.

I mention this – and life insurance – in every program because **these are the two best roads to move the largest amounts of money to tax-free territory.**

There are no limits on how much you can convert to a Roth IRA and under the tax code there is no limit on how much life insurance you can have.

Of course you may be limited by how much you can afford, but you probably can afford more than you think if you tap into the right resources – mainly IRAs and other taxable investments.

Here's my IRA leverage rule:
Use it, leverage it, or lose it to future taxes.

Your IRAs are building a tax liability that will eventually have to be paid. This has to stop, or you will have less later on.

IRAs and other taxable investments should be used now to build tax-free Roth IRAs and life insurance.

Let's start moving them, either in chunks or consistently over time to your tax-free safety zone where they can be earning partner-free money – money you'll never have to share with Uncle Sam.

When you convert your IRA to a Roth IRA, you pay tax on the amount you converted at ordinary income tax rates.

So your first reaction is that it's costing you money. It will raise your taxes. If this will make you angry, then go ahead and do it, and be angry. I'd rather be angry once and move on.

If you don't start withdrawing from your IRA as early as possible, you'll be forced to anyway, after reaching age 70½ and that will make you both angry and miserable, every year for the rest of your life.

With a Roth IRA, you have no required distributions after 70½. You never have to take your Roth money out except when you want to. And the money here grows the fastest because it is never eroded by taxes. You keep it all.

So yes, a Roth conversion will cost you money, but the real power of this plan is in the long term tax free build-up of your Roth IRA.

The taxes are a minor bump in the road. When you take a trip, the goal is to get there. You don't turn around and give up just because you hit your first red light.

Think of paying the taxes upfront this way. You're paying a tax on the seed, but the crop grows for free.

Use your other non-IRA savings to pay the conversion tax. You'll eliminate the taxable income those funds were throwing off, and you'll be able to convert more by not using your IRA funds to pay the conversion tax.

You can do a Roth conversion at any time or any age – even after 70½ if you wish, although the earlier you do it, the more effective it is.

The power of the Roth conversion is the tax free build up over time. If you're going to need the money soon, then a Roth conversion is not for you, since the upfront tax cost won't be worth the benefit.

Also, as you get older it might not pay to convert, given your life expectancy. But it would be worth it if you were converting for your beneficiaries.

With Roth conversions, you also get a second chance, which is rare in the tax code.

How many times in life do you wish you had a second chance?

Here's another rule of mine:

If Uncle Sam gives you a second chance – take it

You have until October 15th of the year after the year you convert, to undo your Roth IRA conversion. That's as close as you can get under the tax code to a money back guarantee.

You don't have to convert all of your IRA – or 401(k) – to your Roth IRA. You can do a little each year over time.

But the most powerful strategy would be to convert it all, and then, before October 15th of the next year – before the deadline to undo it expires – review your tax situation with your tax or financial advisors and see if you want to keep all or maybe just a part of that conversion. Whatever you keep you'll owe tax on.

By the time October of the year after you converted rolls around, you'll have a good handle on your actual income for that year, so you'll know exactly what it will cost tax-wise.

You could undo – technically called a Roth recharacterization – undo all of the conversion and owe no tax on it, like it never happened, or keep just the right amount to pay the lowest tax, for example by filling up lower tax brackets.

It's not how much you convert; it's how much you recharacterize – in other words – how much of the conversion you keep.

The flexibility you have with a Roth IRA conversion is like no other provision in the tax code – because it allows you to bet on a horse after the race is over. Who wouldn't bet on a sure thing?

You can also use your IRA for building a tax-free life insurance fund.

Start this process immediately, but the absolute best time to do this with your IRAs is in your 60s. This is the sweet spot for tax planning. Specifically, I mean between ages 59½ and 70½.

There are no IRA distribution tax rules then, no deadlines, you can't take out too much or too little, you can't take it out too early or too late, you can't get a tax penalty – even if you try. It's a tax free-for-all.

With a traditional IRA, before age 59½ you'll get hit with a 10% penalty for taking your money out early. After age 70½ you'll get a 50% for not taking out enough.

But in between you can do whatever you wish with your IRA funds.

That's why I call this the sweet spot for planning. You have total flexibility to leverage your IRA, using the single biggest benefit in the tax law – the tax exemption for life insurance.

As I say in every program, I don't sell life insurance. I don't sell investments, stocks, bonds, funds or annuities. I am giving you independent and objective tax advice.

I'm a tax advisor and an educator, and once again I am telling you to take advantage of this gigantic tax break, and start using it to fill up your tax-free safety zone.

In the sweet spot, you can withdraw penalty free from your IRA and invest in life insurance. You'll pay tax on those funds at your own rate, but that's not a big deal now. You're planning for long term results. That's just another toll on your road to tax freedom.

If you do nothing, and leave those funds in your IRA, as the balance increases, so does the amount you'll eventually have to share with Uncle Sam.

I've been saying this for years, but I've also heard counter arguments like:

Ed, "Why pay taxes before I have to? Every CPA I talk to says it's always better to defer taxes, put them off – never pay them before you have to."

That's how CPAs are trained. We're hard-wired to always defer and put off taxes as long as possible.

I'm a CPA too, but I'm a recovering CPA and I'm not looking to save you money now. I'm looking to build more for you later – and more of it here – in your tax-free safety zone where no one can touch it but you. Remember, you're the only one with the key.

I don't want to put off a tax bill for a later day, when it'll be larger; just when you it need the most. Doing nothing doesn't mean the problem goes away. That just means it will be a bigger problem later. The taxes will still have to be paid.

Let me ask me ask you something. What happens when we put problems off or bury them under the carpet? Does the problem go away if you ignore it?

My dentist has a warning sign that says "ignore your teeth, and they'll go away." Not a pretty picture. Just like gum disease, taxes will decay your savings.

I want to eliminate the brewing tax problem – permanently. And that means – getting implants – no – it means doing something now.

Get rid of your tax infested IRAs and turn them into tax-free money. The sooner you do it, the more tax-free money you'll have later.

Ed… what if I'm sure I'll be in a lower tax bracket later? Would it still pay to withdraw now?

It won't be lower than zero.

That's what you'll have with my plan. A zero percent tax rate. **No matter how low you think your tax rate in retirement may be, you cannot beat a zero percent tax rate.**

The life insurance leverage can be powerful. Of course it depends on your age, health and other factors. But it could be that for every dollar you invest in your life insurance, your family could be paid 5 times that amount, tax free, or even more in some cases.

I'd do that all day long, to fill up the tax-free safety zone – building tax-free wealth.

It's the most direct route to tax-free territory – your destination – sunshine and rainbows. That's exactly where you want to end up.

But not really where you want to end up, since this happened because you were dead.

But with a special kind of life insurance "permanent insurance", you can have the best of both worlds. You can use it while you're alive or leave it to grow tax free for your family.

With permanent insurance, the value goes in your tax-free safety zone. If you need it, you have the key. You can withdraw what you need tax free. If you don't need it, your family gets the tax-free windfall.

Life insurance can also be invaluable if you have a large IRA and you're worried that your children might squander it when they inherit it. How could that happen?

Clients always tell me "It's not my kids I worry about; it's the ones they marry!"

Do you think that too?

You don't want to work your whole life and your savings ends up with someone you might not even know yet! Your child's inherited IRA could be one divorce away from being lost to an ex-spouse. Is that what you want?

It could take <u>you</u> 40 years to build it up, and take <u>them</u> 40 minutes to blow it!

If you're worried about spending a lifetime saving only to have it disappear right after death, or lost to children's creditors, divorces, lawsuits, bankruptcy or bad financial decisions, you can protect against that.

You could name a trust as your IRA beneficiary and include restrictive provisions. The US Supreme Court recently ruled that inherited IRAs are not protected in bankruptcy under federal law, so we're seeing more trusts being used to protect large IRAs.

The trust works, but it's costly and complicated. There are still required minimum distributions to the trust each year, the trust has to be maintained, specific tax rules have to be followed, annual trust tax returns need to be prepared and after all of that, depending on the trust, much of that inherited IRA could end up being lost to trust taxes – the highest tax rates in the land.

Actually, the tax cost might outweigh the protection you want. Depending on the tax rates, you could be giving more to Uncle Sam than your children all in an effort to protect it for them. So let me understand this. To make sure your children don't blow it, you'd rather give it to Uncle Sam? Really? That's not a good plan.

This is another area where life insurance can be the answer and solve two big problems – the taxes and protecting your children from squandering your IRA money.

In fact, **life insurance can be much better for a beneficiary than an IRA,** it eliminates the complicated tax rules.

Instead of leaving your IRA to a trust, withdraw money now from your IRA, pay the tax, and use the remaining amount for life insurance.

And then – leave the life insurance to your trust. The life insurance is a much better asset to leave to a trust than an IRA.

In fact, you could use less of your IRA to produce more life insurance, leaving more IRA funds for you to use in retirement if you need them.

And unlike the IRA, the life insurance that gets paid to the trust is tax free and the trust can still protect your money from creditors or children blowing it.

Think about it this way – Life insurance is an asset. It's tax free. It doesn't get eroded by taxes. On the other hand, your IRA is a liability – a tax waiting to happen. It's not worth what you think it is because it hasn't been taxed yet.

I know that not everyone qualifies for life insurance due to your age and health. But if you do qualify, don't wait till you don't.

Start piling up your money in the tax-free safety zone – as much as you can. Take it from IRAs or other taxable investments and stockpile it here, through Roth conversions and life insurance, and do it now, before taxes go up.

Using only that money (tax-free money) in retirement will lower your current taxes, lower your future taxes and you'll be rid of Uncle Sam. No sharing anymore.

Coming up I'll reveal the 5 biggest retirement roadblocks so you can steer clear of the danger signs, the dead ends and the wrong turns.

And I'll also show you how to coordinate your IRA planning with your Social Security, so you get the most out of both.

You know where we're going – from ***forever taxed to never taxed!***

Are you starting to see that the land of tax-free retirement is not just a dream? It's a real place and we're almost there, so don't mess it up now. Stay tuned.

Part
3

▶ **Big Message:**

Avoid the 5 Biggest Retirement Roadblocks!

Taking Your Social Security Benefits

When should you begin claiming your Social Security benefits?
For most of you, later is better.

As a general rule, consider delaying your social security benefits until age 70, if you can. You'll get more for the rest of your life.

As a general rule, take your IRA distributions in your 60s and delay your Social Security until age 70. This will allow you to get the most from both and pay the least in taxes.

Be careful to avoid the 5 biggest retirement roadblocks:

1. Not taking care of yourself first – You come first – no detours

2. Moving your IRA funds the wrong way – always use direct transfers

3. Not checking beneficiary forms – update all of them now

4. Not protecting your savings – get an umbrella insurance policy

5. Working with the wrong financial advisor – make sure they're educated in the retirement tax rules

Key Points from Part Three:

Remember my rules of retirement.

Don't lose money in retirement!

You need to manage your investments on the way in, and manage your taxes on the way out.

Your IRA is loaded with taxes. Use it, leverage it or lose it to higher taxes.

"The more you plan, the more you keep" — *Ed Slott*

Part Three

Ok we're back on our trip from *forever taxed to never taxed!*

We're almost there, but before we continue on our journey, let's pull over and address your Social Security options.

The big question is when should you begin receiving your benefits? For most of you, later is better.

However, everyone has different circumstances, so of course you should always run your own situation by your tax and financial advisors to see which option works best for you.

As a general rule:
Consider delaying your social security benefits until age 70, if you can.

You'll get more for the rest of your life, but only for life. If you die early, say at age 73, then obviously you would have received more if you began claiming your benefits earlier. But there's no way of knowing that.

But even if you die early, if you have a spouse that survives you, they'll generally be able to receive your benefit amount.

But what if you stopped working or you need money to live on until age 70?

That's where your taxable IRAs come in, if you have them. It's true that you're not required to withdraw from your IRA until you reach age 70½, but why wait?

If you need money during your 60s, chances are you're in a lower tax bracket and this may be the perfect and least costly time to withdraw your IRA funds.

Yes, taking IRA distributions can increase your current taxable income. But that's ok because you need the money.

So the plan is to take your IRA distributions in your 60s and delay your Social Security until age 70. This will allow you to get the most from all your retirement income sources and pay the least in taxes.

You have most of the road map now, but the biggest bumps in the road may still be ahead. Let's make sure your road map is crash tested to avoid fatal tax mistakes.

You'd hate to mess up now.

Here are the 5 biggest retirement roadblocks – that can stop you from getting to the tax-free Promised Land.

1. Not taking care of yourself first

2. Moving your IRA funds the wrong way

3. Not checking beneficiary forms

4. Not protecting your savings

5. Working with the wrong financial advisor

1. Not taking care of yourself first

You're heading into retirement or maybe already there. When is it your time? I've given you a road map to a tax-free retirement, but there are still some of you who are bogged down with helping everyone else. That's retirement gridlock, and you don't have the time to wait it out. It's a dead end.

There comes a point where you must come first and that time is now. You have only so many years left to enjoy and that shouldn't be put off because you're still worrying about everyone else. What about you?

For example, helping kids or grandkids with college money. That's great if there's plenty to spare. But if it drains the money you put away for yourself, who's going to replace it? Them? They can get a loan for college, but you can't a loan for your retirement. Helping children buy a house. They can get a mortgage for that, but ***you can't get a mortgage for retirement.***

Your priorities have to change now. You first.

If you can't take care of yourself, you can't be of help to anyone else.

This is your time. You've spent a lifetime sacrificing. Retirement can be a long road. Some of you will spend more years in retirement than you spent working. And you need to plan for that.

You first – no detours for others from now on. Got it?

2. Moving your IRA funds the wrong way

Here's an IRA death trap you need to avoid.

When you move IRA money from one IRA to another, that's called an IRA rollover and it's common, and that's fine.

But be careful. Very careful. Think of your IRA like an egg shell. You break it and it's over. The rules are strict and unforgiving. Mistakes here are fatal. They can end your IRA.

If your IRA money is moved the wrong way, your entire IRA withdrawal, which you simply wanted to move to another bank, is now taxable, plus a 10% penalty if you happen to be under 59½. And the funds cannot be rolled over. You've lost your IRA. Gone.

There **are** reasons to move your IRA money from one financial institution or advisor to another. You might be changing advisors, especially after watching this program and realizing how much you weren't told about IRA tax planning. Or you simply might want to change investments or combine your IRA funds.

It's the way you move your IRA or Roth IRA funds that you need to be careful about.

There are two ways to move your IRA money.

One is directly and the other is indirectly. **Always move your IRA funds directly if you can.**

A direct transfer – also called **a trustee-to-trustee transfer** is when your IRA funds move directly from one IRA to another without you touching the money in between. You can do as many of these as you wish without worrying about something called the "once-per-year IRA rollover rule."

With the other method of rolling over IRA funds, an indirect transfer, also called a "60-day rollover," you get a check from your IRA made out to you personally and then you have 60 days from the date you received it to re-deposit that money – roll it over – to another IRA.

Avoid this indirect – 60-day rollover – like the plague.
The problem with the 60-day rollover is that you only get one chance to do this within a year, and it's not a calendar year.

It's 365 days or 12 months. If you accidentally attempt a second 60-day IRA rollover, within the 365 days, the funds withdrawn, which could be your entire IRA account balance, could be subject to tax and possibly a 10% penalty. They can't be rolled over.

That could cause your tax rate to skyrocket and your IRA tax shelter is gone.

Imagine losing a $500,000 IRA because you fell into this trap. That's what I call a wrong turn that could put a serious dent in your retirement plan.

And to make things worse, this is a fatal error. It can't be fixed. It's over.

The rule only applies when you are moving your IRA money from one IRA to another IRA or from one Roth IRA to another Roth IRA.

The rule is even stricter than it was in the past.

For example, if you do a 60-day IRA rollover from one of your traditional IRAs to another, you can't do another 60-day rollover from any of your IRAs or Roth IRAs for the next 12 months.

So why ask for trouble? Avoid this problem altogether.

Always use direct, trustee-to-trustee transfers when moving IRA money.

3. Not checking beneficiary forms

Once again I'll plead with you to update your IRA and plan beneficiary forms.

I mention beneficiary forms in every program, every seminar, every training session, but even with all that, it is still a big problem.

Do you want your retirement savings going to the wrong people? Or to be heavily taxed?

Name your IRA or plan beneficiaries on your beneficiary form, not in your will. Your beneficiary form will trump your will.

Not updating your beneficiary forms could lead to terrible, unintended consequences, like your children being disinherited.

In a U.S. Supreme Court case, after the husband died, his ex-wife ended up getting his 401(k) which he wanted to go to their daughter, and his ex-wife agreed to this. But he neglected to update his beneficiary form after their divorce and remove his ex-wife as beneficiary. She ended up in court against her own daughter for over 8 years fighting over his $402,000 dollar 401(k). The ex-wife won the case because she was still listed as the beneficiary. The daughter was disinherited, not to mention the thousands in legal fees. Can you imagine what that did for their mother-daughter relationship?

In another case, a man's wife died. He had a 401(k) and in this case, he was smart and did update his 401(k) beneficiary form to name his 3 children. But then he made a mistake. He got remarried. Then he died just 6 weeks later. The new wife of 6 weeks got it all. How could that be if he updated his beneficiary form to name his children? This is one case where the federal plan law trumped the beneficiary form.

Under federal law for certain company plans, a spouse is automatically the beneficiary, regardless of who was named on the beneficiary form. The children were disinherited. What should have been done? He should have had his new wife waive her rights to his 401(k), but he didn't know to do that and she walked away with all his money, leaving his children, now without their mother or father, with nothing.

Don't let anything like this happen to you.

Life happens and you need to update your beneficiary forms any time there are changes – what I call life events.

You have a birth, a death, a marriage, a divorce, a remarriage, you had a new grandchild, there's a new tax law, or you simply change your mind and want to change beneficiaries.

Ed, is there still time to fix my beneficiary forms? Yes, but only if you're still breathing! Your beneficiary forms can be changed at any time. Some people still think their choices are locked in. That's not true.

4. Not protecting your savings

Are your retirement savings properly insured? You insure your home, your car, your property or anything else of value, so what about your retirement savings?

What if you get sued? You could have a car accident or someone gets hurt on your property. If you're liable for big bucks, your homeowner's policy might not be enough and you could be wiped out, changing everything.

Get yourself an umbrella insurance policy for at least a million dollars or more, depending on how much you need to protect. It's an excess liability policy that covers you beyond your current home or auto insurance limits.

This is one of the best protections you can have because it covers you for large amounts and it costs very little, in relation to that protection.

In fact, it's so inexpensive; when I got my last policy I actually called the insurance company to make sure the bill was right. Believe me; I wasn't worried about the insurance company making a profit. I wanted to make sure I had the coverage. You should have it too.

Remember that in addition to your retirement savings, which may already be protected under federal law, you have other savings and property to protect. You might be one auto accident away from losing it all.

Protect your savings and your property. Overlooking this simple detail could instantly turn your world upside down.

5. Working with the wrong financial advisor

Protecting your retirement savings means knowing the tax rules or working with an advisor who does.

You need a specialist. The advisor you have may have made you a ton of money, but what does that mean if you lose it all to taxes on the way out?

What I most often hear from those who've seen my public television programs is that their tax planning was never addressed; they say "I wasn't getting this type of information from my current financial advisor."

My "current" financial advisor. What does it mean when you say the word "current?"

That's right. Maybe you need to make a change for the second half of the game.

But you still need to learn all you can here and use this information to demand much more.

My rule: ***If an advisor doesn't invest in their education, then you shouldn't invest with them***

They have to earn your business!

Let's review the 5 Biggest Retirement Roadblocks

1. Not taking care of yourself first – You come first – no detours

2. Moving your IRA funds the wrong way – always use direct transfers

3. Not checking beneficiary forms – update them now

4. Not protecting your savings – get an umbrella policy

5. Working with the wrong financial advisor – make sure they're educated in the retirement tax rules

And of course there's the most important 6th retirement roadblock.

Not following my road map and going off course.

Remember my rules of retirement.

Don't lose money in retirement.

You need to manage your investments on the way in, and manage your taxes on the way out.

Your IRA is loaded with taxes. Use it, leverage it or lose it to higher taxes.

So stuff your tax-free safety zone till it's full – and starve your tax hungry Uncle Sam.

Move your money from ***forever taxed to never taxed!***

Tax free is always better – That's all you need to know. No more sharing and no more partners.

I want you to have more, and pay less.

"The more you plan, the more you keep"   *– Ed Slott*

Add that to my golden retirement rules.

Again – "The more you plan, the more you keep"

You all know of situations where one moment changes everything forever, so you need to do it now.

Got it?

So there you have it… my retirement road map.

Now you can stop worrying about not having a plan or running out of money, and start seeing your savings grow here – in your tax-free safety zone, allowing you to have more, enjoy more and make it last longer.

Part 4

▶ **Big Message:**

Ed Slott's Three Core Principles

In my 30 plus years of experience I have found that there are three core principles you can apply when it comes to building, protecting and preserving your retirement savings. Actually, these principles apply to all things.

1. Focus

What is it that you want to accomplish? What's the most important thing to you?

What keeps you up at night? Focus on those things, and the rest will fall into place.

2. Take the long view

Now that you know what your focus is, don't be short-sighted about getting there.

Focus on the long-term benefit, not the short-term cost. Focus on the big win at the end. The result is what counts.

3. Take action

Nothing will happen if you don't take action. Take consistent action, a little at a time at a pace that is right for you. Otherwise you'll be overwhelmed and you won't stick with your plan. Keep forging ahead and you'll get there. Small steps lead to big victories… in all things.

I wish you all a happy, healthy and ***tax-free*** retirement.

Ed Slott, CPA   Copyright © 2016

DVDs

How to Check Your Beneficiary Forms

The 10 Most important items to check on your Beneficiary forms

Check your IRA and plan beneficiary forms!

It's critically important.

You've heard me say this in every program and every seminar and it is still an epidemic that could cost you and your family. Use my checklist here and nothing will fall through the cracks.

I've seen children disinherited.

I've seen ex-wives and ex-husbands walk away with money that was not supposed to go to them.

I've seen situations where some children ended up with way more than others, when they were all supposed to share equally.

I had that last one in my own family – a relative who never thought to ask me for advice, then died and left a mess to clean up.

These are all due to IRA and Plan beneficiary form mistakes. I don't want this to happen to you or your family. As I always say, life happens and you need to update your beneficiary forms any time there is a change in your life or with your family.

Use my guide to checking your beneficiary forms to make sure everything is correct and current.

Here are the 10 important items to check on your IRA and Plan beneficiary forms

1. Take an account inventory

How many retirement accounts do you have? Make a list and make sure your family has this list. List all your IRAs, 401(k)s , 403(b)s or any other retirement plans you have, and even those you have inherited from others.

Locate beneficiary forms for each account.

Let your beneficiaries know where this information is and how many accounts you have – if they can't find the beneficiary form then it's the same as not having them.

If, like many now, your beneficiary forms are located online or in the cloud, where you may have a code to view them, **let your family know how to access your beneficiary forms online**, so they can find them when they need them, without having to go to court for access to your online account.

As an additional protection, even though it defeats the purpose of cutting down on paper, you should still **print out hard copies of your beneficiary forms** for each account you have. That's not much paper, but it is important paperwork for your beneficiaries to have access to.

2. Are your beneficiary forms current?

Do they take into account life events that would change your choice of beneficiary?

By life events I mean a birth, a death, a marriage, a divorce, a remarriage, beneficiaries to eliminate, marriage of children or grandchildren, children you have adopted, the death of a beneficiary or anything else. See if all of the latest events in your life are taken into account when updating your beneficiary forms.

You need to have your beneficiary forms updated so they are current, and your beneficiaries need to know where to locate them. Make sure your family has the most up-to-date copy.

Make sure any copies at the bank or with your financial advisor are the most up to date. Make sure for example that they don't have old copies on file that might still list the wrong beneficiary, for example, an ex-spouse, or a deceased beneficiary.

3. Have you named both primary and contingent beneficiaries?

It's important not only to name primary beneficiaries but also to name contingent beneficiaries, in case a beneficiary dies or wants to disclaim their interest after death.

Anytime a beneficiary dies, you should update your beneficiary forms, but sometimes people forget. In that case, if you die without updating your beneficiary form, it might help that you had a contingent beneficiary so that your IRA still goes to the beneficiary of your choice.

Have you considered the effect of disclaimers in your planning? Naming contingent beneficiaries is the key to using this strategy.

A disclaimer is a right to refuse the inheritance so that your retirement account will pass to your next named beneficiary, which is the contingent beneficiary you named.

This is a very effective post-death strategy that allows your beneficiaries more flexibility when they inherit. You might name your spouse as primary beneficiary and your daughter as contingent beneficiary. After you die, your spouse may have other funds and wants her share to go instead to your daughter. She can disclaim her interest in the IRA, and the funds will pass to your daughter since she was named as the contingent beneficiary.

Disclaiming must generally be done within nine months of death, and you cannot accept the funds. If you do, you cannot later disclaim them.

Your beneficiaries can disclaim part or all of any inheritance.

But this is a legal process. Make sure to use an attorney to do the disclaimer, and get tax and legal advice before you do.

The point here is to provide a path for a disclaimer after death by naming a contingent beneficiary. If the primary beneficiary disclaims, it can go to the person next in line – a person chosen by you.

That's why **it's essential to name both primary and contingent beneficiaries on all your plans and IRAs.**

Even if the beneficiary does not disclaim, if a beneficiary dies before you do, and you don't get to update your beneficiary form before you die, your IRA will still generally pass to your contingent beneficiary.

4. Have you named your beneficiary on your IRA or plan beneficiary form?

Don't name your IRA beneficiary in your will.

The IRA beneficiary form will trump your will.

If you want a person, such as your children or grandchildren, to be your beneficiary then you must name them on your IRA beneficiary form and not in your will.

If you name them in your will, and not on your IRA beneficiary form, whoever is named on your IRA beneficiary form will get your IRA, even if it's different than the person you named in your will.

But let's say you never filled out your IRA beneficiary form and named your children in your will. Will they still get your IRA? Probably, but why take a chance? Once you name them in your will, you have now turned a non-probate asset into a probate asset.

When you name a beneficiary on your IRA or plan beneficiary form that is a non-probate asset and can't generally be challenged.

If you name your child for example in your will as your IRA beneficiary, it goes through probate, and it can be challenged, say if other children or people come out of the woodwork and make a claim – say children from a prior marriage. Now there's a legal problem that will have to work its way out through the courts – not a good scenario for anyone.

It may be that your children do still inherit your IRA but look at what you put them through.

Even if the correct beneficiaries inherit your IRA through your will, it's still bad. They lose the tax benefits of stretching the inherited IRA out over their lifetime.

The only beneficiaries that qualify for the stretch IRA – the ability to take required minimum distribution over their lifetime, are designated beneficiaries. A designated beneficiary is simply a person – an individual – named on the IRA or plan beneficiary form.

If the beneficiary is not a person, for example, is an estate, a trust or a charity, then there is no designated beneficiary. Some special trusts can qualify as a designated beneficiary.

5. Do you have a designated beneficiary?

A designated beneficiary is an individual who is named on the IRA beneficiary form, not in the will. A designated beneficiary can only be an individual – a person, not an entity like your estate.

If the same beneficiary inherits through the will, under the tax law, it is treated as if the estate was the beneficiary, and since the estate is not an individual and has no life expectancy, the inherited IRA will have to be paid out much sooner to your beneficiaries causing an increased tax bill and diminishing the value of the inherited IRA tax shelter, since it won't be able to last as long.

If a non-person inherits your IRA, such as an estate, a trust or a charity, they cannot use a life expectancy to stretch post-death distributions, because these entities do not have a life expectancy. Only a designated beneficiary can use the stretch IRA to extend distributions over their life expectancy.

Does your beneficiary form name a person (as opposed to your estate, a charity or a trust)?

If not, the beneficiary who does inherit will have to take the IRA funds out much sooner after death.

They will follow the distribution rules that apply when you don't have a designated beneficiary.

Those rules depend on when the IRA owner dies.

If the IRA owner dies before his required beginning date, which is April 1st of the year following the year he turns 70½, then the entire inherited IRA must be withdrawn under the 5-year rule. The IRA balance must be emptied by the end of the 5th year after the year of death. That could cause a big tax in a short amount of time if the account was large enough.

It's even worse with a Roth IRA. If you die without a designated beneficiary on your Roth IRA, the 5-year rule always applies to your beneficiaries who end up receiving your Roth IRA through the will or your estate.

If you die without a designated beneficiary and you die after your age 70½ required beginning date, then your beneficiaries may do a bit better, but not much.

In that case, your beneficiaries still cannot stretch distributions over their lifetimes, because they were not named on the IRA beneficiary form.

They will be stuck taking distributions over your (the deceased IRA owner's) remaining life, had you lived. The longest payout possible there would be only 15 years. That's nothing compared to a 30 year old beneficiary being able to extend distributions out over 50 years.

A Roth IRA has no lifetime distributions, so regardless of your age, whenever you die with a Roth IRA you have died before the required beginning date and your beneficiaries will always be stuck with the 5-year rule if they are not designated beneficiaries.

Remember that these more harsh rules only apply when you die without a designated beneficiary like when you leave your IRA to your estate. That should not happen.

If you neglect to name beneficiaries, your beneficiaries may have a chance to upgrade their status to a designated beneficiary, if the financial institution's custodial document (the bank's IRA rule book, for example) has a default beneficiary.

They have to have a default beneficiary provision. If you neglect to name a beneficiary, they need to know who to pay without a long legal battle.

The default beneficiary only comes into play if you don't have a beneficiary named on your IRA beneficiary form.

The default beneficiary for most financial institutions is your estate – if you neglect to name a beneficiary (or the beneficiary you named died). If the estate becomes your beneficiary by default, then you won't have a designated beneficiary and your beneficiaries will be stuck with those less favorable distribution rules.

Some institutions though have defaults that say, if there is no beneficiary, then it first goes to your spouse, if no spouse, then to your children and if no children, then to your estate. So they have two lines of defense set up for you if you neglect to name a beneficiary.

In that case, say you named your wife as your IRA beneficiary, and wanted your son to be next in line but you neglected to name him as your contingent beneficiary. If your wife died, and you did not update your beneficiary form, and then you died, you would have no beneficiary and the default provision would kick in.

If the default was the kind that said that if you have no beneficiary, it's first the spouse, then your children , then your estate, then in that case, since your spouse is already deceased and you have no contingent beneficiary, it will go to your son as the default beneficiary.

In that case your son will be considered a designated beneficiary as if he were named originally on the beneficiary form.

But you should never plan hoping that the default beneficiary will bail your family out.

If the default in that example was your estate, your son might still inherit, but he won't be a designated beneficiary, since the estate was the beneficiary by default.

Your son might get the IRA but would have to follow the less favorable rules that apply when you don't have a designated beneficiary. Also, the IRA would end up going through probate because it first went to your estate.

In that example, first you should have named your son as contingent beneficiary on the beneficiary form. Then if your wife died, your son would automatically move up as primary beneficiary, without you doing anything.

But even if you named your wife as your beneficiary and your son as contingent on your IRA beneficiary form, once your wife died, you should still immediately name your son as primary beneficiary and name a new contingent beneficiary.

6. Has a beneficiary of yours died?

Then you need to update your beneficiary form.

Anytime a beneficiary dies, the beneficiary form needs to be updated, naming both primary and contingent beneficiaries. This ensures that the people you want to inherit your IRA will inherit it with no legal problems and with the best tax advantages.

The same thing after a divorce. You need to update your beneficiary form to remove your ex-spouse, who will probably inherit if you don't correct this.

7. Will you need to name a trust as your IRA or plan beneficiary?

If you'll be naming a trust as your beneficiary, make sure that trust is named on the IRA beneficiary form.

This is another common mistake. Some people erroneously believe that having the trust automatically takes care of that. No it doesn't. If you don't name the trust on your IRA beneficiary form, some bad things can happen.

First, your IRA might go to the wrong people, and all the time and money spent creating the trust will be wasted since your IRA will never get there.

Chances are that if you are naming a trust as your IRA beneficiary, then you probably have a sizeable IRA you want to protect, and without a beneficiary form naming the trust, none of your intended plan will come to pass.

8. Do you want to leave any of your IRA to a charity?

If yes, then the charity has to be named on the IRA beneficiary form.

Another important tip here: If you are naming a charity as a beneficiary for a portion of your IRA and say your children for the rest, then it's best to split your IRA into two IRAs. Name the charity on the part you want to go to them and name your children on the part you want to go to them.

This is not a requirement. This is just some practical advice from my years of experience. You generally don't want to mix different types of beneficiaries like a charity and children on one IRA.

It will be much smoother after death if the IRAs are separate.

If not, the account will have to be split after death, which is probably no problem, but if there is a delay or other problem and the post-death split is not done in time – by the end of the year after death – then the children will not get the tax advantages of stretching the IRA. They will not be designated beneficiaries if the inherited IRA is not timely split after death.

Also, if there is a problem with the percentage each beneficiary is to receive or it's not clear, you can avoid that possibility by naming the charity and your children each as 100% beneficiary on your separate IRAs.

The same thing goes with spouses and non-spouses.

If you are naming both your spouse and a non-spouse (like a child) as your IRA beneficiaries, each for a portion of your IRA, then the same practical advice applies. Use separate IRAs – one for your spouse and one for your children.

The spouse is entitled to certain advantages, like a spousal rollover, that your non-spouse beneficiaries are not entitled to. But to get those advantages, your spouse must be the sole beneficiary.

It would be easier to have your spouse named as sole beneficiary on a separate IRA for the portion you want to leave that spouse. Then have your children be the beneficiaries on a separate IRA for them. This way it's nice and clean after death.

Like the charity example though, this is not required because the inherited account can be split after death and the spouse can still be considered the sole beneficiary of his or her share.

But once again, what if for some reason there is a family feud or other legal delays, as a practical tip, split your IRA into two separate IRAs and name your spouse for his or her share on one and name your children on the other IRA for their share.

Then go one step further and name contingent beneficiaries on each of those IRAs. The children can be the contingent beneficiary on the IRA you are leaving your spouse. On the IRA you are leaving to your children, you might want to name their spouses or children as contingent beneficiaries so their share goes to their families.

Generally, it's best not to mix different types of beneficiaries.

What if your beneficiaries are all children? Then that's ok to put them together as co-beneficiaries of your IRA since they are the same type of beneficiaries – all non-spouse beneficiaries who will generally follow the same distribution rules after death.

9. Are there multiple beneficiaries? Check the percentages

If you do name several beneficiaries, like your 3 children as co-beneficiaries on your IRA, which is very common and fine, make sure you are clear as to how much each is to receive with either a fraction, a percentage or the word "equally" or "in equal shares" if that applies.

I just had a case where three children were named on the beneficiary form with no statement as to how much they would each receive. No fraction, no percentage – nothing.

In the IRA owner's will he said he wanted each of them to share equally but it didn't say that on the beneficiary form. Because of the way the children were listed, the bank treated only the first child named as the beneficiary and the others as contingent.

That was obviously not what their father wanted, but now they were stuck with a mess. We were able to fix this with gifts and disclaimers to equalize this as best we could, but it was a real mess.

Luckily for this family, the child who was listed first and could have walked away with the entire IRA, with the bank's blessing, did not want to do that.

She chose instead to do whatever possible to honor what she knew her father's wishes were – even though he made the mistake of not including that critical information on the IRA beneficiary form he filled out.

Here's another point on naming multiple beneficiaries.
If you do enter the shares they each get, do they add up to 100%?
Check the math. I have found mistakes here.

If you want your children to share equally, then just say equally as co-primary beneficiaries, so it's clear that they are each a primary beneficiary for an equal share.

If there are percentages, make sure those add up to 100%

Are there multiple contingent beneficiaries?

Who are the contingent beneficiaries? Do their percentages add up to 100%?

10. Do you have a *"per stirpes"* option?

Check to see if your beneficiary form allows a "per stirpes" option, so that if your beneficiary dies before you, that beneficiary's share will go to his or her children and not to other unintended beneficiaries.

But this is only a safety net if the proper planning is not done after a beneficiary dies. It's actually best not to rely on a per stirpes provision, but I mention it so you know about it. It's still best to replace a deceased beneficiary after their death with the beneficiary of your choice leaving no doubt about your intentions for that deceased beneficiary's share to go to *their* family, if that is what you wish.

That said, per stirpes is a Latin term that means that the inheritance will stay with your children's children (their beneficiaries), rather than pass to the other siblings and disinherit that child's survivors, simply because that child died. In other words, to make sure those children can inherit in place of their deceased parent.

However, if you are following my advice here, **when a beneficiary dies, you should replace that beneficiary with a new beneficiary**. Then you won't have to even worry about a per stirpes provision. That will avoid the problem of who gets a deceased child's share if that child dies before you do. If that child dies before you do, then obviously you are still alive to update your beneficiary form to avoid these potential family legal problems.

That's my 10 most important items to check on your beneficiary forms.

And here is an extra piece of advice for your beneficiaries

Do your beneficiaries know to also name beneficiaries when they inherit?

Make sure to inform your beneficiaries to name their own beneficiaries when they inherit, so their remaining share will go to the right people, chosen by them and not a legal process.

The beneficiary's beneficiary is called the "successor beneficiary".

Those are the 10 most critical items to check on your IRA or company plan beneficiary forms.

Make sure you go through this with your family and keep your beneficiary forms for all your IRA and company retirement plans correct and up to date – and in a place where they can be found after your death.

This will resolve lots of problems later on.

You have a great list here, with lots of good practical advice.

But it's only good if you use it. I hope you do.

DVD
Social Security

Getting the Most Out of Your Social Security and Retirement Benefits

Social Security is a benefit that you paid for and have earned and you want to get the most you can out of it.

The big question is when should you begin receiving your Social Security retirement benefits? Some might say, I'll begin as early as I can, so I'll get more. That's sounds good, but for many of you, receiving your benefits later might be better. You'll start later, but receive a higher benefit for life.

Your goal is to try to receive the highest income in retirement, taking all your sources of income into account.

Your social security benefit will be paid to you for the rest of your life. That is an important point to remember. You'll get paid for life.

You cannot use it up, like an IRA for example. With your IRA, even if you only take the required minimum amounts each year, if you live long enough you could still use it up.

Social Security never gets used up.

It's a renewable source of income you can rely on no matter how long you live.

In fact, the very first person to collect Social Security, Ida Mae Fuller, received checks until she died at 100 years old.

So plan on living till at least 100 and make Uncle Sam even angrier as he keeps paying you the maximum every month!

In retirement, you may have several different buckets of money from which to draw from. Social security benefits, IRAs or 401(k) funds, pensions, other savings or hopefully, tax-free Roth IRA funds.

The plan is to choose the right path when accessing these funds in retirement, and avoiding the high tax danger signs. Any road that leads to higher taxes in the long-run should have a stop sign.

44   The goal here is to get the most from each source while paying the least in taxes.

When it comes to claiming your social security, everyone has different circumstances.

Some are married couples where both spouses worked and they each qualify for good benefits on their own. There are some couples where only one spouse had the majority of earnings.

Then there are widows and widowers drawing off a deceased spouse's benefit, and those who are divorced drawing their own or an ex-spouse's benefits – or even those who get remarried.

And – if you have always been single, your situation – believe it or not – is the easiest.

But even though the best options depend on your own situation, there are a few general guidelines that can help you decide when to begin receiving your Social Security benefits.

Before we start talking about those guidelines though, it's important for you to understand some Social Security terminology. The single most important term when it comes to your Social Security planning is probably *"Full Retirement Age."* Sometimes you'll see this abbreviated FRA.

Full retirement age is the earliest time you can claim your full benefit from Social Security. In other words, your monthly payment will not be reduced at all by claiming early.

One thing you should know about full retirement age is that despite its name, it has absolutely nothing to do with your actual retirement age. **Your full retirement age is determined entirely by the year you were born.** So whether you retire early at 50 or work until you are 85, your full retirement age for Social Security benefits is unchanged.

Depending on the year you were born, your full retirement age is anywhere between when you turn 65 and 67. For most baby boomers, your full retirement age will be somewhere between 66 or 67 – there's a sliding chart based on the year you were born.

From the Social Security Website www.ssa.gov

About The Chart

The chart below lists full retirement ages for survivors based on year of birth. It includes examples of the age 62 survivors benefit based on an estimated monthly benefit of $1000 at full retirement age. Click on the year of birth to find out how much the benefit will be reduced if someone begins receiving survivors benefits between age 60 and full retirement age.

Note:
If the worker started receiving retirement benefits before his or her **full retirement age, we cannot pay the full** retirement age **benefit amount on their record**.

The maximum survivors benefit is limited to what he or she would receive if they were still alive.

Year of Birth	Full (survivors) Retirement Age 2.	At age 62 3. a $1000 survivors benefit would be reduced to	Months between age 60 and full retirement age	Monthly % reduction 4.
1939 or earlier	65	$829	60	.475
1940	65 and 2 months	$825	62	.460
1941	65 and 4 months	$822	64	.445
1942	65 and 6 months	$819	66	.432
1943	65 and 8 months	$816	68	.419
1944	65 and 10 months	$813	70	.407
1945 – 1956	66	$810	72	.396
1957	66 and 2 months	$807	74	.385
1958	66 and 4 months	$805	76	.375
1959	66 and 6 months	$803	78	.365
1960	66 and 8 months	$801	80	.356
1961	66 and 10 months	$798	82	.348
1962 and later	67	$796	84	.339

1. If the survivor was born on January 1st of any year, use the information for the previous year.

2. If someone was born on the 1st of the month, we figure the benefit (and the full retirement age) as if his or her birthday was in the previous month.

Note: The full retirement age may be different for retirement benefits.

3. The $1000 benefit would be reduced to $715 for anyone who started receiving survivors benefits at age 60.

4. Monthly reduction percentages are approximate due to rounding. The maximum benefit is limited to what the worker would receive if he or she were still alive. Survivors benefits that start at age 60 are always reduced by 28.50%.

So why is this full retirement age thing so important?

Well there are two big reasons. First, as I mentioned before, your full retirement age is the age you can claim unreduced Social Security benefits, but you don't *have* to claim your benefits then.

You may be able to claim them sooner or you may choose to claim them later. How much earlier or later you claim benefits in relation to your full retirement age will have a big impact on how much you receive from Social Security... for life!

The other reason knowing your full retirement age is so important is that there are a number of advanced Social Security claiming strategies that can't be utilized if you haven't reached your full retirement age yet. I'll tell you more about these a little later in this program.

But before we get to the advanced stuff, I need to make sure you understand some of the basic principles. First, when it comes to your own Social Security benefit, you can generally start receiving payments as early as 62 or as late as 70.

When should you? There's no hard and fast rule, but most Social Security experts agree that **too many people probably claim their benefits too early**.

That might sound counterintuitive. After all, if you claim your benefits earlier, you'll receive payments over more years. That's true, but the downside is that when you claim your benefits before your full retirement age, your benefit will be reduced, a reduction that will carry through for life.

If you wait until your full retirement age, that reduction is eliminated and you can receive the full amount you're entitled to.

You can also wait to claim your benefits beyond your full retirement age too.

Again, this might seem counterintuitive. Why wait to claim an unreduced benefit?

Well, the reason you might do so is that for each year you wait to claim your Social Security benefits beyond your full retirement age, you'll receive an 8% bonus in your future payments – technically called a delayed credit.

That increase is before any cost-of-living adjustment is factored in and it will make your future Social Security payments higher for life.

So the bottom line, when it comes to claiming your Social Security benefit, is that the earlier you claim, the more years you will receive a smaller check. The opposite is also true. The later you claim your Social Security benefits, the fewer years you'll receive higher checks.

If you start sooner and take the smaller checks, you'll have more early on, but over time, if you live long enough, the bigger checks you get by waiting to claim your benefits will amount to more – even though there are fewer checks.

This brings us to our next Social Security concept – the break-even point. This is the age you live to in order to make delaying your Social Security benefits the right decision.

If you die before your break-even point, you would have been better taking your Social Security benefits sooner. If, on the other hand, you live past the break-even point, your decision to wait to claim benefits will have paid off. And each year you continue to live, that benefit will only be enhanced.

So really, the decision of when to claim your Social Security benefits is easy. I can tell everyone exactly when to begin receiving their social security benefits. All they have to do is tell me exactly when they are going to die.

That's the real issue here, and for most of you, that is a big unknown. So in most cases, there's really no way to know for sure whether or not you're making the right Social Security decision at the time you make it.

But there are some general guidelines you might consider following.

If you're single or the higher earning spouse, consider delaying your social security benefits until age 70, if you can.

Don't begin withdrawing at age 62, just because you can.

You can start collecting early but I wouldn't recommend it unless you really need the money because you don't have other sources of savings, or for health reasons you feel you won't live a long time.

The reduction in benefits often doesn't pay, especially if you think you might live about another 15 years or so.

If you receive benefits before that time you could end up with less in 3 different ways:

1. If you receive benefits early and you are still working – your annual benefits could be reduced – but only while you are working and making over a certain amount – around $15,000 or more.

2. You'll also lock in a lower monthly amount for life. Depending on your age, that reduction could be as much as 30%, meaning you'd only be receiving about 70% of the benefit you would have received by waiting until your full retirement age.

Your surviving spouse could also lose. Taking benefits early could reduce the survivor benefits your spouse may be entitled to once you pass away – not a good deal in many cases, unless again you need the money at age 62.

And…

3. Up to 85% of the amount you actually receive could be subject to tax, triggering other taxes – but this could happen even if you delayed taking benefits.

Even if you reach your full retirement age – stay away from your Social Security money until age 70 if you can.

The benefit of delaying your benefits until age 70 simply means you'll get more for the rest of your life.

In fact, it can be a lot more. I call it earning while you wait.

By waiting from age 62 until your full retirement age you'll eliminate the reduction in your Social Security benefits that you would have received by claiming benefits early – the one I just told you about.

But then, it gets even better. **Once you reach your full retirement age, you'll receive an additional 8% increase in your future benefits for each year you continue to delay receiving your benefit, up to when you turn 70.**

That 8% increase is guaranteed by the federal government by the way. Where else could you possibly get a guaranteed 8% annual return these days? Nowhere!

In fact, it even gets better while you wait.

In addition to the 8%, you'll also generally receive annual cost of living adjustment increases. These increases haven't been as high lately, but most long-term estimates peg them at about 3% a year.

Add that to the 8% amount guaranteed by Uncle Sam and that's 11% each year.

And on top of all that, if you have a spouse that survives you, they will generally be able to receive your benefit amount – or the amount you could have been receiving if you die before receiving benefits – if that amount is higher than their own benefit.

Take that deal!

Of course, not everyone should delay until age 70, and not everyone should avoid beginning at age 62 – these are general guidelines.

You're generally better off delaying your benefits until age 70 because you'll receive more for life, but only for life. If you die early, say at age 73, then obviously you would have received more if you began claiming your benefits earlier. But again, you really have no way of knowing that… in most cases.

But what if you have stopped working or otherwise need money to live on until age 70?

That's where your taxable IRAs come in, if you have them.

It's true that you are not required to withdraw from your IRA until you reach age 70½, but why wait? If you need money during your 60s chances are you're in a lower tax bracket and this may be the perfect and least costly time to withdraw your IRA funds.

Also, once you are in your 60s there's no 10% penalty on your IRA withdrawals, because you're in the sweet spot – no early distribution penalties and low taxes. Remember, you cannot get an early withdrawal penalty once you reach 59½.

As we know, IRAs are infested with taxes, so let's get rid of it as early as possible. Yes, you'll pay some tax on it, but at today's lower rates and you'll pay less later, because withdrawing now will lower your required withdrawals after age 70½.

If you do the opposite – which is the conventional wisdom – Delaying IRAs until age 70½ and taking Social Security in your 60s, you'll be reducing your Social Security benefits and increasing your taxable IRA income.

Yes, taking IRA distributions in your 60s can increase your current taxable income. But we're planning long-term here.

Think of this strategy as "buying" a Social Security annuity. That might sound weird. After all, you don't buy Social Security, right? But it's like that with this approach. If you use IRA money to hold off on claiming Social Security for a few years, that's kind of the price you pay to get the higher lifetime benefit. And that higher lifetime benefit is essentially a tax-efficient annuity you've just bought. That's a great deal.

At most, only 85% of your Social Security benefits are taxable, but 100% of your IRA withdrawals are usually taxable. At worst – if you have high income, 15% of your social security retirement benefits will still always be tax free.

Any remaining IRA funds you have – your traditional IRA funds – are subject to required minimum distributions after age 70½ , so you have to take those – unless you followed my advice and have converted your IRAs to Roth IRAs where there are no lifetime required distributions.

The last money you take out should usually be your tax-free money – Your Roth IRA funds since those funds are growing tax free for life.

Roth IRAs have no lifetime required minimum distributions, so you will only take distributions when you need them, and even then, they will be tax free so they won't increase your income and cause your Social Security to be taxed.

Substituting Social Security benefits for IRAs at 70 or older will most likely be a tax saver for the rest of your life, especially if tax rates rise, which is likely.

To be clear, I'm saying **take from your IRAs in your 60s, and then at age 70, start receiving your Social Security.**

You'll likely get the most out of both paying the least in taxes.

2016 Social Security Update

Now remember earlier I told you there were some advanced Social Security claiming strategies that could benefit you as long as you had reached your FRA? Once again, that's your full retirement age – FRA.

Let's talk about a few of those now.

We'll begin by briefly talking about the *file-and-suspend* strategy.

For many years, this was a great strategy that worked particularly well when one spouse was the primary breadwinner. With the file-and-suspend, you would technically file for benefits, but would then tell Social Security not to pay them to you yet.

This would allow your benefit to continue to grow until you're 70, but – and here's the key point – it allowed your spouse to claim a spousal benefit based on your earnings history.

Not anymore! *This has been eliminated.*

Late in 2015 Congress passed a law that eliminated the file-and-suspend strategy beginning in early May of 2016. I still mention it here though, because if you had already filed-and-suspended by that time, you're grandfathered into the old rules.

The same law that eliminated the file-and suspend strategy also eliminated another strategy – the *restricted application* strategy – but depending on your age, you may still have time to use this approach.

If you were 62 or older by January 1, 2016, you are still able to use the restricted application strategy when you reach your full retirement age, or later.

The restricted application strategy is often beneficial when both you and your spouse have a good earnings history. If your spouse has already filed for benefits on their own record, you can use a restricted application to claim ONLY *spousal* benefits you're entitled to.

Again, you can only do this at your full retirement age or later, and only if you were 62 or older by January 1, 2016.

By doing so, you can receive something from Social Security, while at the same time still allowing your own benefit to continue to receive delayed credits until you turn 70.

For example, let's say that you and your spouse are both 66 and your spouse has just filed for their own Social Security benefit. You might want to wait until 70 to claim yours, but you might as well get something in the interim if you can.

And you CAN by filing a restricted application. By doing so, you'll receive ½ of your spouse's benefit at their full retirement age, but your own benefit will be unaffected and will continue to earn delayed credits until you turn 70. At 70 – or earlier if you choose – you can switch over to your own higher benefit.

Your benefit at 70 will be exactly the same as if you had done nothing except waited until 70 to file for anything. That would be foolish though, since using this strategy you could have been receiving a spousal benefit essentially for free.

But remember that ***the tax law has eliminated these two strategies for many of us***.

One final thought on strategies only available once you reach your full retirement age or later.

I'm often approached by people who took their Social Security early – many at 62 – who later regret that decision. While it's often impossible to completely undo that decision and start over, if you've reached your full retirement age, you can still voluntarily suspend your benefits.

By doing so, you'll stop receiving benefits, but you'll be entitled to receive 8% delayed credits for as long as your suspension lasts, up until age 70. Your age 70 benefit won't be as high as if you had never claimed a benefit in the first place, but it will be much higher than if you had not suspended your benefit.

For many, the perfect end game would be to go into your 70's with maximum Social Security and lower required IRA distributions, maximizing your Social Security benefits and lowering your annual taxes.

Of course you should always run your own situation by your tax and financial advisors to see which option works best for you.

One more thing on social security – or I should say one less thing to worry about – There's lots of talk about Social Security going broke. Don't listen to them. It's not going to change much, if at all, for those of you now approaching retirement.

The plan is for you to get the most from all your retirement income sources and pay the least in taxes, increasing your lifetime retirement income.

DVD
Naming a Trust as Your IRA Beneficiary

3-Part DVD Series

Part One

Should you name a trust as your IRA beneficiary?

This is a complex and technical area of the tax code and even most professional advisors are not well versed in this area. I am not an attorney. I'm a tax advisor, but it's the tax rules that are essential when naming a trust as your IRA beneficiary.

You will need to work with a competent attorney to create this type of trust.

That said, if you have a large IRA or even a modest IRA and you are worried that it could be squandered by children or grandchildren, or lost to creditors or lawsuits, divorce or bankruptcy, then you can name a trust to inherit your IRA and provide protection for your heirs.

The same goes for your company plans like your 401(k)s. You can name a trust as the beneficiary of those plans as well.

I'll be using the term "IRA Trust" but that's just a name for a specialized trust set up to be the beneficiary of your IRA or company plan, to protect it for your heirs.

The reason most professionals are not fluent in IRA trust planning is because IRAs are different than most other assets left to a trust.

IRAs have complex distribution rules that don't apply to other assets, like required minimum distributions.

For example, if you leave a home to a trust, there's no rule that the first year after you die and the house goes into the trust, the dining room has to come out, then the second year the kitchen has to come out, then the third year the bathroom comes out and so on.

But IRAs do have rules requiring a portion of the inherited IRA or Roth IRA to be withdrawn each year.

In addition, unlike most other assets, IRA distributions to the trust are generally taxable, but not Roth IRAs, which is why Roth IRAs make a better asset to leave to a trust.

These are just some of the nuances that make IRA trusts a specialized area.

If you are considering naming a trust to inherit your IRA, follow this series of programs to be well informed.

This is not intended for you to attempt this yourself. Don't do that, unless you are already a tax attorney who has the specialized knowledge in this area.

This is information for you to understand the reasons for naming a trust, the process of setting up the right trust for you and to know how the trust will be implemented after death.

I urge you to consult your tax and legal advisors before following any of the information contained in this special DVD series on naming a trust as your IRA beneficiary.

I have set up this program in 3 DVDs, each covering an essential part of the process.

When it comes to naming a trust as your IRA beneficiary, there are 3 essential stages – and I'll cover each of them in a separate DVD.

Stage 1 – Making an informed decision as to whether or not you should name a trust as your IRA beneficiary. I'll cover what's involved and go through who should and who should not name a trust – the advantages and disadvantages. The goal of the first part is to decide if you should name a trust as your IRA beneficiary.

If after going through part one, you decide – again with the help of your professional advisors that a trust is not for you, then you can stop after the first DVD and simply name your beneficiaries individually on your IRA beneficiary form and not name the trust.

But if you later change your mind, you always have the next two DVDs to refer to.

If you decide you need a trust, then continue on to the second DVD, stage two – How to set up the right IRA trust for you.

This is where the complex tax rules come in, but you need to be informed so that you can understand the process and explain it to your beneficiaries.

The 3rd DVD is more of a guide for your advisors and your beneficiaries to make sure that all the planning, the costs and work you and your advisors did to set up the trust plan was not wasted because of mistakes made after death implementing the trust.

This is Stage 3 – Post-death trust implementation.

Also in stage 3 I'll review all the key points and show you how to avoid the most common and costly mistakes. I'll go through some alternatives to a trust that could work out better for you and your family than an IRA trust.

So to review, this program is a 3-part DVD series:

3 Stages – All Essential

1. Should a trust be named?
2. Setting up the IRA trust
3. Implementing the trust after death

Let's begin part one.

Should you name a trust as your IRA beneficiary?

Like anything else – there are pros and cons, advantages and disadvantages.

Probably, the number one reason you are even watching this is because you have a sizable IRA to protect.

Right upfront you should know that a trust is costly and complicated – it will cost several thousand dollars to set up, and you must make sure that the professional you hire to do this has a unique understanding of IRA trusts and their specific tax rules, rules that don't apply to most other assets.

A general trust – sometimes called a "boiler-plate" or "garden variety" trust won't work. This is not a one size fits all situation. You need a customized IRA trust, not one off the shelf, which unfortunately is what most people get who don't know to ask.

It must be a specialized trust set up to inherit the IRA and incorporate the IRA tax rules. Otherwise the trust will fail. Sorry to say, most trusts fail since so few tax attorneys – even estate planning attorneys – are up to speed on IRA trusts.

If the trust does fail, then all the time and money you spent setting up the trust and naming it as your IRA beneficiary will be wasted, and in fact, the taxes could be accelerated costing your beneficiaries more than if you didn't have the trust in the first place.

So with that said – and that is a strong warning to get competent professional advice – let's go through the reasons why you should or should not name a trust as your IRA beneficiary.

Another warning right up front: When I refer to naming a trust as your IRA beneficiary, I mean just that – after your death. An IRA cannot be put in a trust during your lifetime. That would trigger tax on your IRA and end it.

You CANNOT give an IRA away during lifetime through a trust. – Not without triggering an income tax – The trust cannot "own" the IRA.

I mention this because I've seen this happen when people go to living trust seminars. They tell you to protect your assets by putting them in a living trust. That's fine for other assets, but not for IRAs!

This is not for you to put your IRA in a trust during your life, this is about naming a trust to inherit your IRA after you die.

While you are alive, nothing changes, even if you do name a trust as your beneficiary. It's still your IRA and nothing goes to the trust until after death, and even then only the required distributions go to the trust.

Ok, with that said, the first question I ask clients who are considering naming a trust, is why do you think you need a trust as your IRA beneficiary?

And the first two reasons don't count.

1 – Because my attorney said so.
   That doesn't tell me why you need a trust.

2 – To save taxes – these trusts are not meant to save taxes.
   They can, but that is not the primary purpose. There is no tax benefit that can be gained with a trust that cannot be gained without one. In fact, certain types of IRA trusts can actually accelerate taxes at high trust tax rates.

If the trust saved taxes, then everyone would have them.

The main reason you name a trust for your IRA, or any asset you want to protect for that matter, comes down to one word – control – post-death control so you can protect this money for your beneficiaries even after you die. You build in protections so that they don't blow it.

Here are the reasons to name a trust (the advantages)

The main reason is to protect and preserve a large IRA from being lost after your death – and to keep this protection intact for many years, in fact it can be in place for the life of your children or even grandchildren. It could go out for over 80 years depending on the ages of your beneficiaries.

A trust can provide control and management of post-death IRA distributions to your beneficiaries.

If you named your beneficiaries directly, they could withdraw it all right after you die. That will cost them a bundle in taxes, but they might not care because it's found money for them. If that would burn you up, then that is a reason to name a trust.

If you named your children or anyone as your beneficiary on your IRA beneficiary form (without a trust) , they may be able to stretch distributions over their lifetimes adding decades of tax deferral while keeping their current taxes lower each year only taking required minimum distributions.

Remember that inherited IRAs have required minimum distributions each year and that also applies when a trust is the beneficiary.

While the beneficiaries can stretch or extend distributions over their lives, they could still withdraw it all right after death.

If you want to make sure that they stretch it, then that would be a reason to name a trust as your IRA beneficiary. The trust, can limit the distributions your beneficiary receives each year. You can use a trust to ensure the stretch IRA.

A trust can provide asset and creditor protection – for that, use an irrevocable trust. Maybe you are worried about your children or beneficiaries going through a divorce, a second marriage or other lawsuits.

The US Supreme court recently ruled – unanimously by the way , that inherited IRAs are not protected in bankruptcy under federal law – so that might be a reason to name a trust as your IRA beneficiary.

Your child or other beneficiary might be one divorce away from losing your IRA money. So a trust can protect against that.

Remember that it might have taken you 40 years to build a healthy IRA, but it could take them only 40 minutes to blow it.

Another reason to name a trust is if your beneficiary is a minor, disabled, incapacitated, a spendthrift or unsophisticated as to financial matters and possibly vulnerable to financial predators or unscrupulous people who make take advantage of them, or if they are unable to make their own decisions, due to competence or health reasons.

In essence, you don't trust them to handle money properly.

In fact that is a major reason to name a trust for any asset.

Instead of calling it a trust, they should have called it a "don't trust" because if you trusted them, you wouldn't need a trust.

So that is when you name a trust – when you don't trust. When you feel that your beneficiaries will need guidance and protection once they inherit.

A trust may be advisable if an IRA beneficiary is someone who may need help with managing the IRA funds and taking required distributions, even if the beneficiary is an adult.

Another reason to name a trust as your IRA beneficiary could be to secure funds for payment of estate taxes. If a beneficiary inherits your IRA directly without a trust, they can just take all the money out and leave nothing for the payment of any estate taxes that might be due.

Even if there are no federal estate taxes, there could be state estate taxes. A trust can secure that money, so that other estate assets or other beneficiaries don't get left with the bill.

There are also estate planning reasons to name a trust. Under federal estate tax law, there is something called "portability" of the estate tax exemptions for a married couple. For example, after the first spouse dies, the surviving spouse gets the deceased spouse's unused exemption.

So just using round numbers, if the federal exemption is $5 million and the first spouse to die leaves everything their spouse, the surviving spouse can have a $10 million federal estate tax exemption. That's called portability. Any unused amount of the first estate tax exemption can go to the surviving spouse so it is not lost.

But on the state level that might not work since most states don't have portability.

In that case, if you don't use the first state estate tax exemption you lose it.

In that case, you might want to use an IRA to fund a trust at the first death to secure the first state estate tax exemption so that it isn't lost.

If your estate plan calls for a trust at the first death to secure a state estate tax exemption – for a state that does not have the large estate tax exemption that the federal tax system has, then you can use an IRA to secure that exemption or even to secure a generation-skipping transfer tax exemption for grandchildren.

Although other assets may be better for funding that trust (often called a credit shelter trust) than IRAs, since taxable IRAs are not worth their face value due to the taxes on future IRA distributions that must be paid out.

The generation skipping transfer tax exemption – is not portable (like the estate and gift tax exemptions are).

You might want to use a trust if you are charitably inclined and still want to provide for your beneficiaries. You can use a trust to fund charitable bequests. A traditional IRA is the best asset to leave to a charity because it's loaded with taxes.

But be careful here, if you are going to do that with a trust, make sure the trust clearly states that the IRA funds go to the charity. This can backfire if you don't follow the tax rules.

In fact, if your plan is to leave part or all of an IRA to charity, you might not need a trust. You should name the charity directly on the IRA beneficiary form and they'll get the IRA after your death, and your estate will get a tax deduction. But your beneficiaries don't receive any of those funds.

If you want to benefit both the charity and still provide for your beneficiaries you can do both by using a charitable trust, and still have the protection and control you want for your beneficiaries. In fact, this may be a better plan than leaving your IRA to a trust, from both a personal and tax perspective. A charitable trust may be better than a stretch IRA for your beneficiaries. I cover this in more detail on DVD 3 of this series on alternatives to using IRA trusts.

So those are the main reasons to name a trust as your IRA beneficiary.

But as with everything else, there are advantages and disadvantages.

Pros and cons

Here are the reasons _NOT_ to name a trust (the disadvantages)

The biggest reason is the complexity and the cost. An IRA trust will be costly to set up and it has to be done correctly. But that is the cost of the trust protection you want – and that can last for decades if this is all done correctly.

There are many tax rules to follow with an IRA trust. It's not like any other trust.

First it has to be set up properly and I'll cover those rules in the second DVD on setting up the trust.

After death – there are annual tax returns and trust administration.

A big trust drawback is the trust taxes. You have to plan around taxes because trusts have the highest tax rates in the land.

To give you an example, a married couple would not hit the top 39.6% tax rate until taxable income exceeded $466,950 (for 2016), but a trust hits that top rate after just $12,400 of taxable income. That is a huge difference, and a high price to pay for the protection and control you want to have after death, but there are strategies to avoid that.

One strategy is using a Roth IRA to eliminate trust taxes after death.

I'll explain more about that in part 2 – setting up the trust.

Another potential disadvantage of a trust is that the trust's beneficiaries may not be able to stretch distributions over each of their lives as they could do if they were named individually – without a trust.

The general rule for beneficiaries is that if there are several beneficiaries, the post-death required minimum distributions on their inherited IRA is based on the age of the oldest beneficiary or the one with the shortest life expectancy.

The younger the age, the longer the life expectancy and the longer they can stretch distributions on their inherited IRA. For example, a 30 year old could stretch out distributions over 50 years, while a 60 year old could only go out 25 years. In this case, the 30 year old would be stuck using the shorter 60-year-old's 25 year payout term, cutting her tax deferral period by over 25 years.

However there is tax rule called the "separate account rule" that allows your IRA beneficiaries to timely split their shares into separate inherited IRAs so they can each use their own life expectancy.

With a trust there is no separate account rule. Required minimum distributions paid to the trust are based on the shortest life expectancy (if all trust beneficiaries are individuals).

If that is an issue though, you could set up separate trusts for each beneficiary. That would be costly, but if there was a large amount of money at stake, it might be worth it.

When a trust is named as the beneficiary of an IRA, there is only <u>one</u> beneficiary of the IRA – the trust – not the spouse, not the children, only the trust. Your children are beneficiaries of the trust.

Also, a potential disadvantage – or advantage – of naming a trust is that if you do, you must also name a trustee to make sure your wishes and restrictions are followed. Sometimes this can be a problem if you are not sure who to trust. That's something you should discuss with your family and your professional advisors. It could be an advantage if you have the right person looking out for your beneficiaries.

You now have all the pluses and minuses to naming a trust as your IRA beneficiary. You have all the factors to consider.

If you have decided to name a trust as your IRA beneficiary, then make sure that you actually name the trust on your IRA beneficiary form; otherwise your IRA funds may not end up there. Don't name the trust as beneficiary in your will, do it on the IRA beneficiary form.

You should always too, name contingent beneficiaries on your IRA beneficiary form, in case a beneficiary dies or to provide post-death flexibility for your beneficiaries.

For example, let's say you're still not sure if you should name a trust as your IRA beneficiary. You could name your spouse as your primary beneficiary and your trust as the contingent beneficiary. If after you die, your spouse would like to have a trust, he or she could disclaim – refuse – her inheritance and the IRA would pass to the trust since the trust is next in line as the beneficiary. The path is already set up.

It can work the other way too. You can name your trust as the primary beneficiary and your spouse as contingent. If after death, your spouse did not want the trust, the trustee (which might be the spouse) could disclaim the trust's interest and the IRA would pass to your spouse since she is next in line.

Naming a contingent beneficiary gives your family the option of keeping or not keeping the trust as the IRA beneficiary after death.

Now you see why this topic requires 3 parts on 3 DVDs. There are a lot of personal and financial issues to consider and I want you to take this in a little at a time.

That's it for part one – deciding if you should name a trust as your IRA beneficiary.

If you have decided that a trust may be a little much for your family, then still make sure to name your beneficiaries on the IRA beneficiary form, and you don't have to go any further after this DVD.

But you never know what the future holds so you have all the information in either case.

If you have decided to name a trust as your IRA beneficiary, then go on to parts 2 and 3. Part 2 is setting up the trust, and part 3 is implementing the trust after death and providing you with instructions for your beneficiaries and your trustee.

Part Two

Setting up the IRA Trust

To review, there are 3 Stages – All Essential.

1. Should a trust be named?

2. Setting up the IRA trust

3. Implementing the trust after death

Let's begin stage two – setting up the trust.

For whatever the reason is from part one, you have decided you want the added control and protection of naming a trust as your IRA beneficiary.

Now you'll have to meet with an attorney to set the trust up. Do not attempt this on your own! I am giving you the tax information so you are informed about IRA trusts, not to do them yourself.

I strongly urge you to consult appropriate professional advisors here.

That said, here is what you need to know about setting up and designing a trust to inherit your IRA.

Remember, your IRA does not go to your trust during your lifetime.

That would be a taxable event and end your IRA. We are talking about a trust that will take effect after you die, but we're setting it up now, so it will serve your beneficiaries later, according to your wishes.

The trust can be set up under your will as a testamentary trust or set up as a separate stand-alone trust to inherit your IRA. Either way, **remember to name that specific trust as the beneficiary of your IRA on your IRA beneficiary form, not in your will.**

First you need to understand a few IRA trust terms:

See-through trust (also called a look-through trust)

Conduit trust

Discretionary trust (also called an accumulation trust)

I'll explain what these mean in a few minutes.

And you need to know how the money flows from your IRA to the trust, and then from the trust to your beneficiaries (your children or grandchildren) after your death.

And you'll need to make decisions on how much control you want on your beneficiaries – or to put it another way – how rigid or restrictive do you want your trust to be?

You are the boss here. You can make your trust provisions as restrictive or liberal as you wish, as far as how much access your beneficiaries will receive and when you want them to receive it.

But because these are IRA funds, there may be a price to pay in taxes for limiting your beneficiaries' access to the trust funds. You have to balance the post-death protection you want with the tax cost of that protection.

Remember that any taxable IRA funds paid to the trust and not passed out to the trust beneficiaries – your children for example, are taxable in the trust, and trust tax rates are the highest tax rates in the land.

Also, you might want your children to be able to stretch the distributions they do get from the trust, as if they were named directly.

But with a trust, there is no separate account rule so all of your trust beneficiaries will be stuck taking distributions based on the age of the oldest of your trust beneficiaries, who should all be individuals.

The trust won't work if any of your beneficiaries are not individuals, such as a charity or an estate.

Only designated beneficiaries can stretch distributions on an inherited IRA. A designated beneficiary is an individual with a life expectancy – a person. A charity or an estate or most trusts are not designated beneficiaries because they have no life expectancy. They are not individuals.

But there is an exception in the law for so called **"see-through" or "look-through"** trusts. These are special IRA trusts set up to qualify as a designated beneficiary, allowing the trust's beneficiaries to stretch distributions they receive from the trust over their lives, as if they inherited directly, without a trust. But they are really inheriting through the trust.

That's why this special type of trust is called a see-through or look-through trust.

If you want your trust beneficiaries (say your children or grandchildren) to be able to stretch distributions from the trust, then your IRA trust, unlike any other trust, must qualify under the tax rules as a look-through or see-through trust.

The benefits of a see-through trust are that it allows the oldest of the individual trust beneficiaries to be treated as if he or she were named directly. The inherited IRA can be stretched over that person's life expectancy.

If the trust does not qualify as a see-through trust, then the IRA will be treated as if there was no designated beneficiary and the post-death payout will not be based on your trust beneficiary's life expectancy. It will be based on the rules that apply when there is no designated beneficiary for an IRA.

Those are unfavorable tax rules that would negate the long-term tax benefits of setting up a trust. So it's important that your trust qualify as a see-through trust under the tax code.

To qualify as what the IRS refers to as a **"see-through"** or **"look-through"** trust for IRA distribution purposes, the trust must meet the following four requirements outlined in the IRS Regulations:

1. The trust must be valid under state law.

That should be an easy one, since I would hope most attorneys doing trusts would only do valid ones.

2. The trust must be irrevocable or become irrevocable upon death.

This should also be easy. Generally, even a revocable trust becomes irrevocable after death – you can't come back and change it.

3. The beneficiaries of the trust must be identifiable.

Here your trust must be clear who the trust income beneficiaries (the primary beneficiaries) are, and who the remainder trust beneficiaries are (the contingent beneficiaries).

They must be able to be identified. For example, naming a spouse by writing "my spouse" (without naming that spouse by name) could be ambiguous if they are no longer your spouse when you die. Anything that creates ambiguity as to who is the actual beneficiary will create an unidentifiable beneficiary and the trust will fail.

It's always best to name individual names, or you could name a class of beneficiaries like my children or grandchildren, but even then, someone might come out of the woodwork you might not have counted on.

Name names, and leave no doubt.

The IRS does not care who you name, they only want to know who they are so they know what the required payout is after death based on that person's life expectancy.

4. The required trust documentation must be provided by the trustee of the trust to the IRA custodian (or plan administrator for a company plan) no later than October 31st of the year following the year of the IRA owner's death.

Generally this means making sure the IRA custodian – the financial institution holding your IRA assets – receives a copy of your trust by October 31st of the year after your death.

This one also seems simple, but is the most often missed of the 4 requirements and will cause the trust to fail.

In addition to the above 4 requirements, there is the 5th unwritten requirement that, **_all trust beneficiaries must be individuals_** or there will be no designated beneficiary on the IRA and the stretch option will be lost.

If any one of the trust beneficiaries is not a person (for example, an estate or charity), then the IRA may not have a designated beneficiary and the stretch could be lost. The trust will fail.

What happens then? The trust fails as a see-through trust and is not considered a designated beneficiary.

Then the post-death payouts are based on the same rules that would apply if you had no beneficiary or the estate was your beneficiary. Those are not good rules tax wise. They force too much out of the inherited IRA too soon and defeat the long term benefits of the trust.

If the trust fails, for example, if any of the trust beneficiaries are not individuals or the trust does not meet the requirements of a see-through trust, then the post-death distributions are paid out depending on when you – the IRA owner died.

If the IRA owner dies before reaching the age 70½ required beginning date – generally that is April 1st of the year following the year you turn age 70½, then the entire inherited IRA must be paid out under the 5-year rule. The 5-year rule mandates that the entire inherited IRA must be withdrawn by the end of the 5th year following the year of death. That's a short payout.

Your trust was probably set up to preserve your IRA tax shelter for 30 or 40 years or more. If the entire IRA is paid out to the trust within 5 years, the time and effort of setting up the trust will be wasted, and depending on the trust terms, this could cause a huge tax at trust tax rates on the inherited IRA.

This is bad news all around.

Remember that the 5-year rule only applies when you don't have a designated beneficiary (for example, when your trust fails) and you die before your required beginning date.

If your trust fails and you die on or after your required beginning date, then your beneficiaries may do a bit better than the 5-year rule but not much.

They'll still never be able to use their longer life expectancy to stretch out distributions.

If there is no designated beneficiary (the trust fails) and the IRA owner dies after his required beginning date (RBD), the longest possible distribution period for the IRA would be 15.3 years. The inherited IRA would have to be paid out over the remaining single life expectancy of the deceased IRA owner, had he lived.

These are terrible options for long-term planning and protection for your beneficiaries, so it is critical that your trust does not fail by not meeting the see-through trust requirements.

Let's review the four requirements for a see-through trust

1. The trust is valid.

2. The trust is irrevocable.

3. The beneficiaries of the trust are identifiable.

4. A copy of the trust must be provided by the trustee of the trust to the plan administrator no later than October 31st of the year following the year of the IRA owner's death.

In addition to the above requirements, ***all trust beneficiaries must be individuals*** or there will be no designated beneficiary on the IRA and the trust will fail – the stretch option will be lost.

Remember that these are special tax rules **only for IRA trusts**.

To review, the reason you want an IRA trust to qualify as a see-through trust, is to allow the oldest of your individual trust beneficiaries to be treated as if he or she were named directly. This will allow the inherited IRA to be stretched over that person's life expectancy.

If the trust does not qualify as a see-through trust, then the IRA will be treated as if there was no designated beneficiary and the post-death payout will not be based on a beneficiary's life expectancy. It will be based on the rules that apply when there is no designated beneficiary for an IRA.

So we know that you want a see-through trust – most likely, unless you want to see your inherited IRA distributed and taxed soon after death, and maybe at high trust tax rates.

The next issue is how much control you wish to have over the inherited IRA – or how much access do you want your beneficiaries to have? When do you want them to be able to receive the IRA funds from the trust? And how much do you want them to get?

You'll be choosing from one of two trusts

Either a **conduit trust** or a **discretionary trust**. Again, these are specifically IRA trusts.

Which trust do you want? **Conduit Trust or Discretionary Trust?**

The answer will be based on how much post-death control you want your trustee to have over the IRA distributions paid to the trust, and ultimately to the trust beneficiaries.

Conduit Trust

This type of trust is merely a "conduit" to pass required minimum distributions from the inherited IRA, through the trust, and then to the trust beneficiary(s). When a conduit trust is the beneficiary of an IRA, the post-death RMDs are first paid from the IRA to the trust and then from the trust to the beneficiaries of the trust.

No IRA distributions remain in the trust. The beneficiaries of the trust then pay any tax on those distributions at their own personal income tax rates.

Trust tax rates are generally much higher than personal tax rates. **Conduit IRA trusts eliminate any tax at trust tax rates.**

If the IRA is a Roth IRA, then trust taxes are not an issue since all distributions from an inherited Roth IRA will be tax free (if the account was held for at least five years including the time the Roth IRA owner held it).

If the conduit trust does not meet all of the four requirements, then there will be no designated beneficiary. The IRA distributions will still pass through the trust to the trust beneficiaries, but the distributions on the inherited IRA will follow the rules that apply when there is no designated beneficiary.

If the conduit trust qualifies as a look-through trust (which you hope), then only the trust income beneficiaries are considered in determining life expectancy for calculating the annual required minimum distributions.

The distributions will be based on the age of the oldest of those beneficiaries (or the beneficiary with the shortest life expectancy). The life expectancies of contingent or remainder trust beneficiaries are not considered since they can only receive distributions if the income beneficiary dies and there is still a balance in the IRA.

I recommend this trust – a conduit trust – since it eliminates the trust tax problem, but still protects the lion's share of the inherited IRA for beneficiaries, since they only receive the required amounts. And the post-death required minimum distributions are less likely to cause the trust to fail.

You can have additional provisions if you wish to allow special distributions – often called trust invasion provisions – for your children's health, education support or other special reasons. So it is not totally restrictive, if you don't want it to be.

But on the other hand you can include spendthrift provisions so that a beneficiary cannot assign his trust interest to a creditor for example.

Discretionary Trust (also called an accumulation trust)

A discretionary trust (sometimes referred to as an accumulation trust) does not have to pay out all IRA distributions to the trust's beneficiaries. The trustee is given discretion to either pay out some, all, or none of the IRA distributions to the primary trust beneficiaries.

Whatever IRA distributions are not paid out though, are accumulated and taxed in the trust at trust tax rates. After just over $12,000 of income, the trust tax rates jump to the top bracket, currently 39.6%. Plus it could trigger additional taxes on net investment income.

Remember that most people who consider naming a trust as their IRA beneficiary have substantial IRA balances of generally $500,000 or more, otherwise the trust might not be worth the cost and tax complications.

But even a modest IRA balance would have required distributions to the trust of over $12,000 a year, which could trigger high trust taxes if the funds are taxed in the trust because the trustee did not distribute all the IRA funds to the beneficiaries.

This is the price you pay to keep this money protected, but again, that can be eliminated by converting your IRA to a Roth IRA (that means paying the tax on that conversion) and then leaving your Roth IRA to the trust.

There are still post-death required minimum distributions to the trust with an inherited Roth IRA, but those distributions will be tax free, eliminating the potential trust tax problem.

As an alternative to using an IRA trust with all these complications, you might be better off leaving life insurance to the trust instead of an IRA. That too would avoid the trust tax problem and still protect the inherited IRA funds in the trust for your beneficiaries.

That's another great alternative to the stretch IRA for your beneficiaries. You can eliminate both the complicated IRA tax rules, and the trust taxes, and still have the protection you want in your trust.

In part 3 of this DVD series I give you more detail on both life insurance and using charitable trusts as alternatives to an IRA trust – they can each accomplish similar objectives without all the IRA trust tax rules.

IRA owners who want maximum control over the post-death distributions to the trust and to the trust's beneficiaries would set up a discretionary trust.

With a discretionary trust, even annual required minimum distributions can be held in trust until certain trust conditions are met, for example, until a child reaches age 30.

The required amounts must still be paid out from the IRA to the trust, but the trustee does not necessarily have to pay any of these distributions out to the beneficiaries of the trust.

The terms of the trust determine how much or when the trustee will pay out IRA distributions received by the trust to the beneficiaries of the trust.

A discretionary trust must also meet the four trust requirements to qualify as a see-through or look-through trust. If any of the four requirements are not met, the IRA will not have a designated beneficiary and the post-death distributions will be paid out according to the rules that apply when there is no designated beneficiary.

One major difference with the discretionary trust (as opposed to a conduit trust) is in calculating annual post-death required minimum distributions.

With a discretionary trust, you must consider the ages of both the income and remainder trust beneficiaries when you look to see who the oldest beneficiary is (or the beneficiary with the shortest life expectancy). That is the beneficiary whose life expectancy will be used to calculate RMDs on the inherited IRA.

In essence, IRS takes the position that remainder or contingent beneficiaries of a discretionary trust may inherit the IRA because the trustee determines who receives the required distributions.

If any one of those remainder beneficiaries is not an individual – say a charity – the trust fails. With a conduit trust, you don't have to look to remainder beneficiaries, so this is not a problem.

If a trust will be named (or has already been named) as the beneficiary of your IRA, first make sure that the trust qualifies as a look-through trust; otherwise you'll have no designated beneficiary.

This goes for each trust that is named as a beneficiary of your IRA. You'll need an attorney that specializes in this area. There is an epidemic of poorly set up IRA trusts in effect right now. Based on these rules, many trusts may have to be revised or re-done in order for all trust beneficiaries to receive the most favorable distribution options.

If the trust does qualify as a see-through trust, then make sure that all of the trust beneficiaries are individuals (as opposed to a charity). Otherwise there may be a see-through trust but still no designated beneficiary and the trust could fail.

Let's review the two types of IRA Trusts

Conduit Trust vs. Discretionary Trust

There are common features to both Conduit and Discretionary Trusts:

They both must distribute annual required minimum distributions from the inherited IRA to the trust.

They can both qualify as see-through trusts if they meet the requirements – if they don't, there is no stretch IRA. The trust fails.

Depending on the trust terms, distributions to trust beneficiaries can exceed the annual required minimum distribution amount, for example, for health, education, maintenance, support, etc.

Now you need to decide if you want a Conduit or a Discretionary Trust. The answer will depend on how much post-death control you want to have.

A discretionary trust provides the most post-death control.

With a conduit trust, post-death annual required minimum distributions flow through the trust to the trust beneficiaries – no IRA funds are retained in the trust. This eliminates any income tax at trust tax rates.

In a conduit trust, post-death annual required minimum distributions are based on the age of the oldest trust beneficiary but only primary beneficiaries are counted; remainder beneficiaries are not considered.

With a Discretionary (Accumulation) Trust, the Trustee has discretion. The trustee does **not** have to pay out all IRA distributions to the trust beneficiaries. The trustee is given discretion to either pay out some, all, or none of the IRA distributions to the trust beneficiaries.

Distributions from the inherited IRA to the trust that are not paid out to the beneficiaries of the trust (retained by the trust) will be subject to income tax at trust tax rates. Distributions from inherited Roth IRAs will generally be tax free.

With a discretionary trust, post-death required minimum distributions are based on the age of the **oldest** of **ALL** trust beneficiaries (both primary and remainder trust beneficiaries). If any of the trust beneficiaries are not individuals (an estate or charity for example), then the trust fails to qualify as a see-through trust and distributions are based on rules that apply when there is no designated beneficiary.

Once again…
Check to see that the trust is actually named as the IRA beneficiary on the IRA beneficiary form. This is critical.

Review your IRA beneficiary forms to see if a naming a trust as your IRA beneficiary is still appropriate. Situations change with life events.

Check to see if the trust will qualify as a see-through trust. All trust beneficiaries must be individuals.

A testamentary trust (a trust created under the will) is ok as long as this trust is specifically named as the IRA beneficiary – do not name the estate or "as per my will" as IRA beneficiary to get the funds to the testamentary trust.

Here are a few IRA trust warnings:

Avoid trust provisions that require payment of estate debts and expenses. That could cause the trust to fail as a see-through trust since the estate can be considered one of the trust beneficiaries. Trust administration expenses are ok.

Avoid using the term "income" in an IRA trust. That could trigger the use of the Uniform Principal and Income Act resulting in potential payout problems for trust beneficiaries, unless the trust is a QTIP trust, a special type of trust most often set up in second marriage situations to both provide income for a second spouse but protect the remaining trust assets for your children from your first marriage.

If naming a trust as the IRA beneficiary, use a separate, stand alone, irrevocable trust. The trust should inherit the IRA, and only the IRA. Don't mix non-IRA assets and IRAs in the same trust, if at all possible.

Who will be the trustee? Do they know what to do after death? Do they know which professionals to hire to help them? Does the trustee know your wishes especially as to how much and when your children or grandchildren should receive the inherited IRA funds? These are important questions to review with the person you choose to be your trustee.

Trust termination – when will the trust end? That's something you'll have to decide. For example, you could have your IRA held in trust for a term of years, or until your children or grandchildren reach a certain age.

Make sure that your trust has a spendthrift clause to protect the trust assets for your children, for example, so they cannot assign their trust interest to a creditor of theirs.

That's it for setting up your IRA trust but that's a lot to digest so take a break and review this as often as you wish.

Now it's on to part 3 of our 3-Part DVD series on naming a trust as your IRA beneficiary – Implementing the trust after death – and IRA trust alternatives.

Part Three

Implementing the Trust – And Trust Alternatives

Welcome back, to my 3-Part DVD series on naming a trust as your IRA beneficiary.

To review, just in case you jumped in on this program without going through the first two.

There are 3 Stages to naming a trust as your IRA beneficiary – All Essential

Stage 1
Should a trust be named?

There I went through all the personal and tax factors you should evaluate when considering naming a trust as your IRA beneficiary.

Stage 2
Setting up the IRA trust

There we went through the degree of post-death control you want, and described the types of IRA trusts and the tax provisions that must be followed so that the trusts don't fail tax wise.

And now it's on to part 3 – Stage 3 – making sure all the planning you've done was not in vain – by knowing how to put the trust into play after death.

Obviously this is for you to share with your trustee and your beneficiaries so that there are no surprises after death – triggering unnecessary taxes, especially taxes at high trust tax rates.

Once you, the IRA owner, has died, and assuming that the trust is named on the IRA beneficiary form, your beneficiaries and trustee need to know exactly what to do next.

This is one of those areas of the tax law where one mistake can trigger premature taxes on the entire inherited IRA. If you are leaving, say a $1 million dollar IRA to the trust, that would be some tax bill and would completely negate the time and cost of setting up the trust in the first place.

Here's what should and should not be done after death.

First…
After the death of the account owner, the IRA is re-titled as an inherited IRA.

Example:

John Smith (deceased, November 3, 2015) IRA, f/b/o John Smith Family Trust

Still no money has been withdrawn from the inherited IRA – the account has only been re-titled.

Be very careful here. Any funds mistakenly withdrawn from the inherited IRA cannot be put back in.

The IRA is not paid out to the trust. I'll say that again, since this is critical.

Do not pay the IRA out to the trust!

This is the number one most common and costly error made with IRA trusts. This is a fatal tax error that cannot be reversed.

Any funds that come out of the inherited IRA (assuming it's a taxable traditional IRA as opposed to a tax-free Roth IRA) are taxable and this cannot be reversed.

There have been many cases where the attorney who set up the trust was not aware of this specific tax rule that applies only to IRA trusts and it resulted in the loss of the inherited IRA.

The problem believe it or not is that their own estate planning training is working against them. Unless they have specific expertise with IRA trusts they will make this critical error.

As estate planning attorneys, when a property is left to a trust, they will retitle that property into the trust. For example if Mom has a house and the trust is the beneficiary, then after death the attorney will rightly put the house into the trust since the trust is the beneficiary. But you can't do that with an IRA!

Thinking like an estate planning attorney, if the IRA (the inherited IRA funds) is moved into the trust, the entire IRA is gone. It's all taxed and this cannot be corrected.

In fact, if the trust requires that the beneficiaries wait for their money and the distributed IRA funds remain in the trust, not only are those funds taxed, but they are taxed at high trust tax rates, giving Uncle Sam an upfront tax gift of 40% or more depending on any state taxes.

This is the mistake that ends IRAs; Big IRAs that were meant to live on for decades in the trust, but now are taxed in the year of the distribution to the trust.

IRA assets inherited by a trust beneficiary cannot be rolled over. They must be moved as a direct trustee-to-trustee transfer only. Any inherited IRA funds paid out to the trust is a taxable distribution. It cannot be reversed – please don't make this mistake – Also question your advisors on this. It's a fatal error.

Here's what should be done:
As I said, first your IRA is re-titled after death as an inherited IRA.

Then, the only funds that come out of the inherited IRA are the annual required minimum distributions – those distributions are taxable, unless this is a Roth IRA.

Even though Roth IRAs have no required distributions during your lifetime, inherited Roth IRAs do have required minimum distributions, but the distributions are income tax free.

When an IRA is left to a trust, the trust must abide by the IRA distribution rules the same as any other IRA beneficiary. There is still a 50% penalty for missing a required minimum distribution, the same as for any IRA owner or IRA beneficiary.

The required distributions from the inherited IRA depend on if the trust is qualifies as a see-through trust – I covered that in Part 2. It must meet the tax requirements I outlined there.

If it qualifies, then you look to see what kind of IRA trust you have. It is either a conduit trust or a discretionary trust. I covered those terms also in part 2.

If you have a conduit trust, then you need to only look at the ages of the oldest trust beneficiary and the required minimum distributions are based on that person's age in the year after death.

You look up their age on the IRS single life table – you can get this online at www.IRS.gov by looking it up in IRS Publication 590, or you can get that information on my website at www.irahelp.com

For example, if your trust qualifies as a see-through conduit trust and your oldest trust beneficiary is 40 years old in the year after your death, the life expectancy that is used to calculate the required minimum distribution from the inherited IRA is 43.6 years, so roughly 2.3% has to come out of the inherited IRA and into the trust and that amount is distributed to the income beneficiaries – your children or grandchildren.

Your children or grandchildren each pay the taxes at their own personal tax rates, which are often much less than the trust tax rates, unless the children are already at the top brackets.

With a conduit trust, nothing stays in the trust so there is no tax in the trust. That's why I like the conduit trust as opposed to the discretionary trust. It eliminates trust taxes.

Your trustee never has to go back to the IRS table. The next year the life expectancy factor simply drops by one year in this example down to 42.6 years, and then 41.6 years and so on until the inherited IRA is paid out in full to the trust over the 43.6 years, or sooner if there more than the minimums have been withdrawn for other reasons.

If your trust is not a conduit trust, but instead it's a discretionary trust, the post-death required minimum distributions are based on the age of the oldest of *all* the trust beneficiaries – both the income and remainder beneficiaries.

Then, like the conduit trust that distribution amount is paid from the inherited IRA to the trust. But unlike the conduit trust, the trustee will use his discretion based on your wishes in your trust, to see how much if any, of that distribution is paid out from the trust to your trust beneficiaries.

He might pay all of it out, some of it or none of it. Any amounts paid out the children once again are taxed on their own tax returns at their own – usually lower personal tax rates.

Any amount retained in the trust and not paid out to the children, is taxed in the trust at the high trust tax rates – unless this is a Roth IRA.

That's why if you are setting up a discretionary trust it's best convert your IRA to a Roth IRA during your lifetime and leave that Roth IRA to your trust and eliminate the trust taxes on inherited Roth distributions paid to the trust. This is something that only you can do – converting your IRA to a Roth IRA during your lifetime.

Non-spouse beneficiaries, like your children or grandchildren cannot convert their inherited IRA to an inherited Roth IRA. However, if you have a 401(k), your beneficiaries can convert that to an inherited Roth IRA.

As a quick review here:

Only required minimum distributions are required to go from the inherited IRA to the trust annually – these distributions are taxable (unless there is basis or it's a qualified distribution from a Roth IRA). Distributions are taxed to the ultimate recipient; the trust or the beneficiaries of the trust.

If you have a conduit trust – The required minimum distributions pass through the trust and then to the trust's beneficiaries and they pay the tax at their own tax rates.

If you have a discretionary trust – And if distributions from the inherited IRA to the trust are retained in the trust (not passed out to the trust's beneficiaries), the trust pays the tax at trust tax rates. Distributions paid from the trust to the beneficiaries are taxable to the beneficiaries at their own income tax rates.

A couple of other key points on IRA trusts:

Set them up as irrevocable trusts. Some courts have said that the creditor protection is greater than a revocable trust that becomes irrevocable after death.

Your trust should be a specialized IRA trust – not a boiler plate trust that is used for all assets. IRAs have very specific tax rules that require their own special trust.

That trust ideally should be set up to inherit your IRA and only your IRA – not to be mixed with any of your other assets. Use a separate stand alone, irrevocable trust.

Check to see that the trust is actually named as the IRA beneficiary on the IRA beneficiary form. This is critical. If you don't name the trust as the beneficiary on the IRA beneficiary form, your trust will not be the beneficiary and all the time and money you spent planning this will have been wasted.

It seems like a simple detail but I've seen it missed.

Review your IRA beneficiary forms to see if a naming a trust as your IRA beneficiary is still appropriate. Situations change with life events.

Check to see if the trust will qualify as a see-through trust. It must meet the four requirements of a see-through trust, plus all of the trust beneficiaries must be individuals.

A testamentary trust (a trust created under your will) is ok as long as this trust is specifically named as the IRA beneficiary – do not name the estate or "as per my will" as IRA beneficiary to get the funds to the testamentary trust.

Make sure the person you select as the trustee of your IRA trust is provided this information so they know exactly what to do after death and so they don't make any costly IRA trust mistakes.

Also make sure your trustee knows your wishes as to how much discretion there should be for paying out the funds from the trust to your beneficiaries.

Your trustee should know how much access you want your children or grandchildren to have and when the trust will end and payout the remainder of the inherited IRA funds to your beneficiaries.

Avoid trust provisions that require payment of estate debts and expenses. That could cause the trust to fail as a see-through trust since the estate can be considered one of the trust beneficiaries. Trust administration expenses, like investment fees and trust tax preparation fees are ok.

Remember that all of this trust planning is done – now, but nothing goes into the trust until after death.

During your lifetime, nothing changes. You IRA is totally under your control as it always was. No IRA money is moved to your trust during your lifetime.

When I talk about setting up a trust to protect your IRA, I mean naming the trust as your IRA beneficiary – not putting your IRA in your trust during your lifetime. That will end your IRA triggering all the taxes. Don't do this.

I stress this because I have seen this happen and wipe out people's IRAs – all because they were trying to protect them for their beneficiaries.

I had a case years ago where a woman went to an estate planning seminar and they spoke about living trusts, and that's fine. They have their place.

The attorney running the seminar told the people that the trust would not work unless you funded it by putting your assets in it. That's correct – except for your IRA.

She went ahead with the trust which is still all fine and she thought she was following his directions by funding it with all her assets – including her IRA.

That is a taxable distribution. Never take out your IRA funds and put them in a trust. That's ok for other assets, like your home or other non-IRA investment accounts, but not for your IRA.

Luckily, we were able to correct this with IRS mainly because this was her own IRA instead of an inherited IRA.

We had to go through a long expensive process requesting an IRS private letter ruling. The IRS let her roll the funds back to her IRA. That's because an IRA owner can do a rollover. But a non-spouse beneficiary can never do an IRA rollover and a trust is a non-spouse beneficiary.

Don't make this mistake.

That should do it for part 3, implementing the trust.

Let's review:

There are 3 Stages to naming a trust as your IRA beneficiary and they are all essential.

Stage 1. Should a trust be named?
Go through the pros and cons to see if a naming a trust is the right move for you.

Stage 2. Setting up the IRA trust
Once you've decided to go ahead with the trust, you have to decide what type of trust you want – based on how much post- death control you want your trustee to have.

You'll choose between a conduit trust or a discretionary trust.

You'll also want to make sure that whichever trust you go with, that it qualifies as a see-through trust so that your trust doesn't fail.

Stage 3. Implementing the trust after death
Make sure your trustees and your beneficiaries are aware of exactly what happens with your IRA after death.

It does not get paid out to your trust. Only the required minimum distributions get paid out to the trust each year, and then depending on the trust, those distributions get paid from the trust each year to your trust beneficiaries – and if not – the funds are retained and taxed in the trust (unless this is a Roth IRA where the annual post-death required minimum distributions would be income tax free).

IRA Trust Alternatives

Using charitable trusts and / or life insurance

If after all of this, you feel that the IRA trust may be loaded with just too many tax rules to follow and could trigger high taxes or it just seems too overwhelming – and I can understand that – then there are two alternatives to naming a trust as your IRA beneficiary – both of which can accomplish your control, protection and tax objectives.

Using charitable trusts and / or life insurance

Both of them can accomplish the same goals – protecting the funds your heirs inherit and eliminate the complex IRA tax rules that have to be followed.

First is the **charitable trust.**

You can leave your IRA to a charitable trust instead of using an IRA trust. If you are charitably inclined this might be the perfect choice because you can set it up so that after death, your IRA funds can benefit both the charity of your choice and your beneficiaries and still protect your beneficiaries from lawsuits or creditors, or their own bad financial decisions.

But still be careful to make sure the charitable trust is named as the beneficiary on the IRA beneficiary form.

With a charitable trust, after your death, your IRA goes to the charitable trust – without an income tax if the trust qualifies as a charitable trust.

The trust can then pay your beneficiaries income for life or for a term of years. This will be taxable income to your beneficiaries, but they would have had that anyway if they took the required distributions from your IRA.

But here, the funds are protected in the charitable trust. If your children get in financial trouble, these funds cannot be touched by their creditors.

This may actually be a better set up than a stretch IRA, as far as protecting the trust money for your beneficiaries, and guaranteeing them an income for life or for a set term of years.

At the end of the trust term, the charity would receive the balance, but over a long enough period of time, your children would have received annual income that might have been more than the charity ends up receiving, and the funds are creditor protected in the trust.

The reason the charitable trust might be better than the stretch IRA is because the charitable trust avoids all the complicated IRA tax rules. There are no required distributions and the trust has both creditor protection and protections against your beneficiaries squandering the money. They will only get a certain amount each year.

One disadvantage for charitable trusts is that they are irrevocable. They cannot be changed and your beneficiaries cannot take out lump sums – only the annual distributions they get from the trust. But that is probably a good thing for most families.

And of course, the remaining balance does go to the charity, but that may be what you want.

And, as I said, over a number of years and under certain scenarios, the beneficiaries may still end up with more through the distributions from the charitable trust. That's why this set up might even be better than the stretch IRA, as far as protection is concerned.

One word of caution here with charitable trusts – these are not for Roth IRAs.

Never leave a Roth IRA to charity – because you've already paid the tax. So don't leave a Roth IRA to a charity or a charitable trust, since there is no tax benefit here.

The second alternative to an IRA trust is using **life insurance**.

In this case you would withdraw all or a most likely a portion of your IRA – the portion that you would have wanted to leave to your IRA trust – and you'll pay tax on the amount you withdraw.

Then with the remaining funds – purchase a life insurance policy and then leave the life insurance to your trust, instead of the IRA.

After your death, the life insurance gets paid to your trust.

The amount that gets paid to the trust will generally be much more than the amount of IRA used to purchase the life insurance due to the great leverage with life insurance, so you might be able to use less of your IRA to produce more life insurance for your beneficiaries.

After death, the life insurance gets paid to the trust, but unlike the IRA funds, the life insurance payout is tax free – so you don't have to worry about trust taxes.

You can use the same protective trust provisions to make sure your beneficiaries don't squander the life insurance money.

Also with the life insurance, there is not only no tax, but no complicated IRA tax rules, like required distributions and making your sure trust qualifies as a see-through trust.

And the trust can still protect your funds for your beneficiaries and their creditors.

Life insurance is a much more trust friendly asset than an IRA. It's really much better than a stretch IRA both for tax and protection purposes.

Those are two viable alternatives to using an IRA trust.

That's it for part 3 of this 3-Part DVD series on naming a trust as your IRA beneficiary.

As I said on the other DVDs, this is very complex tax law, so take your time and digest this.

Once again, I urge you to consult with a tax attorney with specialized knowledge in advising on, creating and implementing a proper IRA trust.

You have all the information on IRA trusts to make the best decisions for you and your family.

DVD
Is a Roth Conversion Right for You?
2-Part DVD Series

Your Roth IRA Conversion Evaluation
7 Roth Conversion Cautions

Part One

Your Roth IRA Conversion Evaluation

Is a Roth Conversion Right for You? Well, it's time to answer that question now, so you can make the choice that's right for you.

I am a big fan of Roth IRAs and Roth conversions because the money in the Roth grows tax free forever. In case you haven't noticed – I love tax free.

But that said, I'm here for you and I want you to be able to make an informed decision.

This is a 2-part program. In this first part, I'll cover the basics and go through all the factors you should consider before converting to a Roth IRA.

In part 2 – I'll go through the 7 Roth Conversion Cautions – items you should be aware of before you convert to a Roth IRA, so that you do it correctly without hitting any of the tax traps most people don't know about.

So let's begin Part 1 – Evaluating a Roth conversion.

Should you or shouldn't you convert to a Roth IRA?

Let's start with the basics.

Converting to a Roth IRA is where the big tax-free money in retirement will be, but it costs you money to get there. You have to pay tax on the IRA money, or 401(k) money you convert.

You pay the tax at ordinary income tax rates. The amount you convert gets added to your regular income for the year you convert. It will raise your taxes for the year you convert.

Anyone with a tax-deferred retirement account like an IRA, 401(k), 403(b), governmental 457(b) plans can convert those funds to a Roth IRA.

For your IRA, you are in total control and you can convert anytime you wish, even before age 59½.

If you convert before age 59½, the funds you convert are subject to tax but they're never subject to a 10% penalty.

If you want to convert from your plan, like your 401(k) plan, you have to be eligible to take a distribution from your plan. Usually that is allowable when you turn age 59½ or retire, but that's up to your plan, so check with your company.

This is one area where the tax rules are more liberal than your company's own rules.

You can also convert to a Roth IRA from your SEP IRA if you have one.
If you have a SIMPLE IRA, you cannot convert until your SIMPLE IRA is over 2 years old.

There is no age limit to convert. You can convert after age 70½ if you wish, but of course the earlier the better, to give you more time to make your tax cost worth the benefit.

But if you are converting for your beneficiaries, then it would pay since they may be able to keep it going for years after your death.

There are no income limits to convert. Years ago you could not convert if your income exceeded $100,000, but those rules were repealed. There is no longer any income eligibility test.

Also, you do not need to be working or have earned income to convert.

Roth conversions come with a money back guarantee of sorts. It's called a Roth recharacterization and this is the key to your Roth conversion planning.

You can convert all or any part of your IRA and then you have until October 15th of the year after you converted to undo your Roth conversion if your investments tanked or you have second thoughts about paying the tax or for any reason at all.

Once you undo your Roth conversion, you'll owe no tax as if the conversion never happened.

Or you can keep part of the conversion and undo part, whatever you wish – Whatever works best for you tax-wise.

And if you change your mind again, after a waiting period you could re-convert those same funds back to a Roth IRA. Other IRA funds that were not already converted can be converted at any time.

There are no lifetime required minimum distributions for Roth IRA owners, so you are never forced to take your money out if you don't want to. That's a big benefit of Roth IRAs.

When your children or grandchildren inherit though, they are subject to required minimum distributions, but those distributions will generally be tax free.

Note: Although you can convert your IRA to a Roth IRA, your IRA beneficiaries *cannot* convert an inherited IRA to an inherited Roth IRA – but employer plan designated beneficiaries can convert inherited plan assets to an inherited Roth IRA.

This is just something for you to know and tell your beneficiaries about.

Those are the basics. But let's see if a Roth conversion is right for you.

Remember it's not for everyone and this is something of course you should review with your tax and financial advisors.

Here are the 3 key questions to ask in every Roth conversion evaluation:

When, What and Where

1. WHEN will you need the money?

2. WHAT will future tax rates be?

3. WHERE will the money to pay the conversion tax come from?

1. WHEN will you need the money?

If you're thinking about withdrawing your Roth money soon after your conversion then don't do the conversion. There's no benefit. Paying the tax upfront wouldn't be worth the benefit if you're going to withdraw the funds in a few years after you convert.

The power of the Roth IRA is in the longevity – the long term tax-free build up, so the longer your time horizon, the more it pays to convert.

In other words, the younger you are, the more advantageous it is to convert.

Younger people should all be converting to Roth IRAs, while they are likely in lower tax brackets and have relatively lower IRA balances. This would present an opportunity to pay very little for the Roth conversion and have many years to build up tax-free Roth IRA savings.

Remember though that Roth IRA withdrawals are not totally tax free until you have held the account for 5 years and you're are at least 59½ years old.

If you're thinking Roth, you have to be thinking long-term.

Does that mean that older people – say age 70 or older – should never convert?

Probably not, if you are converting for yourself.

Given your life expectancy, the upfront tax cost might not be worth the tax-free benefit. You won't have enough years to make up the upfront cost of the tax benefit.

But if you have other taxable funds, and are in a lower tax bracket it might pay. Again, each situation is based on your particular circumstances. These are only general guidelines.

Once you convert, even at an older age, you never have to withdraw from your Roth IRA, so if you don't need it soon after your conversion, then it might pay.

Even if you are older, if you don't need the money and want to leave your Roth IRA to your children or grandchildren, then it probably would pay to convert, since they can benefit for decades after your death, building their tax-free inherited Roth IRAs.

They will be subject to annual required minimum distributions but those will be tax free.

2. WHAT will future tax rates be? Compared to current tax rates

I believe tax rates can only increase, but you'll have to evaluate your own long term situation.

If your future tax rate will be higher, it pays to convert now, so you don't end up paying more later, when you'll need the money the most.

If you think your future tax rate will be lower, then it might not pay to convert and pay the lower tax later.

The only thing wrong with this approach is that you don't know what future tax rates will be. But whatever they are, they will be assessed on your higher balance at that time.

3. WHERE will the money to pay the conversion tax come from?

Do you have funds available to pay the conversion tax?

If you don't have the money to pay the tax, then you shouldn't be converting.

It's best to pay the conversion tax from non-IRA funds – Don't use your IRA withdrawal to pay the tax. It diminishes the amount you can convert right up front.

You might consider partial conversions though – a little each year based on what you can afford.

Now you have the basics and you've gone through the 3 key questions to evaluate a Roth conversion.

So should you convert or not?

Here are the pluses and minuses – who should and who should not convert:

Who Should Convert?

1. Those of you who will not need the money soon or at all, especially if you plan to pass these funds on to beneficiaries. The Roth conversion is an excellent estate planning vehicle.

   If you don't need the money, you probably should convert. You are not doing the conversion for yourself. You are doing it for your children, grandchildren or other beneficiaries.

2. If you are naming a discretionary trust as your IRA or plan beneficiary – a Roth conversion would be recommended since it removes the trust tax problem.

   If you have a large IRA and are worried about protecting it from your children's creditors, divorce, lawsuits, bankruptcy or bad financial decisions, then you might want to name a trust as your IRA beneficiary.

   The US Supreme Court ruled that inherited IRAs are not protected in bankruptcy under federal law, so naming a trust as your IRA beneficiary could help protect your IRA funds once they are inherited by your beneficiaries.

   Most people who name trusts as IRA beneficiaries do so because there are significant sums at stake. You can convert your IRA to a Roth IRA and then you can leave your Roth IRA to your trust and not have to worry about high trust tax rates, because inherited Roth IRA distributions will almost always be income tax free.

   A trust could help to protect your children from squandering your IRA money right after they inherit.

   But trusts are costly and complicated and I urge you to consult with knowledgeable tax and estate professionals before attempting this.

   A certain type of trust called a discretionary trust offers the most protection for your beneficiary because the trustee has discretion to hold back funds from your beneficiaries and retain them in the trust to protect it for them.

   But those funds will then be taxed at high trust tax rates. Very high tax rates.

To give you an idea how high, a married couple would not hit the top federal tax rates – currently 39.6% – until their taxable income exceeded around $460,000, but a trust would hit that top rate after just $12,000 or so of income.

That's a huge difference. So you're left with a problem. You want to use the trust to protect your IRA funds for your children, but it could trigger huge taxes to do that.

Generally if you have a large IRA of $500,000 or more you might want to consider naming a trust. But the annual required minimum distributions on that large IRA are going to be way more than the $12,000 which would mean high trust taxes would eat away at the inherited IRA funds retained in the trust.

That's not a good plan.

If this is the case, then do all you can to convert your IRA to a Roth IRA during your lifetime. Remember that your beneficiaries cannot convert an inherited IRA to an inherited Roth IRA.

Once you've converted, leave your Roth IRA to your IRA trust. The same tax and trust rules apply, but **leaving a Roth IRA to your trust eliminates the big trust tax problem.** When inherited Roth funds are paid into the trust, they will generally be tax free, and you still get the protection you want for your children or grandchildren.

The Roth IRA is much better than a traditional IRA to leave to a trust. It avoids income tax at high trust tax rates.

Distributions from the inherited Roth IRA to the trust will be income tax free, even if the funds are retained in the trust.

This is a powerful reason to convert your IRA to a Roth IRA – to leave it to a trust, to get the post-death protection and eliminate the high trust tax rates.

3. Another reason to convert is if you expect your future tax rates to be higher – especially those who are worried about future tax rate increases and might be subject to them.

4. You should also convert if you can do it at a low cost by taking advantage of low tax rates due to business losses or high deductions in a particular year.

   You could convert at a low tax rate or maybe at no tax cost if you have offsetting tax losses, deductions or credits.

You can use up low tax brackets, for example the 10% or 15% tax brackets should never be wasted.

You can use up NOLs (net operating losses) from a business.

Any time you can convert for a low tax cost or even for free, you should do it.

For example, let's say you had big business losses that produced negative income of $100,000. Take advantage of that. You could convert $100,000 of your IRA to a Roth IRA tax free, using up the business losses.

Similarly you might have high deductions, tax credits and other tax benefits that can be used to offset Roth conversion income (ordinary income) – but NOT CAPITAL LOSSES! Capital losses can only offset capital gains, and then up to $3,000 of other income like Roth conversion income.

If you are not sure what your income will look like, then convert everything and wait till you know your exact income for the year. Remember, that **you have until October 15ᵗʰ of the year after you convert to undo all or any part of your Roth conversion.**

So once you know how much your conversion will cost, you can recharacterize – undo – the amount of the conversion you wish and keep only enough of a conversion to eat up your tax losses and deductions, and still keep your Roth conversion tax cost low – or eliminate it altogether.

5. If you have ample money in non-IRA funds to pay the Roth conversion tax (not using the converted funds to pay the tax) it will pay to use those funds to convert.

    Don't use the converted funds to pay the tax. This will generally not pay and will be worse for those under age 59½ who could incur a 10% penalty on the amount used to pay the tax, in addition to the tax.

    In addition, if the conversion is recharacterized (undone), the funds taken from the IRA to pay the taxes cannot go back into the IRA as part of the recharacterization process. They will continue to be treated as a taxable distribution and, if under age 59½, could be subject to the 10% penalty.

6. If there is one absolute about converting, it's that young people should convert to Roth IRAs – younger people generally are in a lower bracket and have not yet accumulated large sums in their IRAs or 401(k)s.

Roth IRA conversions for younger people are a must.

Suppose 28-year-old Harry has held various part-time jobs while in school and a couple of full-time jobs since graduation. Ideally, Harry has been contributing to a Roth IRA ever since he started to have earned income. If that's not the case and Harry has a traditional IRA instead, he should convert that account to a Roth IRA immediately.

At this stage of Harry's life, he probably has a small amount in his traditional IRA and he probably is in a low tax bracket, so a Roth IRA conversion will have a low tax cost. Even a small amount can grow considerably by the time Harry is 59½ and is eligible for tax-free Roth IRA withdrawals.

Similarly, Harry has a few thousand dollars in a 401(k) from a former employer. That amount should be converted to a Roth IRA as well.

The same reasoning applies to many young people in the early stages of their careers. A Roth IRA conversion will generate a moderate tax bill now and the payoff might be considerable, in future tax-free income.

7. You should convert if you simply do not want to be paying taxes later, in retirement, when you may need the money more.

A Roth conversion eliminates the uncertainty of what future tax rates will do to your retirement savings.

So you may want to convert now to lock in a zero percent tax rate on your retirement savings.

8. Another to reason to convert is to avoid lifetime required minimum distributions.

If you absolutely can't stand the fact that you must begin required minimum distributions from your IRA after 70½ , then do the conversion before you reach the year you turn age ~~70½~~. 72

Then you'll never be forced to take those distributions from your Roth IRA and you'll never have to worry about missing them or withdrawing the wrong amount, or not withdrawing enough and getting a tax penalty.

All of that can be avoided with a Roth IRA because a Roth IRA has no required minimum distributions. You can leave the funds in there growing tax free for the rest of your life without ever being forced to withdraw them.

That's one of the most common and popular reasons to convert to a Roth IRA. That's one less tax rule to worry about every year. That's one less big tax headache.

Those are the main reasons to convert to a Roth IRA, but again, Roth conversions may not be for everyone.

Here are reasons you may NOT want to convert your IRA to a Roth IRA:

Who Should _NOT_ Convert?

1. Seniors who need the money should not convert.

   No one should go broke converting if they need the funds to live on.

2. Those who believe they will be in a much lower tax bracket in retirement should not convert.

   If you think your tax bracket in retirement will be lower, then don't convert.

3. Those who just cannot bring themselves to pay the tax (especially on large IRAs) or those who don't trust the government to keep the tax-free deal probably should not convert.

   But first a word on that last part. That's the most common question I get from people worried about converting.

   Can I trust the federal government to keep its word about tax-free withdrawals? Many people do not trust Congress to keep their word 20 or 30 years from now.

   There are no guarantees as to what might happen in the future. However, there are some reasons to believe Roth IRAs won't be taxed.

   First of all, it would be a politically risky move since it would be seen as Congress reneging on their promise of a tax-free retirement savings account – a double cross.

   Secondly, Roth IRAs are funded with after-tax dollars. Therefore, the federal government collects taxes upfront. If taxes are imposed on Roth IRAs, there would no longer be any reason to fund them so the government would lose current tax revenues.

The government loves Roth IRAs because they get the tax money upfront and they are counting on that income in their budgets, so it is unlikely they will kill the golden goose here.

Even if the government somehow changes the rules on Roth IRAs to make them less appealing, existing accounts might be grandfathered.

Another reason some people don't want to convert is because the Roth conversion income will increase ordinary income for the year of the conversion – potentially causing the loss of valuable exemptions, credits and tax deductions – but this only happens for the year of the conversion.

For those approaching 70½ [72] – required minimum distributions will soon be required anyway, and they will happen every year.

4. If you don't have non-retirement assets available to pay the tax due on the conversion, you probably should not convert.

5. If you think you will need to tap into your converted funds soon after the conversion then you shouldn't convert. The tax cost won't be worth it.

6. If you are charitably inclined and want to name a charity as your IRA beneficiary, then you should absolutely not convert that IRA to a Roth IRA.

   The charity will not have to pay income tax when they inherit the IRA, so why would you want to pay the income tax on a Roth conversion?

   If you are charitably inclined, a taxable IRA is the best asset to leave to a charity. It's loaded with taxes. But don't leave a Roth IRA to a charity.

   If you want to leave your IRA – part or all of it – to a charity, then don't convert it to a Roth IRA. Paying the tax on the conversion would be a waste of your money.

Those are the main reasons not to convert.

So now you have all the factors you need to consider whether to convert to a Roth IRA or not.

What if you're still not sure?

Then you can still do a few things.

First, prioritize – which of all the benefits or negatives is most important to you?

Which of the results of a Roth conversion (good or bad) mean most to you?

For example if having a zero percent tax rate in retirement is important, it might trump all the reasons not to convert and you should go ahead and convert, because the certainty of avoiding taxes on your Roth IRA money is most important to you.

Or if you absolutely despise the idea of required minimum distributions and you want to avoid them at all costs, then that might seal your decision to convert.

On the other hand if you just cannot stand paying taxes now when you don't have to, that might be the deciding factor not to convert.

One important point to remember with a Roth conversion is that there is no tax or investment risk in converting because of the ability to undo that conversion – a Roth recharacterization, for a limited time after you convert.

You have until October 15th of the year after you convert to undo your conversion – in other words to change your mind.

If after all of this, you're still not certain, then hedge your bets and consider partial conversions over several years.

So there you have it – all the information you need to do a thorough tax evaluation of whether it pays to do a Roth conversion.

Now on to part two of this program – my 7 Roth conversion cautions.

You want to make sure that if you decide to a do a Roth conversion, that you do it right and don't fall into any number of tax traps along the way.

Go ahead now to view part 2 of this special DVD program.

Part 2

7 Roth Conversion Cautions

If you are watching this then either you've gone through all the factors on the first DVD and have decided to convert to a Roth IRA and want to know more, or you have already decided to convert and want to make sure you do it right.

Either way, you have decided to go ahead with your Roth conversion.

And just like everything else in the tax law, there are complicated rules, restrictions and tax traps you need to avoid.

Even if you're still on the fence about a Roth conversion, this would be valuable information to review to help you feel more confident about your decision to convert to a Roth IRA – or not.

Here are my 7 Roth conversion cautions

1. New Roth IRA Accounts Need New Beneficiary Forms

The beneficiary form is, by far, the single most important estate planning document when it comes to IRAs – and Roth IRAs. It controls who will ultimately end up with your money and how long they will be able to keep it.

In fact, when you think about it, the IRA (or Roth IRA) beneficiary form really determines the ultimate value of that account.

While every custodian will have its own procedures for a Roth conversion, a new account is generally established, unless you're converting to an existing Roth account, but even there, check that your beneficiary forms are current.

Just like any other new retirement account, the new Roth IRA will need to have beneficiary forms.

What's more, **not having beneficiary forms for a Roth IRA is even worse than not having them for a traditional IRA** (although neither is good and shouldn't happen).

97

Why? An individual who inherits an IRA without being named on the beneficiary form will not be considered a designated beneficiary. In such a case, if you die before your required beginning date – age 70½ – the account must be emptied within five years. If you die after your required beginning date, then your beneficiary can only take distributions over your remaining single life expectancy, had you lived.

But a Roth IRA has no required distributions! That means that a Roth IRA owner can never reach their required beginning date, so if there is no designated beneficiary, the account will always have to be emptied within five years after death.

Specifically, the inherited Roth IRA would have to be emptied by your beneficiaries by the end of the 5th year following the year of your death. This is known as the 5-year rule, and it's not a good plan for your beneficiaries.

This includes when the estate is named as the default beneficiary, which is common in many plan documents and IRA custodial agreements.

An estate has no life expectancy and is never a designated beneficiary. Even though the same beneficiary (your child, for example) might ultimately inherit the account through the estate, he or she will not be considered a designated beneficiary – since they are not really a beneficiary of the IRA, but rather of the estate.

And on top of that, a Roth account grows tax free. While the tax-deferred growth of an IRA is generally better than a taxable account, ultimately, those earnings will all be taxed as ordinary income. Not the Roth though. All that growth can come out tax free, so the longer it can be compounded and grow the better.

You've already paid the tax upfront to do the conversion and you want your beneficiaries to have the longest time possible to keep it growing tax free.

In fact, the driving force behind many older people converting is the ability of their beneficiaries to stretch out tax-free distributions over their lives. They might never live long enough on their own to make the conversion profitable, but by incorporating the next generation into the mix, it becomes a great planning strategy and wealth transfer vehicle.

All that planning is for naught though, if there's no beneficiary form and the account has to be withdrawn in five years after death.

Check that new beneficiary forms are in place for all new Roth accounts created, and check the beneficiary forms for your existing Roth accounts, and all your IRAs and 401(k)s for that matter.

2. 60-Day Rollover Mistakes

Technically, when you convert to a Roth IRA – that is a rollover. It's a rollover from your IRA – or plan – to a Roth IRA. And that means you have to follow the IRA rollover rules.

Like any transfer between retirement accounts, the best way to move money from an IRA to a Roth IRA is by trustee-to-trustee transfer (a direct transfer).

But some company plans or IRA custodians don't offer this option, or you might not know to ask about it.

Instead, they will simply write a check to you and if they do, you now have triggered several rollover problems that could have been avoided if you simply did the direct transfer from your IRA to your Roth IRA.

If the distribution is made to you, you have only 60 days to re-deposit those funds to your Roth IRA.

If you miss the 60-day deadline, then the funds become taxable and are no longer eligible to be converted. They would have been taxable anyway if you converted them, but now you're paying the tax and you can't convert the funds because you didn't complete the conversion within the 60 days.

The only fix for this is a private letter ruling, and those can be both costly and time consuming – and even then, there is no guarantee that IRS will rule favorably.

If the bank or your financial institution insists on giving you a check rather than doing the direct transfer to your Roth IRA, then one way to avoid this problem altogether is to see if they will make the check payable, not to you personally , but instead to your new Roth IRA. Such a check would be considered a direct transfer and would not fall under the 60-day rule.

Eliminate these complications and potential tax traps and do your Roth conversion as a direct trustee-to-trustee transfer.

3. Partial Conversions Involving After-Tax Money – The Pro-Rata Rule

What if you have after-tax funds in your IRA and you want to convert part or all of your IRA funds to your Roth IRA?

After-tax funds in your IRA mean that those funds have already been taxed and should not be taxed again when you convert.

After-tax funds in your IRA can come from two sources.

Nondeductible IRA contributions you have made or from after-tax funds rolled into your IRA from your company plan, like your 401(k).

Your IRA is subject to something called the pro-rata rule, which applies when your IRA includes some after-tax funds.

If you have no after-tax funds in your IRA, this rule does not apply to you, because all the IRA money you convert is 100% taxable, so there is no allocation.

But if your IRA does contain after-tax funds, then this pro-rata rule applies. It basically states that you cannot just convert the after-tax IRA funds and pay no tax, even if they are all in a separate IRA. For this rule, all of your IRAs are considered one big IRA.

The pro-rata rule states that when you take a withdrawal from your IRA, for example, to convert it to a Roth IRA, part of that distribution will be tax free and part will be taxable depending on how much of your IRA contains after-tax funds.

It's a percentage. If for example, you have a total IRA balance of $100,000 and that balance includes $20,000 of after-tax funds, then any distributions from that IRA will be 20% tax free and 80% taxable. If for example you convert the entire $100,000 IRA to your Roth IRA, $20,000 will be tax free and $80,000 will be taxable.

If you convert only say $30, 000, then $6,000 (20%) will be tax free and $24,000 (80%) will be taxable.

You want to make sure that you are not paying tax on the after-tax funds when you convert them, since you already paid tax on that money.

And you want to make sure you pay the correct amount of tax on the conversion to avoid future IRS problems.

So remember this pro-rata rule when converting from your IRA to your Roth IRA if you have after-tax funds in your IRA.

If you are converting from your company plan – say your 401(k) – and there are after-tax funds in your 401(k), there is a different rule that actually allows you to roll your plan's taxable funds to an IRA and then convert your plan's after-tax funds to a Roth IRA tax free.

In this case the rules are tricky and you should review them with both your financial consultants and your company plan to see if you're eligible to convert your plan money to a Roth IRA and how to properly allocate and take your distribution to maximum benefit, for example to be able to convert the part of your plan distribution that is after-tax funds, tax free to a Roth IRA.

4. Required minimum distributions cannot be converted – It's the law

Required minimum distributions from your IRA are not eligible rollover distributions. Only eligible rollover distributions can be converted. Your required minimum distribution must be taken before converting.

If you are subject to required minimum distributions, for example after age 70½, then the first dollars withdrawn from your IRA are deemed to be your required minimum distribution, until that amount is satisfied. Once the required minimum distribution is withdrawn, then the remaining IRA balance can be converted.

For example, if your required minimum distribution amount is $7,000, then the first $7,000 you withdraw from your IRA cannot be converted, but then any of the remaining balance can be converted, but only for the rest of the year, since next year you will also have a required minimum distribution.

Once you take your required amount, then you can convert the rest in that year.

Here's another example

A 78 year old with a $100,000 IRA would be required to withdraw almost $5,000 for the year. So he could only convert the remaining $95,000 that year. He would owe tax on the full $100,000 distribution – the $95,000 converted plus the $5,000 required minimum distribution.

Mistakenly "converting" a required minimum distribution could result in an excess contribution to the Roth and would result in a 6% excise penalty for each year it remained in the account.

Although the required minimum distribution itself cannot be converted – that's just the law – once those funds have been withdrawn, they are no longer IRA funds and you can use them pay the tax on any additional funds you want to convert to a Roth IRA. Or if you qualify for a Roth IRA contribution, say you're still working, you can use those funds to contribute to your Roth IRA, up to the annual limit – but they cannot be converted.

5. Some Funds are Not Eligible to be converted to a Roth IRA

You might think that just because anyone can convert, it means that anyone can convert anything! Not so. The tax code allows only eligible rollover distributions to be converted to Roth IRAs. That means that besides required minimum distributions, which we now know cannot be converted – that was my 4th Roth conversion caution – remember? – There are other items that cannot be converted and you should know them.

How about cash? You can't simply take $100,000 from the bank or from the sale of an asset and convert it to a Roth IRA. That $100,000 is not an eligible rollover distribution. It didn't come from your IRA or company plan.

You may be able to contribute those funds up to the annual limit to a Roth IRA, if you qualify, but you cannot just take gobs of money and convert that to a Roth IRA.

Regardless of where the funds come from though, if excess or ineligible amounts end up in a Roth IRA, they will be subject to the 6% excise tax for excess contributions for each year they remain there.

There are some other items that cannot be converted.

An inherited IRA cannot be converted to an inherited Roth IRA.

However, an inherited company plan can be converted to an inherited Roth IRA, so go figure how that came to be.

Non-spouse plan beneficiaries who convert inherited plan balances to an inherited Roth IRA must be aware that the funds cannot go into their own Roth IRA.

They must go to a properly titled inherited Roth IRA. The name of the deceased plan participant must be in the title of the account, and the title must also indicate that it is an inherited Roth IRA. The beneficiary cannot make contributions to this inherited Roth IRA.

Let your beneficiaries know that if they inherit your IRA, they cannot convert it to a Roth IRA.

However, if your spouse inherits your IRA he or she can convert it to her own Roth IRA, but a non-spouse beneficiary, like your child cannot do this.

All IRAs, including SEP IRAs and SIMPLE IRAs, are eligible for conversion to a Roth IRA. But unlike a traditional IRA or SEP IRA that can be converted anytime without penalty (even for those under 59½), SIMPLE IRAs present a dangerous trap.

SIMPLE IRAs have a two-year holding period. The two year clock is unique to each participant and starts once they have made their first contribution. Funds that leave a SIMPLE IRA in the first two years are treated as a taxable distribution that is NOT eligible for rollover other than to another SIMPLE IRA.

They cannot be converted to a Roth IRA. In addition, if the employee is under age 59½ at the time of the distribution, the 10% early distribution penalty is increased to 25%; unless an exception to the penalty applies.

If you have a SIMPLE IRA and want to convert it to a Roth IRA, make sure you wait out the 2-year period to avoid this costly error.

6. The 10% Penalty Trap

The 10% early withdrawal penalty applies when funds are withdrawn from an IRA before age 59½ and no exception applies (age 55 for a plan, if separation from service occurred at age 55 or older). The Roth conversion is an exception to the 10% early withdrawal penalty.

IRA or plan funds withdrawn at any age are not subject to the 10% penalty if those funds are converted to a Roth IRA, but two tax traps can still trigger the 10% penalty.

One of these traps is if some of the funds withdrawn are used to pay the conversion tax. That's a bad move. Since funds used to pay the conversion tax are not actually converted to the Roth, they will be subject to the 10% penalty in addition to income tax.

The second trap occurs when funds converted to the Roth are withdrawn within the first five years and the Roth IRA owner is still under age 59½. You can't avoid the 10% penalty by first converting to a Roth IRA and then withdrawing converted Roth funds to pay the tax. In general, using IRA funds to pay a conversion tax isn't worth it, but paying a 10% penalty makes this a terrible and costly tax move.

In addition to being a poor tax move, paying the conversion tax from the IRA funds means that less of the Roth conversion can be recharacterized – undone – since only funds that are actually converted to a Roth can be recharacterized.

There can also be a different type of 10% Roth conversion caution. It involves withholding tax on a Roth conversion. This can be a trap.

When you convert your IRA to a Roth IRA you generally don't want any of that IRA distribution withheld for taxes because then those withheld funds cannot be converted and you still pay tax on them.

Some financial institutions though require you to opt out of the 10% withholding on an IRA distribution. If you don't know to opt out, they will withhold 10% of your IRA distribution and now you'll only have 90% of the money to convert.

The remaining 10% will still be taxable but you can't convert it. You would then need to make up the shortage from other funds you may have and get that amount converted to your Roth IRA within 60 days. If you miss the boat on this, and you also happen to be under age 59½, the withheld amount could be subject to penalty, in addition to the tax.

Make sure to opt out of any withholding on an IRA distribution that you want to convert to your Roth IRA.

7. The Loss of Tax Benefits in the Year of Conversion

This one is not so much a trap but a reminder that when you convert to a Roth IRA, you increase your income and that could mean the loss of other tax benefits, like deductions, credits and exemptions. A conversion could also increase the tax on your social security, but again that only happens in the year of the conversion, so that is the one year price of admission.

Under the tax code, there are a slew of tax benefits that get phased out or otherwise eliminated as income increases. When choosing to make a Roth conversion, you should take this into account, but still I wouldn't let it deter you from doing the Roth conversion, because you are converting for the long term tax-free build up.

The short term cost will become insignificant over time in comparison to the long term benefits you receive.

One strategy to minimize the impact of the Roth conversion is to do partial conversions – a little at a time over several years.

That could help you keep below the various income limits where the tax benefits start to phase out or where new taxes start to kick in.

Potential Loss of Financial Aid

One non-tax item that you might want to also consider is the possible loss of financial aid, due to your increased income for the year of your Roth conversion.

A Roth conversion will cause a spike in income for the year or years where the income is included. While this additional income is an aberration and does not represent typical income levels, it can cause a loss of valuable financial aid.

Parents of students who are receiving, or who hope to receive, financial aid may want to hold off on converting until their child no longer needs assistance.

Those are my 7 Roth conversion cautions.

One more important big caution though

Keep track of your Roth recharacterization date.

It's October 15th of the year after you convert. The ability to undo a Roth conversion well after the fact is a key part of the Roth conversion planning process. It's a second chance to get this perfect.

Don't miss this date.

For example, if you converted to a Roth IRA anytime in 2016, you have until October 15, 2017 to undo that conversion like it never happened, or you could undo part of it to get you to the exact amount of the conversion you want to keep.

Make a note of your Roth recharacterization deadline.

Well that was a ton of Roth conversion information. Go back and review it as often as you wish so you can make the right choice and steer clear of any tax traps on your Roth conversion.

You now have all of the information you need to make the right choice on whether to convert to a Roth IRA.

Choose wisely – and consult your tax and financial advisors before making this important financial decision.

DVD
2016 Retirement Tax Update

Yes, once again Congress, the Courts and IRS have made several changes to the retirement tax rules that you need to know. Some of these items were in effect for 2015 and some go into effect in 2016.

Even the Social Security rules changed for 2016, eliminating some of the benefit options.

The tax rules are constantly changing, so for the latest updates, go to my website at **www.irahelp.com**

Social Security – Two Strategies are Phased-Out

The new changes regarding your Social Security benefits are a big deal since this is a major source of retirement income for many.

The budget bill signed into law in November 2015 changed Social Security planning for millions. I cover this in more detail in the separate DVD on Social Security planning included in this Program Guide, but this is too important to leave out of this 2016 Retirement Tax Update, so here are key items you need to know.

Two key Social Security claiming strategies designed to increase your benefits have been **_eliminated_**.

The file-and-suspend strategy is eliminated, effective for suspension requests submitted after May 1, 2016.

Instead of family members being allowed to receive a benefit off of your earnings record after you've merely _filed_, the new law makes it necessary for you to actually be _receiving_ benefits for them to do so.

So if you are planning to use the file-and-suspend strategy as part of your planning, you are faced with a more difficult choice.

On one hand, you could hold off on receiving your own benefit until as late as 70. That would make your benefit as large as possible, but would prevent other family members from receiving benefits based on your earnings until that time.

On the other hand, you could begin receiving benefits sooner. That would reduce your benefit, but would also allow other eligible family members to claim a benefit off of your earnings record sooner.

Another strategy, ***the Restricted Application Strategy, will also be eliminated.*** You may be eligible to receive a retirement benefit based on your own earnings record and a spousal benefit based on the earnings record of your husband or wife.

By filing a restricted application, you are essentially telling Social Security "pay me *only* my spousal Social Security benefit, not my own retirement benefit."

By utilizing this approach, you can receive at least some Social Security benefits, while still allowing your own retirement benefit to earn delayed credits until as late as 70. At that time, you could switch over to your own, higher, benefit. But the restricted application strategy has been eliminated for most.

You will no longer be able to file solely for your spousal benefits while allowing your own benefit to continue to compound and grow. However, you will be grandfathered into the old rules if you turned age 62 by the end of 2015 (technically, if you turn 62 on January 1, 2016, you will also qualify).

If you turn age 62 afterwards, you will be deemed to be simultaneously applying for ***both*** your retirement and spousal benefit when you apply, regardless of the benefit for which you're actually applying.

You would not be able to file solely for your spousal benefits while allowing your own benefit to continue to compound and grow. Instead, you would be forced to either wait until as late as age 70 to receive a higher benefit, but receive nothing in the interim, or you could begin receiving smaller benefits sooner. Neither option is as attractive as the restricted application strategy was.

These changes limit your claiming choices and make it more likely that your best option now to receive the largest monthly checks is to hold off claiming your benefits until age 70, if you can. That may mean working longer, reducing expenses or using other savings until age 70, when your higher Social Security benefits kick in.

For more detail on these new rules and other Social Security claiming strategies, go to the section of this Program Guide on Social Security, "***Getting the Most Out of Your Social Security and Retirement Benefits.***"

Given the new more restrictive rules, you'll want to learn all you can on this to maximize your benefits.

The New MyRA Retirement Account

Do these words interest you?

Safe

Affordable

No risk of losing money

No fees or costs

Guaranteed principal protection – backed by the United States Treasury

That's the new MyRA account.

In November 2015, the US Treasury expanded access to the new retirement account called a MyRA which is My R A or My Retirement Account. It's a new account created for those just starting to save for retirement, so this might be good to mention to your children or grandchildren just beginning to save for retirement. It's perfect for new savers with modest earnings from wages or self-employment income.

MyRAs have no fees, no risk of losing principal and no minimum balance or contribution requirements. These accounts remove the common barriers to saving, and give people an easy way to get started.

The Treasury Department has expanded the ways you can fund a MyRA, making these accounts an option for millions more savers nationwide. Originally, you could only open a MyRA if your employer offered direct deposit of your paycheck.

You can now also fund your MyRA from your checking or savings account or direct all or part of your federal tax refund to your MyRA when you file your taxes.

The MyRA is now available to all workers with just a few restrictions. It is a special type of Roth IRA. That means that all the normal rules for Roth IRAs will apply to MyRAs as well.

For instance, you need earnings from work to qualify. MyRA contributions will be limited to $5,500 per year or $6,500 per year for those ages 50 or older (though in reality, few who can afford to make contributions in these amounts are likely to use MyRAs – They would probably simply use Roth IRAs).

In addition, the Roth IRA contribution income limits will apply, but those limits are so high that lower income workers looking to fund MyRAs will qualify.

Furthermore, MyRA contributions will be coordinated with the overall annual Roth and IRA contribution limit, so you cannot fund both a Roth IRA and a MyRA with $5,500 each, since the overall limit is $5,500.

MyRA contributions, like other Roth IRA contributions will not be tax deductible, but contributions may be withdrawn at any time tax and penalty free. Earnings generally can be withdrawn tax and penalty free as well after five years and reaching age 59½.

A MyRA account can have a maximum balance of $15,000 or a lower balance for up to 30 years. When either of these limits is reached, the money is transferred to a Roth IRA. You can also choose to transfer or roll over your MyRA into a Roth IRA at any time.

MyRAs will be invested in a new United States Treasury security, which will earn interest at the same variable rate as investments in the government securities fund for federal employees. This investment is backed by the United States Treasury and the account carries no risk of losing principal. It will never decline in value.

The biggest benefactors of the new MyRA will be young savers just starting out in the workforce and those with very modest incomes who can't afford to save much, but also can't afford to lose anything.

That's because, in addition to the opportunity to withdraw contributions at any time without a tax or penalty, the MyRA will offer two big benefits.

First, there are the no minimum contribution limits. MyRAs can be opened with an initial contribution as low as a few dollars a month. This gives those with even very modest income the ability to contribute at least something in each pay period.

Secondly, the Treasury Department has said that there will be no maintenance or custodial fees for the MyRA that might otherwise eat into small contributions made to privately held accounts.

To learn more or to establish a MyRA, visit the Treasury Department's website at **www.myra.gov.**

Supreme Court Ruling Grants Rights to Same-Sex Marriage

In a landmark 2015 case, the United States Supreme Court ruled that the US Constitution guarantees a right to same-sex marriage.

The Court ruled that the 14th Amendment requires that states license same-sex couples to marry and recognize same-sex marriages lawfully performed in other states. This was the ***Obergefell*** case. Same-sex couples who are legally married under state law were already recognized as married for federal tax purposes after the ***Windsor*** case in 2013 and subsequent IRS guidance. But now, all states must license same-sex couples to marry and recognize same-sex marriages lawfully performed in other states.

Although the *Windsor* decision was a big step forward for same-sex couples in terms of marriage equality, the decision didn't offer an opinion as to whether or not states had to allow same-sex couples to get married. It simply said that the federal government had to follow a state's lead.

In *Obergefell*, the Supreme Court took it a step further. Now, states still are vested with the rights to determine marriage law, but those laws cannot discriminate against same-sex couples. No laws can conflict with the U.S. Constitution.

It's important to remember the *Obergefell* decision relates to married couples and married couples only.

In some states that previously did not allow same-sex couples to marry (as well as some that did), such couples were sometimes able to enter into other legal relationships, such as domestic partnerships and civil unions, which afforded them various rights.

These relationships do not constitute a marriage, even if that relationship was afforded many of the same rights as marriage at the state level.

Now, under the new ruling, more same-sex couples will have access to lifetime IRA benefits such as spousal contributions and the ability to use the Joint Life Expectancy Table to calculate required minimum distributions. More same-sex spouse IRA beneficiaries will be able to complete a spousal rollover and enjoy special rules for inherited IRAs.

More same-sex couples will have access to qualified plan benefits, including spousal protection under ERISA and the QDRO (Qualified Domestic Relations Orders) exception to the 10% penalty in divorce situations.

For some married same-sex couples, the most significant positive impact of the decision will be on Social Security. They are now able to qualify for benefits that were previously denied to them in some states.

They can now take advantage of federal tax benefits such as married-joint tax rates (although that can sometimes cause a higher tax with the so called "marriage penalty").

Legally married same-sex couples MUST file their taxes as either married-joint or married-separate federal returns, but they can no longer file as two single individuals.

Key estate planning benefits that married same-sex couples gain include favorable estate and gift tax treatment, enhanced guardianship and adoption rights, and greater ability to make medical and end-of-life decisions.

Legally married same-sex couples are able to use estate tax portability to make use of each spouse's estate or gift exemption. They can make unlimited property transfers to their spouse free of gift or estate tax.

They can take advantage of all the federal tax planning benefits for married couples that I mentioned in this 2016 retirement tax planning update.

More Public Safety Employees Qualify for Penalty-Free Access to Their Retirement Savings

Two New Tax Laws Expanded the 10% Early Distribution Penalty for Public Safety Employees

Two tax laws, a trade bill signed into law in June 2015, and the extenders bill, signed into law in December 2015, included provisions that will allow more public safety officials to take early distributions without penalty from more of their government-sponsored retirement plans. These changes are effective for 2016 and beyond.

Early distributions from retirement plans are generally subject to an IRS 10% early distribution penalty. However, there are a number of exceptions to this penalty. Of course, not all exceptions apply to all types of retirement plans.

Currently, the law provides an exception to the 10% early distribution penalty for withdrawals from company retirement plans for individuals who separate from service at age 55 or older.

For obvious reasons, this is commonly referred to as "the age 55 exception." Another, less publicized exception, known as the "age 50 exception," is available for some public safety officials.

Now remember, ***these early distributions are still subject to income tax***. The exceptions I am referring to here are only for the 10% penalty, not the tax, but that still can provide much needed savings for some.

Certain public safety officials, such as state and local policemen, firemen and EMS workers, who separate from service at age 50 or older, are exempt from the 10% early distribution penalty. The exception applies only to distributions from these workers' government-sponsored defined benefit (pension) plans.

The exception is not available for distributions from IRAs or from other plans.

For instance, a public safety employee who has an IRA and a governmental defined benefit plan may qualify to take a penalty-free distribution from their defined benefit plan at age 50, but any distribution from the IRA would be subject to the penalty (unless another exception applied).

The new laws expand the definition of "public safety official." Under prior law, public safety officials only included state or local public safety employees. Federal public safety workers, even those who had essentially the same jobs as their state and local counterparts, were not eligible.

The first change to this provision in 2015 largely resolved this obvious discrepancy, expanding the term public safety worker to include federal law enforcement officers and firefighters. Other federal workers, such as certain customs officials, border protection officers and air traffic controllers were also given the ability to use the exception.

The second change, made in December of 2015, further expanded that list to include certain nuclear materials couriers, or any member of the U.S. Capitol Police, Supreme Court Police or diplomatic security special agent of the State Department.

As a result of the 2015 changes, the age 50 exception is also expanded to include distributions from governmental defined contribution plans. Previously, the exception applied only to distributions taken from governmental defined benefit plans.

This will allow not only federal public safety employees, but also state and local public safety workers to access a wider range of retirement plans without penalty after retiring at age 50.

To qualify for this exception, your distribution will have to occur in 2016 or later, but your separation from your company **must have occurred in the year you turned age 50 or older**.

It's generally best not to tap into retirement funds early, but if you do need the money and this new exception to the 10% early distribution penalty applies to you, it's good to know that you can access your company plan retirement funds penalty free. The funds you withdraw of course are still taxable, but no 10% penalty if you qualify for the new exception.

ABLE Accounts

ABLE = Achieve a Better Living Experience

Tax-Favored Savings Accounts for Families with Disabled or Special Needs Children.

If this does not apply to you, please pass this valuable information on to someone you know who can benefit from this.

A new account called an ABLE account was created by Congress and was passed into law late in 2014.

ABLE is an acronym that stands for **Achieve a Better Living Experience**

What are ABLE accounts?

ABLE accounts are a brand new type of tax-favored savings account created to benefit young disabled people. They are not taken into account for qualifying for federal welfare benefit programs.

ABLE accounts – also known as 529A accounts – have begun to be provided by certain states in a manner similar to the way states operate 529 plans for education savings.

Since these accounts are still relatively new, not all states have established ABLE account programs, but many that currently do not offer programs will be establishing them in the years and months ahead.

Furthermore, if a disabled person's home state does not offer an ABLE account, as a result of a change in the law in late 2015, an ABLE account may be established for that beneficiary using any other state's program. Keep in mind, however, that a person can generally only have one ABLE account established for their benefit. Multiple ABLE accounts are generally not allowed.

In order to qualify for an ABLE account, an individual must have a significant physical or mental impairment that severely limits their ability to function. In addition, the impairment must be expected to result in the person's death or, at the very least, be expected to last continuously for a period of 12 months or more. Blindness can also be used to qualify for an ABLE account.

There is also an age requirement for ABLE accounts. Regardless of the condition an individual uses to qualify, the condition must occur before the person turns 26 years old.

ABLE Contributions

Contributions to ABLE accounts must be made in cash. Cash includes actual cash, as well as check, money order or even credit card payments.

Contributions to an individual's ABLE account can be made by anyone, but the total contributions made by all individuals on behalf of one ABLE account owner are limited to the annual gift tax exemption amount.

For 2016, that amount is $14,000, per year. In the event that an ABLE account receives more contributions than is allowed during a single year, the excess contributions (along with any attributable earnings/losses) must be returned to the contributors on a last-in, first-out basis.

If this return of excess is not completed by October 15th of the year after the contribution, then the ABLE account owner will be assessed a 6% excess contribution penalty for each year the contribution remains in the account.

ABLE Distributions

Distributions from ABLE accounts that are used to pay for qualified disability expenses are completely tax-free. If, however, distributions are not used to pay for qualified distributions, the earnings portion of the distribution will be taxable and subject to a 10% penalty.

Qualifying ABLE Expenses

The list of expenses that can potentially qualify as qualified disability expenses is fairly liberal, including education, housing, transportation, employment training and support, assistive technology and related services, personal support services, health, prevention and wellness, financial management and administrative services, legal fees, expenses for oversight and monitoring, and funeral and burial expenses. These are all in included in the tax rules as well as other expenses that may be identified in future guidance published by IRS.

ABLE accounts remaining after the owner's death will first be used to repay State-provided funds. So in some cases, beneficiaries of these accounts will not receive any benefits, even when a balance remained at death.

Up to $100,000 can be accumulated within an ABLE account without impacting any means-tested federal programs (other than housing expense distributions under SSI). If a beneficiary's ABLE account exceeds $100,000, then their SSI will be suspended, but their Medicaid treatment will remain unaffected.

As with any tax-related program, there are more technical rules that must be followed, but this is a good starting point.

There are some drawbacks and in some cases you might still be better served with a special needs trust where much larger sums can be saved, but the special needs trust is not as tax efficient. ABLE accounts are not required to file tax returns (like trusts are), and the income earned in the account will generally not be subject to income taxes.

Make sure you discuss this with a knowledgeable attorney, tax or financial advisor before going ahead with the new ABLE accounts or using special needs trusts.

The main thing here is that you know this exists. It's new.

Now I want to remind you of some recent retirement tax rule changes that have **already been in effect since 2015** – you need to know these:

The Once-per-year IRA Rollover Rule

This is a major shift in the law which began in 2015 so be very careful when you are moving your IRA money

The once per year IRA rollover rule states that you can only do one 60-day rollover per year from your IRAs – that's not a calendar year – it's 12 months or 365 days.

In the past – before 2015 – if you had separate IRAs, this rule applied separately to each IRA – so you could possibly do several 60-day rollovers within a year from different IRAs.

But that is not the rule anymore due to a major tax court case that decided the issue. Now the once-per-year IRA rollover rule applies to *all* your IRAs, not to each one separately. The new stricter interpretation of the once-per-year IRA rollover rule states that you can only do one IRA rollover per year, 365 days.

If you do a second IRA rollover of your taxable IRA funds within the 365 days, that is a taxable distribution and it cannot be fixed. It cannot be rolled over. If you happen to be under age 59½ it can also be subject to a 10% early withdrawal penalty. This is a fatal tax mistake and cannot be fixed. You've lost your IRA.

Don't do these 60-day rollovers. Instead do only direct, trustee-to-trustee transfers when moving IRA funds from one IRA to another. These strict rollover rules do not apply to direct IRA transfers. You can do as many of these direct transfers as you wish.

I'll say it again – Do only direct trustee-to-trustee transfers when moving IRA money.

The new rules state that Traditional and Roth IRAs are combined for purposes of the once-per-year rule.

For example, if you do a 60-day IRA rollover from one of your traditional IRAs to another, you can't do another 60-day rollover from *any* of your IRAs or Roth IRAs for the next 12 months.

Checks made directly to receiving IRAs will qualify as trustee-to-trustee transfers, so that will be ok if the check is not made out to you, but to the new IRA instead.

Don't violate this rule. IRS has no authority to provide relief.

The once-per-year rule only applies when you are moving your IRA money from one IRA to another IRA or from one Roth IRA to another Roth IRA.

There are Exceptions:
Trustee-to-trustee transfers don't count
Rollovers from plans to IRAs, don't count, and vice versa
And Roth conversions don't count

Be careful when moving your IRA money. I don't want you to lose it to this new strict tax rule. I've already heard several horror stories, and some of them from financial advisors who were not up on the new rules.

After-Tax Plan Funds Can be Converted to Roth IRAs Tax Free

If you have after-tax funds in your 401(k), you now may be able to convert those funds to your Roth IRA tax free.

New IRS rules state that if you have both pre-tax and after-tax funds in your 401(k) and you are eligible for a distribution from your plan, you can roll the pre-tax funds to your traditional IRA tax free. They'll be taxed later when withdrawn from your traditional IRA. And then you can convert the after-tax funds in your plan, tax free to a Roth IRA.

For example, let's say you have $100,000 in your 401(k) plan. Assume that $80,000 of those funds were your pre-tax funds (not yet been taxed) and $20,000 of those funds are after-tax funds (already taxed funds).

If you were eligible for a distribution from your plan, say when you retire, you can do a direct rollover of the $80,000 tax free to a traditional IRA and then convert the $20,000 of after-tax funds to a Roth IRA, tax free.

Your plan has to make the allocation for you.

What you *cannot* do is simply withdraw only the after-tax funds from your plan and convert those funds to your Roth IRA and pay no tax, while leaving pre-tax funds in your 401(k).

Be careful though, the process involves tax rules and you should only do this after consulting with competent tax or financial advisors and run this by your company plan administrators to make sure these rollovers and conversions are done correctly under the tax law.

One more thing. ***These new rules do not apply to IRA distributions***. If you have after-tax funds in your IRA, any IRA distributions will still follow the pro-rata rule, where every IRA withdrawal is a percentage taxable and tax free.

QLACs – Q-L-A-C-s, stands for Qualifying Longevity Annuity Contracts

QLACs are a new type of retirement annuity that became effective July 2, 2014.

As I always say, life is short, but retirement may be long and you don't want to run out of money.

There's a relatively new type of annuity product that can provide income if you live a long life, and it includes benefits for IRAs. In its most simple terms, a longevity annuity begins paying you income at an advanced age, say at 85, for the rest of your life.

The theory is that if you live that long, you could run out of money by then, so this income kicks in just at that time.

Qualifying Longevity Annuity Contracts – QLACs – are fixed annuities that offer insurance against living too long and outliving your money

QLAC distributions must start by age 85.

There are IRA benefits for QLACs.

With IRAs, once you reach age 70½ you need to begin taking your required minimum distributions. Those are calculated on your IRA balance.

But if you have a longevity annuity that won't start paying you income until age 85, you still must include the value of that annuity in your total IRA balance you use to calculate your required minimum distributions, even though you won't access those funds until age 85.

That increases your required minimum distributions each year, increasing your current taxes and leaving you less in your IRA growing tax- deferred.

QLACs solve that problem. The QLAC value is NOT included in your IRA balance when calculating your IRA and plan required minimum distributions.

But there are limits to this benefit.

Your QLAC amount is limited to the lesser of 25% of your retirement funds or $125,000.

The QLAC must be fixed annuities. Variable annuities, equity-indexed annuities and similar products will not qualify.

And the QLAC may not offer any commutation benefit, cash surrender value or similar feature.

QLACs are not for Roth IRAs because Roth IRAs don't have required minimum distributions – so there is no problem with that here.

You could still have longevity annuities in your Roth IRA if you wish, but they won't specifically be QLACs under the new law.

Once again, do not go ahead with QLACs without consulting a financial advisor. These are new products, so even some financial advisors might not be up to speed on them yet.

Inherited IRAs are NOT Protected in Bankruptcy Under Federal Law

Are you worried that your children or other beneficiaries might lose your IRA money when they inherit it? Maybe to bad financial decisions, lawsuits, divorce or even bankruptcy?

Well now it may even be worse and you should know about this new development with inherited IRAs.

In June 2014, the U.S. Supreme Court ruled unanimously that inherited IRAs are not protected in bankruptcy under federal law. This is now the law of the land.

Some states have bankruptcy protection for inherited IRAs, but not many.

If you are worried about this, you might want to look into naming a trust as your IRA beneficiary in order to protect the funds your heirs inherit, from lawsuits, creditors, ex-spouses, bankruptcy or even themselves.

But IRA trusts, as they are known, have several drawbacks, mainly the complex tax rules and the high trust tax rates.

So the problem is, is it worth it to pay high trust taxes in order to protect the inherited IRA funds from creditors. It might not be, but there are at least 3 possible solutions.

1. **Use Conduit IRA trusts**

   This is a special type of IRA trust that passes annual required minimum distributions from the inherited IRA directly through the IRA trust and to the trust beneficiaries, so that no inherited IRA funds are retained in the trust. This eliminates the trust tax problem, but it does pass a minor amount of IRA funds to your beneficiaries each year that cannot be protected. That's not a bad trade off and I recommend using the conduit IRA trust for inherited IRAs that need the trust protection.

2. **Roth conversions**

   Your beneficiaries cannot convert an inherited IRA to a Roth IRA, but you can convert your own IRA to a Roth IRA during your lifetime. You'll have to pay the tax to convert, but then you leave your Roth IRA to your trust and eliminate the trust tax problem even if the inherited Roth IRA funds are retained in the trust – to protect it for your beneficiaries. The required distributions from the inherited Roth IRA paid to the trust will be tax free.

3. **Life Insurance**

   Instead of leaving your IRA to a trust, turn it into tax-free life insurance first. You could withdraw your taxable IRA funds down and pay the tax, and then use the remaining funds to purchase life insurance. Then leave the life insurance proceeds to the trust. That would eliminate the trust tax problem even if funds were retained in the trust, since the life insurance would be income tax free. Better yet, the insurance also eliminates all the complicated IRA tax and trust rules. Life insurance is a much more trust-friendly asset than an IRA – both tax-wise and creditor protection wise.

That's it for my 2016 Retirement Tax Update. There is plenty here that you and your family may benefit from.

Remember that when it comes to tax planning for retirement, it's what you keep that counts, after taxes, so take advantage of all you can, by knowing all the latest tax rules.

And always consult with professional tax, legal and financial advisors when it comes to your tax and retirement planning.

DVD

How to Avoid the 5 Most Costly Stealth Taxes

5 Sneaky Taxes That Can Cut Into Your Retirement Savings

In the last few years there were several critical retirement tax rule changes that went mostly under the radar.

Although these are lesser known, they will impact most people with retirement savings.

You need to know how your retirement savings and other income are really being taxed. When it comes to retirement, it's all about what you can spend, that is, what you keep, after-taxes.

Since most retirement funds are tax-deferred as opposed to tax free, there is a cost to accessing your retirement savings whether they are in a traditional IRA or 401(k) or similar account.

Remember there is a huge difference between tax-deferred and tax-free.

All you need to know is that tax free is always better!

Our government constantly needs to raise taxes but no congressman wants to admit that they are raising your taxes, so what do they do? They raise them anyway in ways they hope you won't notice.

But I am going to make sure that you do!

Most of you have probably already noticed that your taxes in retirement are increasing but can't understand why, since Congress keeps telling us that they have not raised our taxes, or that they have even lowered our taxes.

The truth is that Congress can actually say that the tax rates have not increased, but since 2013, you may have been paying more. How can that be?

That's because they are actually raising taxes in ways they hope you won't notice.

Many of the biggest tax increases you're facing are hidden. These are items that tax professionals call **"stealth taxes"** because they are under the radar, so it is harder to see them coming and plan for them.

Instead of raising your tax rates, the actual tax you pay, depending on your income can still be more because of these so called "stealth taxes."

Stealth taxes are tax increases that result from taking away tax benefits, like deductions, exemptions and tax credits. These tax breaks that would normally reduce your tax bill, are now getting phased out, which in the end increases the actual amount of tax you pay.

Congress loves these "phase-outs" because it's a sneaky way of raising your taxes without saying they are raising taxes.

But the bottom line is you pay more, so to me that's a tax increase.

For example, required minimum distributions are one of the biggest generators of stealth taxes because they increase your income which sets a host of new stealth taxes in motion

The tax law that first took effect in 2013 was loaded with these stealth taxes – hidden tax increases – and they are now entrenched into the system.

The key to retirement tax planning for many years to come unfortunately comes down to what I call **Stealth Tax Management**.

Stealth taxes can have a long-term crippling effect on your retirement planning

It's not about the taxes or the rates we see. It's about the unfair tax increases that are camouflaged.

But we all have to deal with this and I will guide you through some tax tactics and strategies to reduce your exposure to these stealth taxes and help you keep more of your hard-earned retirement money.

First let me review the 5 biggest stealth taxes and then give you strategies to avoid them some other stealth taxes too. Remember that these began in 2013 so they still might be relatively new to some of you seeing them for the first time.

These are all based on income limits, many of which change each year. And for the most part, the stealth taxes target higher income people.

To see all the actual income amounts where these stealth taxes kick in, please refer to the companion piece – my printed 2016 Tax Update guide which is included with the gifts you received with this program.

All the specific dollar amount details are there, so you can use that to follow along as I go through the 5 big stealth taxes now.

Here are the 5 big stealth taxes you need to know:

1. The phase-out of personal exemptions

2. The reduction of itemized deductions

3. Increased tax on net investment income

4. Increased tax on earned income – Salary and self-employment income

5. The decrease in deductible medical expenses

In general, stealth taxes are essentially the loss of tax benefits depending on your income.

Like medical deductions – numerous types of tax credits and tax deductions – even ability to contribute to a Roth IRA are – based on income.

How much of your Social Security is taxable, Medicare Part B and D premiums – all based on income.

And of course, the most insidious of all – the Alternative Minimum Tax – which is,

as the name states – an alternate universe of taxation based on income and the amount of deductions claimed.

Stealth tax management in its simplest form comes down to keeping your income as low as possible for the long-term. I emphasize long-term because short-term solutions won't help.

Lowering income in one year might cause a bubble of income in the next year and cost you more in the long run. You need more permanent relief.

And that may mean raising your income initially to clean out the items that increase your income and trigger these stealth taxes each year – so you can benefit from lower taxable income and in turn much lower taxes in your retirement years. That's when you want to reap the benefits.

First let me explain the 5 biggest stealth taxes.

1. The phase-out of personal exemptions

These are the exemptions you get for yourself, your spouse and, perhaps, others that depend on you for support, like children.

Effective since 2013, these valuable exemptions are being phased out as your income increases beyond certain limits that change each year.

This can result in a 100% loss.

In other words:
When your income exceeds the upper phase-out limit based on your filing status, you lose 100% of your personal exemptions

---

2016 Personal Exemption Phase-Out Limits:

Phase-out of Personal Exemptions (up to 100%)

Impacts **married-joint** filers with AGI in excess of $311,300 and fully phased-out at $433,800

Impacts **individuals** (single) filers with AGI in excess of $259,400 and fully phased-out at $381,900

Impacts **Head of Household** filers with AGI in excess of $285,350 and fully phased-out at $407,850

You cannot avoid this phase-out with the typical itemized deductions – like the deductions for mortgage interest, state taxes or charitable contributions. That's because the income limit is based on your adjusted gross income which is calculated before being reduced by any of your itemized deductions. They already thought of that.

Losing personal exemptions increases your tax bill without raising your actual tax rate. That's what a stealth tax is.

2. The reduction of itemized deductions

This provision reduces your overall total of itemized deductions if you are over the income limit.

The reduction is 3% based on your Adjusted Gross Income.

So, for every dollar of income you have above your applicable threshold, you're going to lose three cents of itemized deductions. This 3 cents per dollar reduction can eliminate up to 80% of your itemized deductions!

The income limits for having your itemized deductions reduced are the same as the income thresholds for losing your personal exemptions, except that there is no total phase out.

2016 Itemized Deduction Phase-Out Limits:

3% of AGI reduction of overall itemized deductions (up to 80%)

Impacts:
Married-joint filers with AGI in excess of $311,300

Individuals filers with AGI in excess of $259,400

Head of Household filers with AGI in excess of $285,350

To make it even more complicated, there are certain itemized deductions such as medical expenses, casualty and theft losses, gambling losses and investment interest expense that are not affected by this limitation because they are subject to their own limitations.

The way it works is that once your income exceeds the income thresholds, your overall total of itemized deductions – other than the exceptions – will be reduced by 3% of the amount your income exceeds the income thresholds for your filing status.

For example, if your adjusted gross income exceeds your threshold amount by $100,000, then your itemized deductions will be reduced by $3,000, that's 3% of the $100,000 in excess of the income limit – but you cannot lose more than 80% of your itemized deductions.

Unlike the phase out of the personal exemptions which can lead to 100% of your exemptions being lost, the reduction in itemized deductions is limited to 80% which is still serious but that only would be the case for those with extremely high income – or those with very little in the way of itemized deductions to begin with.

But once again, this is a stealth tax that increases the actual tax you pay.

It's amazing how convoluted the tax law gets just to find a way to increase your tax without calling it a tax increase.

3. The additional tax on net investment income

Although the tax code includes a top ordinary income tax rate of 39.6% and a top long-term capital gains rate of 20%, this provision effectively increases those rates.

This is a 3.8% tax on net investment income. This raises the top ordinary tax rate from 39.6% to 43.4%. It can also raise lower income tax brackets.

It also raises the top long-term capital gain rate from 20% to 23.8%, the 15% capital gain rate too, can be increased to 18.8%.

To see the full impact here I have to veer off a bit to yet another income limit. Yes, believe it or not there is another income limit to see if you will hit the top 39.6% income tax rate and the long-term capital gain rate of 20%.

This is not only another income limit, but a different type of income.

Instead of adjusted gross income or modified adjusted gross income, this limit is based on taxable income. That's your income after exemptions and itemized deductions.

The top income and long term capital gain rates kick in when taxable income exceeds around $466,000 for married filing joint and $415,000 for singles.

These are the amounts where the top 39.6% income tax rates apply as well as the 20% long-term capital gain rates apply – but again these rates can be increased by the 3.8% tax on net investment income.

This is classic stealth tax since the stated 20% top long-term capital gain rate is paid by virtually no one. If you are subject to this rate, you are almost certainly going to be paying 23.8%, but you won't see that rate published anywhere – but you pay it.

Only those with high income will be affected by this 3.8% surtax.

But to keep this utterly confusing, high income for this provision is different from the definition of high income for the other two stealth taxes we've talked about so far, and different from the high income amounts for paying the top regular income and long-term capital gain rates.

For this provision, the threshold amounts are $250,000 for those filing married jointly and $200,000 for single taxpayers. If you file married-separate the limit is $125,000 for each spouse.

MAGI Threshold Amounts for 3.8% Surtax on Net Investment Income

Married Filing Joint	$ 250,000
Individuals	$ 200,000
Married Filing Separate	$ 125,000
Trusts and Estates	$ 12,400*

*The 3.8% surtax kicks in at much lower income levels for trusts that retain this income. The threshold for trusts and estates is the amount at which the top trust tax bracket takes effect. This amount is $12,400 in 2016. All other threshold amounts are NOT indexed for inflation.

The tax applies only to net investment income, not to your other income.

Investment income can include your interest, dividends, capital gains and other passive types of income (as opposed to earned income like wages) – don't worry there is a separate extra tax on earned income too – I'll get to that next.

To get to what "net" investment income is, you can deduct your investment related expenses from your investment income. These are items like investment management fees, brokerage fees, investment interest, financial advisor fees, expenses related to rental and royalty income and even a portion of state income tax related to the investment income.

As I said, the tax on net investment income does not apply to earned income like wages and self-employment income from a business. Luckily for retirees, the tax does not apply to distributions from retirement accounts like IRAs and 401(k)s, so Roth conversions will not be subject to this additional tax.

In addition, municipal bond interest, proceeds of Life Insurance Policies and Social Security and Veterans' Benefits are exempt from the tax.

3.8% Tax on Net Investment Income

For this provision, investment income includes:

Interest, Dividends, Capital Gains (long and short)

Annuities (but not annuities in IRAs or company plans)

Royalty Income

Passive Rental Income

Other Passive Activity Income

NOT Investment Income

Wages and Self-Employment Income

Active Trade or Business Income (including interest, dividends, capital gains)

Distributions from IRAs, Roth IRAs, and Company Plans
 – Including Net Unrealized Appreciation

Excluded Gain from the Sale of a Principal Residence

Municipal Bond Interest

Proceeds of Life Insurance Policies

Veterans' Benefits

Social Security Benefits

Gains on the Sale of an Active Interest in a Partnership or S Corporation

Taxable income from items that are *NOT* investment income can push taxpayers over the income threshold and cause investment income to be subject to the 3.8% surtax.

The really sneaky part is that although the extra 3.8% tax does not apply to some types of income, if they produce taxable income for regular income tax – like taxable IRA distributions, they still raise your income.

The increase in your income from these taxable income sources (which are not subject to the 3.8% extra tax) for example, required distributions from your IRA can trigger the 3.8% tax on net investment income – so in effect, even the income that is exempt from this tax can cause the tax to apply.

To review, the tax only applies to net investment income and only when your income exceeds the threshold amounts of $250,000 for married joint and $200,000 for singles.

If you have named a trust as your IRA beneficiary – and there are good reasons for that – the trust might call for certain portions of the inherited IRA required minimum distributions to be kept in the trust for a period of time.

If that's the case, what's the trustee going to do with those funds? Put them under a mattress? No! Chances are the trustee is going to invest those funds, producing interest, dividends, capital gains… you get the point.

And when you combine that income with any required minimum distributions the trust may take and hold, if the total is over around $12,000, the trust money will be eaten away, at least in part, by the 3.8% surtax in addition to regular income tax. You need to plan for that.

There are a few ways around this which I'll give you in a few minutes in the planning phase.

There is another version of this tax on net investment income and it is number 4 on my list of new stealth taxes.

4. Increased tax on earned income

If by some chance you think you may be out of the woods on this investment income tax since almost all of your income is from wages or self-employment – think again – you didn't really think our Congress would leave you out of the stealth tax game did you?

Remember when I said that the tax on net investment income did not apply to your salary or your self-employment income from a business?

Well that's because Congress created an additional tax on earned income to cover that.

It's a .9% surtax on earned income – that's point nine percent or almost one percent, so it's a bit less than the investment income tax of 3.8% but for many, especially those of you still working that have high earned income, it can apply to a much larger amount.

The income limits are the same as those for the net investment income tax, but the only income that counts here is earned income.

Technically this is an additional 0.9% Medicare tax on wages and self-employment income over the threshold amounts $250,000 for married-joint filers and the $200,000 for individuals. But the tax is only assessed on the amount of your wages or earned income over these amounts.

If you are single and your wages are $199,000 or $1,000 under the limit, then this tax does not apply to you. If your wages instead were $210,000 then the .9% extra tax would only apply to the $10,000 over the limit.

Now for the extra bad news – if you have both investment income and earned income over the limits, you can get hit with both taxes – though technically not on the same income.

5. The decrease in deductible medical expenses

This one can hurt those who have high out of pocket medical bills, and particularly those with high medical bills and high income.

When deductions are decreased, taxes are increased. This is a classic back-door or stealth tax increase.

Retirees generally have higher unreimbursed medical bills so this stealth tax increase hits retirees harder.

Effective for 2013 and later years, to deduct your medical expenses, they must now exceed 10% of your adjusted gross income (up from 7.5%). There is a temporary exception if you or your spouse is age 65 or older – then the higher 10% won't apply until 2017.

This stealth tax is the only one of the group that is not based on income. This affects everyone who pays taxes, even if you have low income – but the lower your income the less this provision will impact you.

The 10% limit also applies to the medical expense exception to the 10% penalty on early IRA or plan withdrawals – which only affects those under age 59½.

Those are the 5 stealth taxes you have to deal with. The strategy is to keep taxable income as low as possible to minimize the impact of these stealth taxes.

The big master plan is to lower your taxable retirement income by consistently moving your money to tax-free territory. However, that generally costs money, but I am telling you that this is money well spent if your income will subject you to higher taxes each year.

Use the right money to pay the cost of moving your money to tax-free territory.

You have to begin reducing assets that would be exposed to the stealth taxes and build a retirement fund that you can access tax free so your taxable income will stay low for life.

Remember that the price you pay to keep your taxable income low is paid only in the year or years you move those funds. From then on you can really make a dent in reducing your income taxes and the related stealth taxes by having your assets in tax-free containers.

But you have to take the long term view – to keep taxes low for your retirement years.

For example:

A Roth conversion – convert your traditional IRA to a Roth IRA.

That will only raise your income in the year of the conversion because you pay tax on the taxable amount of your conversion.

It's true that a Roth conversion could trigger some of the stealth taxes I just warned you about – but that is only for the year of the conversion. Look at what happens in the long run. Once converted, the funds in your Roth IRA are growing tax free.

Also, Roth IRAs have no required distributions during your lifetime, so if you don't need the money, the fund can continue to grow tax free.

Even if you did need to tap into some of that Roth money in retirement, the distributions for most people will be tax free – that means less chance of higher income taxes and stealth taxes for the rest of your retirement years. That's a great payoff for just one year of biting the bullet and doing the conversion.

You don't have to convert all of your IRA or other retirement funds to a Roth. If the tax hit is too big for you all in one year, then think amount making partial conversions over many years.

If you don't do the Roth conversion, then your IRA will continue to build tax-deferred and you'll be building a tax problem since you are forced to withdraw required distributions from your IRA after age 70½ and that will continue for the rest of your life or until you have no IRA funds left.

This means that you have a good chance of getting hit with stealth taxes as well as regular income taxes for all your retirement years. That's not a good plan.

Since a Roth conversion requires you to pay a tax on the taxable amount you convert, another strategy would be to **pay the tax from funds that would otherwise be exposed to these stealth taxes.**

For example, it might pay to sell some stocks (if you were going to sell them anyway during your lifetime) that will produce big capital gains and/ or dividends and be subject to the net investment income tax if your income is too high. That would also increase your current income for the year of sale but would remove the income from exposure to taxes for the rest of your life.

Also, if you really like the stock and believe it has great upside potential, then once you convert your IRA funds to your Roth IRA, you can buy the stock back in your Roth IRA. Then if the stock appreciates all of that appreciation is income tax free for life because it is in your Roth IRA. If the stock throws off great dividends, that's all tax free now too!

By using funds that would be subject to stealth taxes – in addition to regular income and capital gains taxes – for Roth conversions, you make out in two ways:

1 – You remove those assets from being exposed to future income and stealth taxes.

And

2 – You remove your IRA funds from future income tax exposure.

All the gains and income piling up in your Roth IRA are income tax free for life

All for taking the plunge for just one year – that's a valuable payoff.

One more point – with Roth conversions, for a limited time, you can get a do over if this is not working out for you. Let's say you decide that you don't want to pay the tax or you need the money or your investments tanked after you converted.

The tax law includes a provision called a Roth Recharacterization allowing you to undo part or all of your Roth conversion. You have until October 15th of the year after the conversion to undo all or any part of it for any reason at all.

For example, if you converted your IRA to a Roth IRA at any time in 2016, you have until October 15, of 2017 to undo your Roth conversion for any reason at all. That's a good tax opportunity and one you should consider with your tax or financial advisor.

In the long run, a current Roth conversion can reduce your taxable income for the rest of your life. You'll likely pay less tax and have more tax-free money to last longer during your retirement years.

Another strategy to reduce stealth tax exposure:

Leverage your IRA distributions to tax-free vehicles. Again, this means increasing income up front but really you are just changing pockets from taxable to tax free.

If you don't do this now, you will be forced to withdraw those taxable IRA funds after age 70½ when your balance and your tax rate might be higher – if taxes continue to go up – which is likely.

It's what I always advise – move your money from accounts that are forever taxed (like IRAs and taxable investments) to accounts that are never taxed (like Roth conversions and life insurance).

It's important that you review all of this information with your tax or financial advisors.

Similar to Roth conversions is the tax-free benefits of life insurance.

As I say on every program – just so you know you are receiving objective and unbiased advice.

I do not sell life insurance. I do not sell stocks, bonds funds, insurance, and annuities. I am a tax advisor.

But as a tax advisor, I am telling you that the biggest single benefit in the tax code is the tax exemption for life insurance. Life insurance is more valuable as tax laws begin to raise your taxes. And can be even more valuable at keeping your retirement income low to avoid the stealth taxes.

As long as you have enough funds to live on, don't hesitate to use retirement funds to pay for life insurance – or use other funds that if they went unused would just be exposed to the stealth taxes every year.

Remember my IRA Leverage Rule:
Use it, leverage it, or lose it to future taxes

One of the best ways to leverage your IRA is with life insurance. One dollar of IRAs produces many more dollars of tax-free life insurance.

Plus with permanent insurance, if you need to access your life insurance during your life, those funds will be tax free, keeping your retirement income low and avoiding those stealth taxes.

Once again, review this, and all these strategies with a professional insurance advisor.

Here are even more ways to lower your income and avoid the stealth taxes: .

Give to charity – that gives you a tax deduction. It also reduces your taxable income to see if the top income tax rates will apply, but it does not reduce your adjusted gross income for the other stealth taxes. But giving property away that throws off taxable income can reduce stealth and income taxes for the long term.

Give your IRA to charity – The charitable IRA rollover provision – a "qualified charitable distribution" (QCD) expired after 2014, but the 2015 Tax Act extended this provision permanently. The QCD was renewed retroactively for 2015 and made permanent for 2016 and all later years.

The QCD counts toward your annual required minimum distribution (up to the annual $100,000 limit).

Now that the tax law has made this provision permanent, you can plan with certainty, earlier in the year. If you are charitably-minded, the QCD provides you with a greater tax benefit. While you do not receive a tax deduction for your contribution, the direct transfer from your IRA to the charity is excluded from your income. This lowers your income and the actual cost of making the contribution.

You have to be age 70½ to take advantage of this, and this only applies to your IRA funds or inherited IRA funds.

Make gifts to family members if that is right for you.

You don't get a tax deduction for gifts to family but gifting creates 3 immediate benefits.

1 - It removes the property from your estate.
2 - It removes the appreciation of the property from your estate.
3 - And it removes the income from your estate – once again lowering your taxes, including some stealth taxes long term.

But please – first discuss this with your tax or financial advisor to make sure you are making gifts of the right property.

For example, you might not want to gift a house or stocks that have appreciated substantially since you have owned them. These are assets you might want to instead **hold until death so that your beneficiaries can get the step-up in basis** and be relieved of the income tax on the appreciation during your lifetime.

While a lot of the material I covered in this program might make your head spin, just remember the big picture master plan.

It's to keep your taxable income low during retirement. It will help to avoid or at least lower your exposure to these insidious stealth taxes.

Using funds from tax free vehicles like Roth IRAs and life insurance will result in lower taxable income and that means lower taxes – and – it increases your chances of coming in under the various income thresholds where the stealth taxes begin to kick in.

Congress doesn't want you to know that they are raising your taxes, but I do – and now you know.

Stealth taxes are sneaky and meant to be undetected – under the radar.

Not anymore.

Now you know the 5 biggest stealth taxes and how to avoid them for good!

Please view this again and again until it sinks in. This will save you a ton in taxes.

DVD
Big Mistakes Made by Banks, Brokers and Financial Advisors

They may make the mistakes… but *YOU* are responsible!

Here are the biggest mistakes I see made by financial institutions like banks, brokerage firms and fund companies – and by financial advisors, on your retirement savings.

I'm not talking about investments here. I'm talking about administrative and tax mistakes that can be costly and some of them cannot be corrected.

I'm hoping that by reviewing this information, you'll be able to recognize and avoid some of these so they don't happen to you. Remember that even if these mistakes are made by your bank, broker or financial advisor, **you are responsible and the loss will be yours.**

When it comes to the tax rules on your retirement savings, they are not only complex but sometimes unforgiving. That's why you need to be educated so that these mistakes don't impact your IRA, 401(k) or other retirement savings.

Unfortunately a majority of financial advisors or representatives of even the biggest financial institutions do not have expertise in these tax rules and can make costly mistakes – and you will pay the price.

They might know investments but they are generally not trained on the tax rules.

For example, many of them run expensive ads about IRA rollovers, but some of the biggest mistakes involve the mishandling of these rollovers or not knowing about the changes in the tax rules.

The bad news is that this creates a dangerous situation for you if you are relying on untrained advisors. Running afoul of these tax rules can often take the biggest bite out of your retirement savings so I'm glad you're watching this program.

Rollover Mistakes

Let's begin with rollover mistakes which are very common and in some cases can cause you to lose your entire IRA.

Rollovers occur when you move retirement funds from one account to another.

As a general rule, you should be careful anytime you move retirement money because it's easy for you and the financial institutions to make an error here.

First, you should know the difference between what I am referring to as a "60-day rollover" and a direct transfer (also called a trustee-to-trustee transfer). The bottom line here is when you wish to move your IRA or plan funds to another bank or advisor, always instruct your financial advisor or institutions to move the funds as a direct transfer where you don't touch the funds.

A 60-day rollover occurs when you have a check made out to you personally, and then you have 60 days to deposit that in another IRA or retirement account. These are dangerous, even more so now because of the new more rigid IRA rollover rules.

Under new rigid rules that began in 2015, you can only do one 60-day rollover per year (that's 365 days from receipt – not a calendar year) from all your IRAs including Roth IRAs.

If you attempt a second 60-day rollover within the one year, it is not eligible to be rolled over and can become a taxable distribution. This error cannot be fixed. You are stuck.

That is why I covered this new stricter rule in the program you watched and in several other books and DVDs you received. I don't want you to miss this and I want you to make sure that your bank, broker or financial advisor does not make this mistake. They are not as up to date on the new rules as they should be.

In fact, after the new rule was in effect I polled advisors at training programs I was presenting at and on average only 10% of the advisors knew about this new rule.

Every advisor should know this since they all handle IRA rollovers, but they don't. That is scary especially since these are advisors, who, to their credit are at least attending training programs on the tax rules – and only 10% of these advisors were familiar with the rule change.

Most other advisors don't take training at all on the tax rules, so your IRAs are at high risk of being lost when working with advisors who are not up to speed.

If for some reason your IRA financial institution accepts a second rollover because either they didn't know the rules or were not aware you already did one 60-day rollover from some other IRA or Roth IRA during the year, then you not only have a distribution that may be taxable, but also an excess IRA contribution that carries a 6% annual penalty until corrected.

This is serious so you need to be vigilant about checking that your IRA or plan money is moved the right way – as a direct transfer.

This is one of the most common mistakes made by banks and advisors and many times it's because they were not given specific instructions to move the money as a direct transfer.

Make sure you give them those instructions and put it in writing, and then follow up that it was done properly as a direct transfer. Make sure they do not issue you a check made out to you personally.

A check make out to the IRA or plan where your retirement funds are moving to is ok, because you can't cash that check, so it qualifies as a direct transfer.

Be clear in your instructions to your advisor or your financial institution that your money moves as a direct transfer, and then check that it was done properly.

You can do an unlimited number of direct transfers. This is the better way to move retirement funds.

Inherited IRA Mistakes

The next item on my list of advisor and financial institution errors is the advice they give your beneficiaries on their options when they inherit. Please make sure you share this information with your beneficiaries now.

Often after the death of a loved one, your family may be relying heavily on advisors or representatives at financial institutions that may provide incorrect advice that cannot be later corrected. So share this with them now, so they can be better prepared to make the right choices when the time comes.

Spouse Beneficiary

The #1 mistake made by spousal beneficiaries is failing to properly choose between:

Remaining a beneficiary, and

Moving the funds to their own IRA, better known as a "spousal rollover."

139

Now earlier I just told you to avoid 60-day rollovers and this applies to spousal rollovers too, so when I talk about spousal rollovers, make sure they are done as direct transfers – not as 60-day rollovers.

Here are the general rules:

If the surviving spouse is under age 59½, then setting up an inherited IRA is almost always the correct option. Once the spouse turns 59½, a spousal rollover (as a direct transfer) can be completed.

If the surviving spouse is 59½ or older, a spousal rollover is almost always the right move.

If your spouse inherits, most advisors and financial institutions will tell your spouse to do a spousal rollover, but that might not be the best option in all cases. In some cases, the spousal rollover is done automatically and it cannot be corrected.

A spouse who inherits an IRA has a choice, he or she can do a spousal rollover (again, as a direct transfer) to their own IRA (this is the most common choice) or remain a beneficiary, but this option is not as well known, even to professional advisors.

If your spouse inherits when she is younger than 59½ it is generally better to remain a beneficiary to avoid a 10% early withdrawal penalty if funds are needed.

If she were to do a spousal rollover to her own IRA, then the funds inherited would be treated as her own IRA funds and if she needed to withdraw before reaching age 59½, she would be subject to the 10% early withdrawal penalty. But by remaining a beneficiary instead, she would not be subject to the penalty no matter when funds are withdrawn.

Once the spouse reaches age 59½, and the 10% penalty no longer applies, she can do a spousal rollover. A spousal rollover can be done at any time.

Some banks and advisors don't know this and will automatically do the spousal rollover which could cause unwanted penalties. Also, ***once the spousal rollover option is chosen, you cannot go back and change it to an inherited IRA***.

If the spouse who inherits is already over age 59½, then the spousal rollover is the best choice in most cases, but you should still question your advisors on what the right choice is for you.

Non-spouse Beneficiary

If your beneficiary is not your spouse, but a non-spouse, like your child, children, grandchildren or other people, then there is no 60-day rollover option.

A non-spouse beneficiary can never do a 60-day rollover. That would be a mistake that cannot be corrected causing a taxable distribution of the inherited account.

Make sure that once your child (or other non-spouse beneficiary) inherits, they do not take funds from the inherited account or attempt to roll it over to their own IRA, even if the bank or broker offers them a check. They should never be offering them a check of the inherited IRA funds, but some beneficiaries might not know this and request the check.

Make sure that a financial institution or advisor does not pay out the balance in the inherited IRA to your non-spouse beneficiary. This is what I call a "fatal error". It cannot be fixed.

If that happens, the entire inherited IRA is deemed distributed and cannot be reversed. You should educate your beneficiaries now that no distributions should be taken without consulting a knowledgeable advisor, so that an unwanted and premature tax bill can be avoided.

Instead, beneficiaries should have the financial institution set up the inherited IRA as a ***properly-titled inherited IRA***, meaning that the name of the deceased IRA owner remains in the title of the inherited IRA and that the account shows that it is an inherited or beneficiary account.

It should look something like this:

John Smith (Deceased 11/15/16) IRA, f/b/o John Smith Jr., beneficiary

Then your beneficiary will take only the required minimum distributions each year, or they can take more, but whatever is withdrawn will generally be taxable unless there are after-tax funds in the inherited IRA or it's an inherited Roth IRA.

If your beneficiary wants to move the inherited funds to a new advisor or new financial institution, make sure they do not take a check from the account made out to them personally. Only move the funds as a direct transfer to the new inherited IRA.

5-Year Rule Mistakes

A still too common mistake that financial institutions and some advisors who are not up on the tax rules make is telling IRA beneficiaries that their inherited IRA must be withdrawn in 5 years.

That is not usually the case. Any individual who is named on the IRA beneficiary form is a designated beneficiary and can usually extend their required minimum distributions over their lifetime. This is the stretch IRA which most financial institutions will allow.

However, I still see cases where representatives of these institutions are telling beneficiaries that their inherited IRA must be withdrawn in 5 years under what's known as the "5-year rule." That rule only applies when there is no designated beneficiary, for example, when the estate is the beneficiary.

And even then, the 5-year rule only applies if the IRA owner died before his required beginning date which is April 1st of the year following the year he turned age 70½.

Let your beneficiaries know that if they are named on the IRA beneficiary form, they will generally be able to use the stretch IRA and extend distributions over their lifetime.

The 5-year rule will not apply to them.

They should take distributions over their life expectancy factor based on their age using the IRS Single Life Expectancy Table for IRA beneficiaries. This table can be found in IRS Publication 590-B for IRA distributions.

If there are several individuals named as beneficiaries, for example, your three children, they can each use their own age if the inherited IRA is split out to one inherited IRA for each child. The split must be done by the end of the year after the year of death, so that gives them plenty of time to split the account and each stretch their portion of the inherited IRA over their own lifetime.

IRA Trust Mistakes

One of the most costly errors made is when a trust is the IRA beneficiary and the IRA is paid out to the trust after death. That is the death knell for the inherited IRA.

Naming a trust as the IRA beneficiary is not the problem. In some cases a trust is necessary if you want some control over your IRA funds after your death.

This is usually the case when there is a sizeable IRA (say $1 million or more) and you want make sure that there is control and professional management after death, especially if your beneficiary is a minor, disabled, a spendthrift, unsophisticated or a spouse you wish to be protected from those who might prey on a vulnerable widow or widower, or to protect children you have from a first marriage.

A trust can also provide asset and creditor protection after death. So there are reasons to name a trust as your IRA beneficiary, so that is not the mistake.

The big mistake I see is after death when either attorneys, financial institutions or other advisors make the mistake of paying out the inherited IRA funds to the trust.

This is the number one most common mistake made even by experienced estate planning attorneys because they are not familiar with the specialized tax rules that apply to IRA trusts – that is, trusts that are created to inherit an IRA. These rules are different than the tax rules for most other assets and these mistakes are by far the most costly.

Paying out the inherited IRA funds to the trust after death is a fatal error.

It triggers immediate taxation of the entire IRA and possibly at high trust tax rates (depending on the trust terms) but worst of all, the entire IRA is gone. Your beneficiaries will only have what's left after the massive tax bill, and the funds will no longer be tax-deferred in the IRA tax shelter.

I've seen hundreds of thousands of dollars paid out prematurely in taxes from this error.

Here's the mistake: Once the funds are paid out of the inherited IRA to the trust, they are taxable (unless this is a Roth IRA) and this mistake cannot be reversed. The mistakenly distributed funds cannot be rolled over back into the inherited IRA because a trust is a non-spouse beneficiary and a non-spouse beneficiary can never do a rollover. This is a fatal error.

What should be done? Upon death, a properly-titled inherited IRA should be set up as I explained earlier here.

For a trust though, the title should read:

John Smith (Deceased 11/15/16) IRA, f/b/o John Smith Family Trust as beneficiary

But no IRA funds are distributed.

Your IRA is merely retitled as an inherited IRA. The only distributions from that inherited IRA now should be the annual required minimum distributions or maybe some extra distributions if the trust allows. But that's it.

In a recent case, an attorney advised a terminally ill IRA owner to change the IRA beneficiary from his wife to a newly created IRA trust. So far, so good. The trust was needed to help the future widow manage and protect the IRA funds.

When the IRA owner died, the attorney advised the bank to distribute the entire $608,000 IRA to this IRA trust. This was the classic fatal error!

Result: Over $200,000 in immediate unnecessary taxes and the tax deferral on the inherited IRA was lost forever. The mistake could not be corrected. It was not caught until the following year by the accountant who was preparing the trust tax return.

The only amount that should have been paid to the trust was the annual required minimum distribution (only about $24,000 in this case), NOT the entire IRA account balance!

The attorney here was the attorney who created the trust, but did not know how to properly implement it according to the IRA trust tax rules, and the damage was done.

This was a huge loss to the family and worst of all, the deceased IRA owner's plan which was so carefully created to protect his IRA for his family was never carried out as it should have been.

Once again, so your family or their advisors never make this mistake – After the IRA owner dies, ***if a trust is named as the IRA beneficiary, the IRA balance SHOULD NOT be paid to the IRA trust***.

After the death of the IRA owner, only the required minimum distribution has to be paid from the inherited IRA to the trust, NOT the entire IRA account balance.

Required Minimum Distribution (RMD) Mistakes

The next area where I see big mistakes is on calculating required minimum distributions (RMDs), both for IRA owners and beneficiaries.

While the financial institutions are required to provide you with the required minimum distribution on your own IRAs, they are not required to provide you the ***right*** amount! They can make a mistake, sometimes because they don't have the right information or they calculate incorrectly.

But in the end, YOU are responsible for taking the right amount once you turn age 70½ and if you are short, it's a 50% penalty on the amount you did not take.

In fact, I just came across a case where this was done wrong for 8 years before the mistake was realized. In this case, thousands of dollars in unnecessary taxes were paid because too much money was withdrawn that didn't need to be.

In this case the IRA owner's spouse was 15 years younger than him, but the required minimum distributions were calculated using the regular chart for most IRA owners.

But in this case, much less could have been withdrawn if the brokerage firm made the correct calculation.

This is rare, but there is a special rule that if your sole beneficiary for the entire year is your spouse and he or she is more than 10 years younger than you, you can use the Joint Life Expectancy Table for calculating your annual required minimum distributions which will produce a lower RMD each year. You can find that table in IRS Publication 590-B, for IRA distributions.

The financial institution will generally use the regular "Uniform Lifetime Table" if you don't let them know you qualify to use the joint table.

The rule to remember is that during lifetime when a spouse is more than 10 years younger than the account owner and is the sole beneficiary for the entire year, the Joint Life Expectancy Table can be used for calculating RMDs. You have to let the financial institution know this. Even if they should see this from the beneficiary form it doesn't mean they'll pick it up.

Other common advisor mistakes with required minimum distributions occur when you have several different types of retirement accounts. For example, you might have a 401(k) and 3 traditional IRAs at different banks.

In a recent case, the financial advisor had the IRA owner take the total required amount from his 401(k) and IRAs all from his IRA. That is a mistake. You cannot do that.

For IRAs, you calculate the RMD from all your IRAs and you can take that total amount from any one or a combination of your IRAs, but you cannot take it from the 401(k).

If you happen to have several 403(b) accounts, then those RMDs can be taken from any of the 403(b) accounts, similar to the rule for IRAs. But again, you cannot take a withdrawal from your 403(b) to satisfy a required distribution from your IRA or vice-versa.

You also cannot withdraw from the IRAs to satisfy the required amount from your 401(k). That required amount must come only from that 401(k).

When you withdraw the entire amount from your IRAs, you have taken too much from your IRA and not enough from your 401(k). There is no penalty for taking too much out, other than an unnecessary tax bill, but there is a 50% penalty for not taking enough out of the 401(k) or IRA.

Along these same lines, if in addition to your IRA you also have an inherited IRA, you cannot combine those for required minimum distributions. You must calculate the required amount from your IRA and your inherited IRA separately and take the required amount from your IRA and your inherited IRA separately.

If you happen to have several inherited IRAs inherited from the same person though, those can be combined and the required amount can be taken from any one of the inherited IRAs inherited from the same person.

You can see how even professional advisors and financial institutions can easily mess this up.

Remember that under no circumstances can a required minimum distribution from one type of retirement account be taken from a different type of retirement account.

Beneficiary Form Mistakes

Now let's turn to common errors made by financial institutions on beneficiary forms.

It is your responsibility to keep your beneficiary forms up to date, but you need to check on your IRA financial institution (or company plan – with your 401(k)) to make sure that they have a copy and it is the most current copy.

We have seen banks and brokers produce old, outdated beneficiary forms that may list dead beneficiaries or unwanted beneficiaries, like an ex-spouse.

Check that every institution has the most current version of your beneficiary forms and that you have a copy of that.

As you should know by now, the wrong beneficiary can wreak havoc with the family such as having no beneficiary named and having your IRA or retirement plan be paid to your estate.

Every time you have a change in your life, for example, a birth, a death, a marriage, a divorce – in fact – *especially a divorce*, or a remarriage, or a new grandchild or even a change in the tax law, you should update your beneficiary forms for all of your IRAs and any company retirement plans you have. This is critical if you want to make sure your retirement savings go to the people you want them to.

In addition to naming the right beneficiaries, make sure that all of your beneficiary forms name contingent beneficiaries in case your primary beneficiary dies or wants to disclaim his or her share to the next in line beneficiary, maybe their children.

Check that each financial institution where you have your IRAs or plan funds has the right beneficiary form on file and that you have a copy.

Here are some actual cases where beneficiary forms were botched and what to do about it.

A mother wanted to leave her IRA to her son and daughter equally. When establishing the IRA, she misread the beneficiary designation form and named her son as primary beneficiary and her daughter as contingent beneficiary.

The bank never noticed or questioned this. The son could have walked away with the entire IRA with the bank's blessing and the daughter would be disinherited, even though that is not what mom intended.

In another case, a father wanted to name his three children as equal beneficiaries of his IRA. The beneficiary designation form required that when he named beneficiaries he include the percentage each beneficiary will inherit. He listed each child as receiving 30% of the IRA, so that left 10% unaccounted for.

These are easy problems to fix, if caught while you are still alive.

Simply contact the custodian (the bank, broker, Fund Company or advisor) and complete a new beneficiary designation form and make sure you have a copy of the updated form.

This is much more difficult after death. However, if the beneficiaries have a good relationship and all believe that the parent's intent was to split the funds equally, many custodians will allow the beneficiaries to sign an agreement accomplishing this. Advisors and IRA custodians share an interest in avoiding a court battle over the IRA.

Ineligible Rollover Mistakes

Here's another problem:

What if the financial institution accepts rollovers that were not allowed? That has happened. These are *ineligible rollovers*.

For example, an annual required minimum distribution is not eligible to be rolled over, but sometimes the bank or financial advisor won't know the rollover you are giving them is not eligible and they deposit the funds in your IRA with them anyway.

Now you have a problem. You have a taxable distribution, not a rollover, and an excess contribution to your IRA. That's a 6% penalty each year on the excess, until that amount is removed.

In this case, the tax is not the big problem because your required distribution would have been taxable anyway. The problem is the ineligible rollover and the excess contribution penalty.

Another version of an excess contribution (the 6% penalty) occurs when an ineligible rollover is made to your IRA, for example if you mistakenly do a second 60-day IRA to IRA rollover within a year.

Those funds cannot be rolled over. But the bank or advisor may not know this and roll the funds over anyway. In that case, the distribution is taxable (since it cannot be rolled over) and the rollover creates an excess contribution subject to the annual 6% penalty for each year the funds are not removed.

The penalty can be avoided by removing the excess IRA funds (the funds that were not eligible to be rolled over) plus the earnings on those funds by October 15th of the year after the excess contribution.

IRA and Roth IRA Contribution Mistakes

Now I'll move on to IRA contribution mistakes we see made by advisors and financial institutions.

First you should know that ***not everyone is eligible to make an IRA or Roth IRA contribution***, but some institutions will accept contributions without checking if you are eligible to make them. Once again, this can cause an excess contribution problem subjecting the ineligible contribution to a 6% penalty each year until the excess IRA contribution is removed.

For both IRAs and Roth IRAs you need to have earned income in order to make an annual contribution. There is an exception if you are married and have no qualifying earned income but your spouse does. In that case you can contribute to what's known as a spousal IRA (or spousal Roth IRA) based on the working spouse's earned income.

Other than that though, you need to have earned income to be eligible to contribute to an IRA or Roth IRA. Earned income is generally wages or self-employment income. It is not pension income or investment income. But strangely enough, alimony qualifies as earned income here.

After the earned income test, traditional IRAs and Roth IRAs have different eligibility rules.

For traditional IRAs there is no income limit. No matter how high your income is, you can always contribute to a traditional IRA, as long as you have earned income.

The reason there is confusion about an income limit for traditional IRAs is because there is an income limit for those who are active in a company retirement plan, like a 401(k). But that income limit is only for deductibility. If you are active in a company plan and your (or your spouse's) income is too high, you can still make an IRA contribution, but it will not be deductible.

While there is no income limit for making a traditional IRA contribution, there is an age limit. Once you reach age 70½, you can no longer contribute to a traditional IRA for that year or for future years.

Roth IRA contribution eligibility for some strange reason works the opposite way. There are income limits, but they are high enough so most workers will qualify.

But unlike traditional IRAs, there is no age limit for making a Roth IRA contribution, so you can continue Roth IRA contributions even after age 70 1/2, as long as your income is under the limit and you have earned income.

However, the financial institution or the advisor you are working with will sometimes make the mistake of accepting an IRA or Roth IRA contribution even when you don't qualify, *so it's up to you to make sure you qualify before making an IRA contribution.*

Many financial institutions accept IRA contributions online without checking to see if you qualify. They will probably have you sign forms where you state that you do qualify, but of course you don't read or understand all the legalese and sign the forms anyway. So make sure you qualify if you are making an IRA contribution. It is your responsibility.

In addition, a sharp tax preparer will notice if you made a traditional or Roth IRA contribution when you did not qualify. Most professional tax programs will spot this and flag it based on income and age restrictions, but I still see situations where even experienced CPAs have let tax returns get prepared with IRA and Roth IRA contributions that should not have been allowed, based on income or age.

That creates an excess contribution.

Form 5329 Mistakes

Excess IRA contributions bring me to a serious error that many CPAs and tax preparers are not aware of. It has to do with IRA and other retirement account tax penalties.

These are the 10% early distribution penalty, the 6% excess contribution penalty and the 50% penalty for not taking a required minimum distribution. These penalties are all reported on **Form 5329**. The name of that form is ***Additional Taxes on Qualified Plans (including IRAs) and Other Tax-Favored Accounts.***

That's a mouthful, but basically it's the place where you must report these penalties when they apply. Due to several landmark tax court cases a few years ago, Form 5329 has become a critical area where hefty penalties can mount without you even knowing about it.

That's because most CPAs don't know that as a result of these court cases, Form 5329 is treated as a separate tax form. It even has its own signature line on the bottom of page two of the form.

If a penalty applies and you do not file this form, there is no statute of limitations. Penalties can grow over years to significant sums.

Normally with taxes, once you file, there is a 3-year statute of limitations, meaning that IRS cannot go back and open an old year (except if there was a tax fraud).

But since Form 5329 is treated as a separately filed form, no statute can begin to run if it is not filed, which means the penalties can mount for years building a liability that can grow exponentially when interest and other penalties are added.

Some tax preparers make the mistake of not filing this form, for example, if they didn't know you didn't qualify for a Roth IRA contribution or did an ineligible rollover. Those situations can cause an excess contribution – the 6% penalty – and you must file that form until the excess is removed.

The form can also be missed if your tax preparer or other advisors did not realize that you didn't take your required minimum distribution for the year (or were short due to an incorrect calculation).

That would generate a 50% penalty on the amount of the required minimum distribution not taken. If Form 5329 is not filed, that 50% penalty liability plus interest and other penalties continue to grow for all the back years since there is no statute of limitations.

CPAs are shocked when they learn about this, so I am informing you now that if any of these penalties apply, make sure you file Form 5329, to avoid the escalation of these tax penalties and accrued interest.

Relief on the 50% Penalty for Missing an RMD

Just so you know, the biggest penalty, the 50% penalty for not taking a required minimum distribution is one that can be waived by IRS for good reason. A good reason can simply be a financial advisor or bank error, a medical problem, a death in the family or confusion on the tax rules.

To get a waiver, you first must make up the missed required distribution and then file Form 5329 with your explanation. This goes as well for beneficiaries who miss a required minimum distribution from their inherited IRAs or inherited Roth IRAs.

You don't have to pay the 50% penalty with the form. Just give your explanation on the form and file it with your tax return.

Don't ignore Form 5329. It never goes away.

Beware of Untrained Advisors!

Probably the biggest financial advisor or institution errors are those that are made by not knowing the tax rules for retirement accounts and not keeping up to date when these rules change.

Many of the tax rules in the retirement area change even when no new tax laws are passed. For instance, the new stricter version of the once-per-year IRA rollover rule came from a court case and an IRS announcement that has the effect of law, not from a new tax law.

IRS also issues revenue rulings, notices, revenue procedures and other technical guidance that has the effect of law and your advisors need to be aware of these changes so that they can advise you properly.

Unfortunately ***most advisors are not well trained in this area***, so you should make sure you are working with an advisor who is.

For your reference:

Here is how to find advisors that have gone through our highest level of training. These advisors are members of ***Ed Slott's Elite IRA Advisor Group***, an advanced education program focusing on tax and estate planning for retirement savings. You can find these advisors on our website at: **www.irahelp.com**.

They are not the only advisors to consider, but they have been exposed to my training and have access to our team of IRA experts when they have questions.

Question everything and check these critical issues on your retirement savings to avoid these common errors.

Now you know where the biggest risks lie.

DVD
Strategies for Volatile Markets

Use the Tax Code to Turn
Lemons into Lemonade

I hope you'll never need this, but unfortunately, I know that you will at some point. We all do!

Here is what to do about stock market volatility. We all worry about it, but after watching this program I'm hoping you can worry less and plan more.

Next time the market takes a dive, do nothing. Touch nothing. Watch this program first! It will save you a bundle and save you from making mistakes and panicking.

So what is your reaction to market volatility? This is something we have to live with and here are some strategies for when the market takes a big drop – as we all know happens from time to time.

Probably the best advice for most people is to do nothing. Panicking won't help. Historically markets go up and down and even when they have really tanked, over time they have always come back. But you might be saying, what if I run out of time?

So the first thing you should do is an assessment of your risk tolerance and focus more on *when* you will need those savings – your time horizon.

If risk tolerance is a problem, maybe the market is not for you. Remember that, in general, the greater the risk, the greater the reward. But when you look at when you'll need the funds, maybe the risk is not as great as you thought, depending on your time horizon.

If you cannot deal with the risk of principal loss at all, you probably shouldn't be in the stock market, especially if you are older and cannot afford to lose money in retirement and change your lifestyle.

In that case you should first educate yourself on stock market alternatives and sit down with a knowledgeable financial advisor. Discuss options that might eliminate or reduce your exposure to market risk.

For example, insurance company products like life insurance and annuities can eliminate market risk, because you are paying for guarantees. Ask about the various types of products in this category that might lock in a certain return that is guaranteed. But again, there is no free lunch. You pay for these features.

Funds within a permanent life insurance policy can be structured to grow tax free and if held to death, they will pay a tax-free death benefit to your heirs. And many permanent life insurance policies eliminate market risk.

Annuities can offer guaranteed lifetime payments in retirement, and if those are held in your Roth IRA, those payments can be tax free too. So in that scenario, you can eliminate both the tax risk *and* the stock market risk.

This might help you sleep better at night, and peace of mind is a nice feeling – not worrying about the stock market, or even taxes, with this strategy.

But no matter where you put your money, you'll find that every investment vehicle has up and down sides.

For example, you can invest in certain bonds that pay a stated rate of interest, but the value of that bond could go up or down depending on interest rates. If interest rates rise, your bond is worth less if you want to sell it before maturity. In addition, the company or municipality behind the bond could default, so there might be risk there as well.

US Government backed securities are probably the most solid when it comes to eliminating risk of loss, but they generally return less.

You could look to real estate, but that is subject to its own risk of property values and like anything else, you have to know what you are doing. The benefit of real estate is that even if you're using non-retirement account money, the appreciation in value is not taxed until the property is sold. And if the property is held until you die, your beneficiaries receive a step-up in basis and the income tax bill on the lifetime appreciation is eliminated.

That goes as well for stocks and other property you have that has appreciated – but not for anything you own in your IRA or other tax-deferred retirement plan. Those funds never receive a step up in basis.

But maybe you should look a bit differently at a market decline. ***There are some ways you can benefit from a down market***.

Remember that this will happen, we just don't know when and by how much the market will drop – and we don't know how long it will take to recover. But history has told us to expect it at some point, so be prepared to deal with it and turn lemons into lemonade.

Let's first start with some things you should not do when the market takes a hit.

Don't panic. Don't overreact. Take a breath and make no immediate moves.

Chances are whatever you do will be out of emotion and not in your best interests. Remember that everyone is feeling what you are feeling and they are equally worried.

First thing is that ***you haven't lost anything until you sell***.

Selling immediately in a panic at a loss to stop the bleeding is generally a mistake if you are looking long term. You might miss out on an upswing that often follows declines and then you'll feel even worse.

In fact, the opposite reaction might be better. That is, buying or investing more to buy more funds or stock at lower values.

That is something that could benefit you long-term. This is like dollar cost averaging which means continually buying shares with a long term vision regardless of changes in price. When prices are lower, your money will buy more.

But let's get back to ***what*** and ***when***.

What you are saving for, and when will you need that money? You need to know what your end game is.

What is the purpose of this money?

For example, a great saying I heard to make this point is from **Joel Goodhart**, an experienced and knowledgeable financial advisor in **Plymouth Meeting, PA** .

Joel has a good calming way about talking to his clients when markets drop and he shared some of this good advice with me.

He tells his clients:

> ***"If you need the money on Thursday, you shouldn't be in the stock market. If you need the money in 30 years, then you shouldn't have it in the bank."***
> *– Joel Goodhart*

That makes it clear that you have to know what your end game is.

Joel Goodhart calls this a ***"Financial GPS."*** In other words, tell me where you want to go and when you want to get there. Only then can you know where the right investments are for your time horizon and risk tolerance.

Remember that a market decline is a good time to buy, not to sell. You have incurred no loss until you sell.

A market decline is a great time to get in, <u>NOT</u> to get out.

If you think about it, when markets are down, everything is on sale. Who doesn't like a sale? Buying low is the key to selling high. When you panic and sell, you're selling low and losing.

This should all be common sense, but sometimes you need to hear this when you hear that the market has taken a big dip and your savings are affected.

Don't make things worse, or like the medical schools teach – the so called Hippocratic Oath – "first do no harm" to yourself or your savings.

If anything, a market correction (the nice way of saying the market has taken a significant drop) should be a sign to do more long-term planning, so that market gyrations won't have an impact on your long-term plan.

For example, you should know what money you'll need and when.

You should invest differently for short-term needs and liquidity for short term expenses and have different investments for your long-term needs.

For example, money that may be earmarked for your heirs has a much longer time horizon and a market decline in the short run is just a bump in the road.

The problem is when your money is in the wrong place at the wrong time, for example when short-term money – money you will need soon for income – is invested with too much risk in the market.

Short-term money should be more secure.

The time you will need your money dictates where and how you invest. This is something to review with your financial advisors and get started on that now.

What's the purpose of the money? If it's 30-year money, the best thing you can do is nothing. So don't worry. Go back to whatever you were doing and ignore the stock market.

The key is the financial GPS I mentioned earlier. You have to know what the purpose of your money is and where you want to end up.

In a previous Public Television program I talked about beginning with the end in mind. It's the same thing here.

In that program I compared this to a 1,000 piece jigsaw puzzle. That can be overwhelming when you see all those pieces. Where do you begin? That's how many of us feel about our retirement savings, but you need to address this now and create a plan… a solution.

You have to have a plan, because as I always say, "If you don't have a plan, you get the government plan, and that is not a good plan."

Like that puzzle, you have to know where you want to end up.

Begin with the end in mind.

With the puzzle, you see the picture on the box and you know what the solution looks like…you know where you want to end up.

In my Public Television program a few years ago I referred to the 75th anniversary of the classic *"Gone with the Wind"*. It took author Margaret Mitchell 10 years to complete the book, but what was interesting was that she wrote the last chapter FIRST. She had a plan and she began with the end in mind.

It's the same thing here.

So the bottom line is to work with a knowledgeable and objective advisor. I say this because you are sometimes too emotional and not objective with your own point of view or may have an emotional attachment to your investments which might cause you to make the wrong moves at the wrong time.

It's best to work with someone knowledgeable who you trust to give you independent advice, keep you calm and avoid making rash decisions when the market gets jumpy, as we know it will at some point.

That's the best advice I can give you for volatile markets. Stay calm. Do nothing rash, but do create a plan for the future based on what money you will need and when you will need it.

That said, here are some tax moves you can make to turn lemons into lemonade when the market declines. You may as well have Uncle Sam share your pain.

Let's start with **Roth IRA conversions**

What if you converted, say, early in 2015, but then after the summer your account value went down when the market took a hit. Well now the funds you converted and will be paying tax on are not worth what they were. You'll be paying tax on value that no longer exists.

Thanks to the tax law, you can recharacterize – or undo – reverse – that Roth conversion so you won't be on the hook for value that no longer exists. You can eliminate that tax liability.

But wait. It gets better. Like I said earlier, you can take advantage of this situation.

Remember I said that low values mean there's a sale on? Well that's true here. You can turn around after a waiting period and re-convert those same funds back to a Roth IRA at an even lower cost than you originally paid. Or you can convert other IRA funds at the lower value.

Since your Roth IRA is likely long-term money, you can wait it out and when the market comes back, all of those gains will be earned tax free in your Roth IRA. If not for the market decline, you would have paid a lot more in tax for that Roth IRA. The market crash turned out to be an opportunity that you took advantage of. You re-converted at a lower tax cost.

Here's a simple example of how this can work for you.

Let's use round numbers. Let's say Jack converted $100,000 to his Roth IRA in January 2015. That means that when Jack files his 2015 taxes, in 2016, he'll have to add that $100,000 conversion to his income. He'll owe the tax on that $100,000.

But let's say that when Jack goes to have his taxes done in March 2016, the market value declined and his $100,000 Roth took a real hit and was only worth $60,000.

Jack still owes tax on $100,000 Roth conversion even though it's actually only worth $60,000. Let's say Jack's tax rate on that conversion (when added to his other income) is a combined Federal and state rate of 40%. So Jack would owe $40,000 in tax on an account worth only $60,000. That is obviously a bad situation.

But it can be fixed, thanks to a provision in the tax law that allows a Roth conversion to be reversed – a **Roth recharacterization.**

Jack can have the entire conversion reversed like it never happened. Like a bad dream. He directly transfers the remaining $60,000 back to his traditional IRA. Now he now no longer owes the tax on his $100,000 conversion. The tax liability is eliminated. Jack's account is still down, but at least he's off the hook on the tax bill.

But now is the time to buy, when the value is low. After waiting 30 days, after he recharacterizes, Jack can re-convert the $60,000 to his Roth IRA, now paying tax on only $60,000 which might even drop his tax rate to maybe 35% or less.

When the smoke clears, Jack has $60,000 in his Roth IRA and paid a lower tax to get it there. Over time, assuming the market comes back as it usually does, Jack's $60,000 goes back up to the original $100,000 or even higher. But now all of that gain from the $60,000 on is tax free in Jack's Roth IRA.

He only paid tax on $60,000 but long-term he'll have $100,000 or more growing tax free. This is exactly what I mean by turning lemons into lemonade.

Just so you know, the waiting period to re-convert the previously converted funds back to a Roth IRA is the ***later*** of:

30 days after the recharacterization (as was the case here),
Or
The year after the original conversion.

In Jack's case the original conversion was in 2015, so he would have to wait until the later of the year after the conversion – which would have been January 1, 2016 or 30 days after the recharacterization – which is 30 days after his March 2016 recharacterization. In Jack's case, the 30-day rule applied.

If Jack had done the same conversion – in January 2015, but recharacterized say in August 2015, then he would have to wait until January 2016 to re-convert.

But this strategy can get even better. This waiting period is only for funds that were previously converted.

Other IRA funds that were never converted before can be converted at any time. If Jack had say another $80,000 of IRA funds that he did not originally convert, he could convert those too, without a waiting period, when the market values were much lower and get those converted funds on sale too.

If it turned out that the market dropped further, those funds could also be recharacterized and reconverted to get the best tax deal.

Market volatility here can be your friend, but only for a limited time. The window for a recharacterization closes on October 15th of the year after the year of conversion, but that can still be a long window.

In Jack's case, since he converted in January 2015, he would have 21 months, until October 15, 2016 to undo – recharacterize – his 2015 Roth conversion.

Jack can even try a better strategy to maximize the benefit of conversions that may have declined in value.

He can **convert different investments to different Roth IRAs**. This brings up a key strategy for converting.

It's best to do all conversions to **separate NEW Roth IRAs** that have no other Roth money in them. This way you can cherry pick losers and winners to recharacterize and get even more benefit out of the conversion, recharacterization and re-conversion cycle, when stock values decline…or rise.

Here's an example:

Let's stick with Jack who converted $100,000 to his Roth IRA in January 2015. Let's further assume that Jack converted only two stocks; Stock A and Stock B to his Roth IRA.

To simplify this example and emphasize the point here, let's assume that each stock was worth $50,000. So Jack converted $50,000 of Stock A and $50,000 of Stock B to his Roth IRA, making up the full $100,000 conversion.

Now let's say that Stock A doubled in value to $100,000, but Stock B became worthless and is now worth zero, zilch, nothing.

The value in Jack's Roth IRA is the same $100,000, but all in Stock A. Because Jack converted both stocks to the same Roth IRA, he will get no tax benefit for the loss in Stock B by recharacterizing, because you have to combine the gains and losses in the Roth IRA account when you recharacterize.

The gain was $50,000 on Stock A, but the loss was also $50,000 on Stock B, so there was no net loss in the Roth, so there would be no tax benefit to recharacterizing. Jack cannot cherry pick the loss and just recharacterize the loser since they are both in the same Roth IRA account.

But you can cherry pick the loser if each stock was converted to a separate new Roth IRA that had no other Roth IRA funds in there.

If that was done, Jack would have converted $50,000 of Stock A to one Roth IRA and $50,000 of Stock B to another, different NEW Roth IRA.

Now, Jack could recharacterize only the Roth IRA with Stock B and eliminate the tax on that $50,000. He could leave that other Roth IRA with Stock A because that is worth $100,000.

The result is that Jack has the same $100,000 in his Roth IRA, but only paid tax on $50,000. If both stocks were converted to the same Roth IRA, Jack would have the same $100,000 but would have paid tax on the full $100,000. That's a big difference, so be aware of this strategy too.

That's how to use market volatility to your advantage with Roth IRA conversions.

You can also do this when making your annual Roth or traditional IRA contributions if you qualify. By contributing when the market is down, you are getting more for your money, again, buying on sale.

In addition to the above items, your required minimum distributions can be lowered if the value at year-end is lower. But that benefit won't happen until the following year.

For example, if your December 31, 2015 IRA value was lower due to a market decline, then you won't be able to lower your 2015 required minimum distribution, because that is based on the previous year's December 31st value.

But your 2016 required amount will be lower since that is the distribution that is based on the December 31, 2015 IRA account value, even if your IRA balance rises in 2016.

Tax Losses

Let's now talk about tax losses.

If you do feel that some stocks should be sold, maybe if you need the liquidity for short-term income, it might pay to sell certain losing stocks and take the tax loss.

The tax loss can offset capital gains dollar for dollar plus up to $3,000 of other ordinary income like income from a Roth conversion or income from required minimum distributions.

Work with your financial advisor and see how much in gains and losses you might end up with for the year. You can use the losses to offset large amounts of gains.

For example, maybe you sold a piece of property for a $50,000 gain, during the year. You can use $50,000 of losses to offset the tax on the $50,000 property gain.

If you have inherited property that receives a step-up in basis as I referred to earlier, and later that property, say stock, declines in value, you can deduct the loss on that property, generating a capital loss.

For example, your dad bought stock for $10,000 and held it for many years before he died. At his death it was still unsold and now worth $70,000. You inherit it at the $70,000 getting a step-up in basis from the original cost of $10,000 to the $70,000 value at the date of death.

If you sold right after death when the stock was still worth the $70,000, there would be no income tax due, since your cost would be the $70,000 stepped up basis.

If on the other hand, the market declines after death and that stock is worth only $50,000, and you sell it at the $50,000, you can claim a $20,000 capital loss which can be used to offset $20,000 of gains or up to $3,000 of ordinary income.

The same with other property like a house or land. But remember that IRAs, 401(k)s, annuities or other similar items which are known as items of income in respect of a decedent, never receive a step-up in basis.

For example, if your dad had an IRA he invested the same $10,000 in, and it was worth the same $70,000 at his death, you would owe tax on all $70,000 if you withdrew the funds when they were worth $70,000. There is no step-up in basis on inherited IRAs.

If the value went down to $50,000 like in the stock example where you had a $20,000 capital loss, with an IRA you would owe tax on the full $50,000 IRA value withdrawn.

Alternate Valuation Election for Estates

Here's another possible benefit of a falling market, but one that will only benefit your heirs – not you – because this one can only apply after you die.

Let's say the value of your estate declined substantially soon after death. Your executor should know about a special provision designed to lower your estate tax on the value of an estate that declined. It's called electing **alternate valuation**.

Normally the value of estate property is determined on the date of death. But alternate valuation can be elected which allows the estate to use the value of assets on six months after the date of death if the asset values declined, so your heirs can reduce

the estate tax owed. You can only use this if it reduces the estate tax liability and it must be elected on all assets of the estate, including any IRAs or retirement plans in the estate.

Your executor would have to know to elect alternate valuation on your federal estate tax return (Form 706) to gain this benefit.

Net Unrealized Appreciation (NUA) – When Markets Decline

There is a tax break for net unrealized appreciation in employer securities – called NUA for short.

NUA sounds complicated but the mechanics of the tax break on net unrealized appreciation of company stock are relatively simple.

If a lump-sum distribution from a company plan includes highly appreciated stock, you are permitted to roll it over to an IRA, but you may not want to.

Although conventional wisdom says do the rollover, there is an exception that applies to company stock and works best when that stock is highly appreciated from the date the company plan (for example, a 401(k) plan) acquired it.

The higher the appreciation and the lower the cost basis in the company shares, the more advantageous the NUA tax break is.

Under the special NUA tax rule, you can withdraw the stock from the plan and pay regular (ordinary) income tax on it, but only on the original cost to the plan and not on the market value, that is, what the shares are worth on the date of the distribution.

The difference (the appreciation) is called the ***net unrealized appreciation (NUA)***. NUA is the increase in the value of the employer stock from the time it was acquired by a plan to the date of the distribution to the plan participant – you.

The plan participant can elect to defer the tax on the NUA until he sells the stock. When he does sell, he will only pay tax at his current capital gains rate. To qualify for the tax deferral on NUA, the distribution must be a lump-sum distribution and all the assets in all like plan accounts must be distributed out of the plans, and all in one calendar year.

For example, say the value of shares of company stock in your 401(k) is $100,000, but the original cost was only $10,000 years ago when you purchased the stock in the plan. Then the NUA would be the $90,000 of appreciation.

If you transfer those shares as stock (in kind) to a taxable brokerage account as part of a qualifying lump sum distribution, then you will pay ordinary income tax on the $10,000 cost but no tax on the $90,000 of NUA until those shares are sold.

But when they are sold, the gain is long-term capital gain regardless of how long the shares are held. This is an exception to the one-year holding period for long-term capital gain treatment. Since most CPAs don't even know about this special tax rule, the authority for it is from **IRS Notice 98-24**.

But what would happen if the situation were a bit different and the market value of the shares declined substantially.

Let's say instead, the value of your company plan shares is the same $100,000, but the original cost is $90,000. You would typically not be a good candidate for the NUA tax break because it's usually not worth paying ordinary income tax on $90,000 just for the extra $10,000 of NUA benefit.

But let's say now the market crashed and the value of your company shares went down to $20,000 (I hope not, but just to make a point). It might pay to sell the shares in the plan and buy them back at the low $20,000 value. Then hopefully over time they go back up to the $100,000 or even higher.

Once the shares have rebounded over the years to $100,000 or more and you qualify for a lump-sum distribution by separating from service or reaching age 59½, the NUA benefit is more appealing because your new cost is now the lower $20,000 cost you locked in by buying the shares when they declined to that lower value.

You used the loss in value to your advantage and may now receive a bigger tax break under the NUA provision.

Benefit with Gifting When Markets Decline

Here's another way to take advantage of a market decline using the same principle I spoke about earlier when I said that stock is on sale when it's worth less. You can buy more of it for the same money.

That works the same way for gifting.

Gifting can be advantageous if you are doing the gifting to remove property from your estate or pass it on to your family. One caveat though – *you generally don't want to gift property that has appreciated in value*. It's best to hold that property until death so your heirs get the step-up in basis to eliminate the tax on the appreciation during your lifetime.

But if you have stock for example that has declined in value, it might pay to gift that property to your child, for example, so you can gift more of it.

For instance, say you wanted to give $14,000 of stock as your annual gift to your child. If the value of the stock declines, more shares can be gifted under the $14,000 annual limit. Just something to be aware of.

Just a note: if you want to make a gift to a charity, only gift stock that has appreciated in value.

Lets' hope a volatile market doesn't give you the jitters, because it will happen.

But now you know what to do. Don't panic. Use the advice I gave you here and take advantage of the market decline and have Uncle Sam share your pain now, while you gain later.

Remember to get a handle on when you will need your money.

Your time frame is the key to where you will invest for short term liquidity, income or long-term gain or even to leave to your loved ones.

Begin with the end in mind. Create your plan now.

And always run all of this information by your tax, legal and financial advisors.

Everyone's situation, risk tolerance and time horizon is different. You have to focus on what's best for you. Create your plan now so you can sleep better later, no matter what happens in the stock market.

But when the market does decline, as we know it will, that's your signal to look to the tax code, as I have done for you here to **_turn stock market lemons into lemonade_**.

DVD

The Biggest Retirement Tax Loopholes

How to make the Tax Code work for YOU!

Here are some great ways to make the Tax Code work for you by taking advantage of all you can. I've got **over 20 tax-saving loopholes** for you, so let's get going.

1. Roth Recharacterization

One of the best deals in the Tax Code is a Roth recharacterization because it gives you a second chance to change your mind about your Roth conversion.

It allows you to undo your Roth conversion.

Are you thinking about a Roth IRA conversion for this year? If so, the funds must leave your traditional IRA or company plan by the end of the year. This may seem risky because the deadline requires you to convert before the year is over, before you may have complete awareness of your tax situation for the year.

But there is no risk to you because you can always recharacterize. The recharacterization is one of the rare second chances granted by the Tax Code and allows great flexibility in your financial and tax planning. In the simplest of terms, a Roth IRA recharacterization is an "undo." In volatile economic times, tools that allow you a "do over" are more valuable than ever. It erases a Roth IRA conversion, and the conversion is treated as if it never occurred.

The deadline is October 15th of the year after you convert so that gives you plenty of time to undo your Roth conversion. You can recharacterize all or only a part of your conversion and you can recharacterize for any reason at all. In fact, you don't even need a reason.

Why would you want to recharacterize? The main reason people voluntarily recharacterize is because the account has declined in value. A recharacterization cancels out the conversion and the conversion tax is eliminated. When tax time rolls around if you get a case of buyer's remorse and don't want to pay the tax on the conversion, that's perfectly ok.

The Roth recharacterization is treated as if the Roth conversion never happened at all.

How do you recharacterize? Since a recharacterization reverses a Roth conversion, you would have to transfer the converted funds back to a traditional IRA and that transfer must be done as a direct, trustee-to-trustee transfer.

This means that the funds must go ***directly*** from your Roth IRA to the traditional IRA. You cannot withdraw the converted funds from your Roth IRA and then deposit them back into your traditional IRA. You can do either a full or partial recharacterization.

You can even get your tax money back after you've filed! If you recharacterize after you have already filed your tax return for the year of conversion, that's still ok.

In that case, you will need to file an amended return so the IRS, and your state, know that you are no longer responsible for tax on the conversion. If you've already paid all or a portion of the tax, you'll get those amounts back... plus interest!

2. Back-Door Roth IRA Conversion

Although the income limits for Roth conversions are repealed, the Roth IRA contribution income limits still exist, but you can easily bypass them by using the ***"Back Door Roth IRA Conversion"*** strategy.

Here is how it works. If your income exceeds the limits for contributing to a Roth IRA, you make a non-deductible contribution to a traditional IRA and then convert that traditional IRA to a Roth IRA.

4 Cautions When Using this Strategy:

1   You must have earned income – such as wages or self-employment income.

2   You cannot be over age 70½ (traditional IRA contributions can no longer be made for the 70½ year and later years).

3   The pro-rata rule will apply. All your IRAs, including SEP and SIMPLE IRAs, are included in the pro-rata calculation.

This could mean that some of your back-door Roth conversion will be taxable if you have other pre-tax funds in any of your IRAs. That's still not a bad thing because that tax would have been paid anyway eventually, and now you are getting more money growing tax free in your Roth IRA.

4   The funds that end up in your Roth IRA through a back-door conversion are **_converted_** funds, **_NOT_** Roth IRA contributions. This makes a difference for you if you are under age 59½ because you must wait 5 years for penalty-free access to those funds. If the funds went in as Roth IRA contributions, you would be able to access them immediately, tax and penalty-free.

But Roth money should be for the long-term, so hopefully you will not be withdrawing before age 59½.

3. Mega Back Door Roth IRA Conversion

Next up here is another Roth-related item known as a Mega Back Door Roth IRA Conversion –where you can use after-tax funds in a plan to beef up your Roth IRA, with little or no tax.

If some is good, more is better, right? If you feel comfortable with the **_Back-Door Roth IRA Conversion_** strategy and you have additional discretionary income, you may want to see if there's the potential to take this strategy to the next level with another related strategy that has been dubbed by some as the *"Mega Back-Door Roth IRA Conversion."*

Your ability to potentially take a distribution of your after-tax employer plan (your 401(k), for example) contributions, along with the earnings on those funds, at any time, gives rise to the *"Mega Back-Door Roth."* In order for you to take advantage of the mega back-door Roth strategy, three conditions must be satisfied:

1) Your employer plan must allow you to make after-tax contributions.

2) You must have enough disposable income to make after-tax contributions to your plan.

3) Your plan must allow for periodic in-service distributions of your after-tax money and earnings.

Here's how the strategy works… There is a requirement that distributions from a plan must be made on a pro-rata basis – meaning a proportionate amount of each distribution includes earnings and principal. You generally cannot just convert the after tax funds in a plan and pay no tax, except possibly for this strategy. That said, the pro-rata calculation for the distribution can only include funds you are eligible to take a distribution of at the time.

With that in mind, if you are young (under 59½), you can make after-tax contributions to your plan on an ongoing basis (provided your plan allows this). Then, periodically and preferably before there are significant gains on those amounts, you can take a distribution of those funds and have them converted to a Roth IRA. Since the pre-tax and/or Roth salary deferrals you have, along with their earnings, would generally be inaccessible, the pro-rata calculation would typically only consider your after-tax funds and their respective earnings.

Therefore, your converted funds will be all or mostly after-tax money, and the conversion will be virtually tax-free. That's powerful and not well known.

4. NUA – Net Unrealized Appreciation in Employer Securities

NUA is short for **"Net Unrealized Appreciation"** of employer securities. It's the difference between the cost basis and the market value of employer securities held inside your company plan, for example your 401(k).

The special tax break for NUA allows you to pay long-term capital gains rates on the growth of your shares instead of ordinary rates, and you will not owe that tax until the shares are sold outside the plan. This can create up to a 20% tax savings.

If your company plan includes highly appreciated company stock, consider withdrawing the stock and rolling the rest of the plan assets over your IRA.

This way you will pay no current tax on the NUA or the amount rolled over to the IRA. The only tax owed would be on the cost of the stock when acquired by the plan.

How do you know if you are a candidate for the NUA tax break?

First ask these 2 Questions:

1. Do you have stock of the company you work for in your 401(k)?

2. Is it highly appreciated?
(What was the cost when the shares were put in the plan – and – what is today's value of those shares?)

The mechanics of the tax break on net unrealized appreciation of company stock are relatively simple.

If a lump-sum distribution from your company plan includes highly appreciated stock of that company, you are permitted to roll it over to an IRA, but you may not want to.

Although conventional wisdom says do the rollover, there is an exception that applies to company stock and works best when that stock is highly appreciated from the date the company plan (for example, a 401(k) plan) acquired it. The higher the appreciation and the lower the cost basis in your company shares, the more advantageous the company stock tax break is for you.

Under the special tax rule, you can withdraw the stock from the plan and pay regular (ordinary) income tax on it, but only on the original cost to the plan and not on the market value, that is, what the shares are worth on the date of the distribution.

The difference (the appreciation) is called the net unrealized appreciation (NUA). NUA is the increase in the value of the employer stock from the time it was acquired by your plan to the date of the distribution to you.

You can elect to defer the tax on the NUA until you sell the stock. When you do sell, you will only pay tax at your current capital gains rate. To qualify for the tax deferral on NUA, the distribution must be a lump-sum distribution.

A lump sum means that all the assets in all like plan accounts must be distributed out of the plan within one calendar year. Partial distributions spanning more than one year won't work.

Before using this NUA tax break, it is essential that you consult with knowledgeable professional tax and financial advisors to make sure all the tax rules are followed precisely. Also consult the administrators of your company retirement plan.

5. Still Working Exception to RMDs from Plans

Here's a way to delay those pesky required minimum distributions (RMDs) after age 70½.

It's called the *"still working"* exception, but it only applies to the company plan of the company you are still working for. It never applies to IRAs, so continue your RMDs, from your IRAs, even if this exception applies to your company plan.

Generally, you must begin taking your RMDs from your retirement plan by April 1 of the year following the year you turn 70½ years old. For example, if you turn 70½ years old in 2016, you will have a required beginning date of April 1, 2017.

However, if you have a 401(k) or other company plan you may be able to delay your RMDs until April 1st of the year following the year you finally retire by using the "still working" exception.

You are eligible for this exception if you meet certain criteria:

You are still working for the company where you have the plan, and…

You don't own more than 5% of the company, and…

Your plan allows "a still working exception." This provision is optional on the part of the plan. They are not required to have a "still working exception."

This rule applies to RMDs from employer plans only. It does NOT apply to IRAs. It also does not apply an employer plan if you are not currently working for that employer.

6. Catch-up Contributions

Here's a nice benefit for those age 50 or older.

You can contribute more to most retirement plans using catch-up contributions.

The IRA or Roth IRA contribution limit is $5,500 per year if you are under age 50, and $6,500 if you attain age 50 during the year.

The extra $1,000 is called a *"catch up contribution,"* based on the idea that those near retirement may need to contribute more to "catch up" on retirement savings.

This higher contribution amount is available to you even if you're not behind and catching up. This is sometimes missed so take advantage of this benefit.

You may begin the higher contributions at any point in the year you attain age 50 and you do not have to wait until your 50th birthday to make that first $6,500 contribution.

You and your spouse may both be potentially eligible to make catch-up contributions to your IRAs for a combined total of $13,000 in contributions.

7. Spouse as Beneficiary Tax Breaks – Delayed RMDs

Here are some little known tax breaks for spouses who inherit an IRA from their spouse.

A spouse who inherits may delay RMDs on an IRA inherited from a spouse who was not yet 70½ years old. Spouses often get breaks when it comes to the retirement account rules.

Here is a rule that can be very helpful if you are a spouse beneficiary and your younger spouse passed away before his or her required beginning date – before age 70½.

If you choose to remain a beneficiary (instead of doing a spousal rollover), you'll have to take beneficiary payouts based upon your life expectancy, recalculated if you are the account's sole beneficiary.

But you may delay these payments until the *later of* the year after the year of your spouse's death, or the year your spouse would have attained age 70½. You may be able to delay taking RMDs for years.

For example, let's assume you are 75 years old, and your spouse passes away at age 65. If you choose to be a beneficiary, you would not have to start RMDs on the inherited IRA until the year your deceased spouse would have attained age 70½.

You would not have to draw down for another five years. A spousal rollover or transfer would mean you would have to begin withdrawals by December 31st of the year following death.

8. Spouse as Beneficiary Tax Breaks – Penalty-free Distributions

Here's a benefit for a young spouse who inherits:

You may be eligible for penalty free distributions from inherited IRAs if you are a young spouse who inherits an IRA and remains a beneficiary.

If you inherit your spouse's IRA when you are under age 59½, you may consider ***not*** doing a spousal rollover and instead, taking advantage of a rule that allows you to stay as the beneficiary of the IRA until you are safe from the 10% early distribution penalty.

Here is how it pays to remain as the beneficiary if you are younger than age 59½.

Let's use an example where your spouse passes away when you are both 40 years old. If you are 40 years old and do a spousal rollover, the account would be treated as your own IRA. If you want to take any money out before age 59½ there would be a 10% penalty which is assessed on retirement plan owners who tap into their retirement plan accounts before age 59½.

But this *10% penalty does not apply to retirement plan beneficiaries.* In this case, if you are younger than 59½ years old, it would pay to be treated as a beneficiary because you could take distributions without incurring the 10% penalty. You still pay the income tax of course, but no 10% penalty.

After reaching age 59½, you would still have the spousal rollover option available.

Choosing to remain a beneficiary does not restrict you from being able to roll over to your own IRA later on. You can do a spousal rollover at any time.

But it doesn't work the other way. Once you do a spousal rollover, you cannot go back and be treated as a beneficiary with an inherited IRA.

9. Increased Contributions with Sideline Income

You can increase your retirement contributions if you have sideline income in addition to 401(k) contributions from a regular job.

Many people work two jobs. You may have a regular job and run a business on the side. Why not consider increasing your retirement contributions by setting up a retirement plan for your small business.

This loophole lets you do both. The IRS has essentially said, "Yes, you can set up a SEP (that's a Simplified Employee Pension) for your self-employed business even if you participate in your employer's retirement plan at another job."

You can make the maximum contributions to your 401(k) *and* fully fund a SEP plan for your small business.

If you are self-employed, you must use a special formula to calculate your compensation. A worksheet with the calculation can be found in **IRS Publication 560.**

10. SEP Contributions After 70 ½

Here's something that most people don't take advantage of:

You can contribute to a SEP after 70½ (even though you can no longer contribute to a traditional IRA after age 70½). If you reach age 70½ during the year, you may not make a traditional IRA contribution for that year. But this limitation does not apply to SEP IRAs.

There are no age restrictions for SEP IRA contributions. If you have a SEP IRA plan for your small business you may continue to make SEP IRA contributions if otherwise eligible for the year you reach age 70½ and for years thereafter.

Remember though, you will still need to take RMDs beginning by April 1 of the year following the year you attain age 70½ because the "still working" exception that applies sometimes for employer plans does not apply to SEP IRAs.

11. Extensions for SEP Contributions

Here's another way that SEP IRAs differ from traditional IRAs, even though they are both IRAs.

SEP IRAs can be established and funded until the tax-filing deadline ***including extensions***. That gives you until October 15th to set up and fund your SEP IRA for the prior year.

There is no extension beyond the regular April 15th deadline to make IRA or Roth IRA contributions for the prior year.

Are you self-employed or a small business owner? You may not know how profitable your business will be from year to year. Take advantage of the rule allowing a special late deadline for establishing and contributing to a SEP IRA.

This rule allows you the advantage of waiting to assess your business' performance before deciding how much to contribute to a SEP IRA plan. If your business has a good year, you can contribute a higher amount. In a bad year, you can contribute a smaller amount or even nothing at all.

Here is how it works. The deadline for making a SEP IRA contribution for the year is the business' tax-filing deadline, including extensions. If you have an extension to file your 2015 federal income taxes until October 17, 2016, you are still eligible to establish and make a SEP IRA contribution until that date.

This deadline is different than the deadline for traditional IRA and Roth IRA contributions, which is the tax-filing deadline, not including any extensions.

Your SEP contribution may be made to an IRA under an existing SEP IRA plan or you may still establish a new plan for the year. Remember, you may only establish a SEP IRA plan if you are an employer.

12. Roth IRA Contributions *After* 70 ½

Here's a nice break for Roth IRAs that's different from the traditional IRA rules. You can contribute to a Roth after 70½, even though you can no longer contribute to a traditional IRA for years you are age 70½ or older.

Traditional IRA contributions are no longer permitted once you reach the year that you attain age 70½. There is no such rule in the tax code for Roth IRAs. If you are age 70½ or older and still working (you have earned income) you can continue to make Roth IRA contributions.

Even if you are well into your retirement years, your age will not prevent you from contributing to a Roth IRA. If you are 80 years old with a part time job and working a few hours a week you may consider making a Roth IRA contribution.

Keep in mind that the income limits for Roth IRA contributions would still apply, regardless of your age. But those limits are very high allowing most workers to contribute to Roth IRAs.

13. Spousal IRAs

Here's a nice loophole allowing you to contribute to a traditional or Roth IRA even if you have no earnings. It's called a **spousal IRA**.

If you are retired, you may think that your days of contributing to an IRA are behind you. This may not be the case if you are married and your spouse has earnings from a job or self-employment income.

You can make an IRA contribution to the IRA of a spouse who is not working (or has very little income) providing you file a joint tax return and you have sufficient income to cover the contributions for your retired spouse, plus any contributions made for you.

If you are retired and your spouse's compensation at least $13,000 for, you can each go ahead and fully fund a $6,500 IRA contribution for the year (assuming you are both age 50 or over).

You do not both have to contribute to the same kind of IRA. You might contribute to a Traditional IRA and your spouse might contribute to a Roth IRA.

However, you still must meet all the other contribution rules for that IRA, such as age and income limits.

14. Roth IRAs AND Company Plans

Did you also know that you can still fund a Roth IRA if you participate in company plan? It's true, although most people don't know this.

You are eligible to fund a Roth IRA if you or your spouse have earned income for the year and your income is below the income limits for Roth IRA contributions.

Your participation in a company plan has no impact on your ability to fund a Roth IRA. You can contribute the maximum amount permitted to your company plan and still fully fund a Roth IRA.

The reason most people, even advisors, get this wrong is because there is a limitation if you are working for a company and participating in their retirement plan, but that is only for a traditional IRA, not a Roth IRA. You never get a tax deduction for Roth IRA contributions.

That rule still does not affect your ability to contribute to a traditional IRA. It only affects your ability to deduct that traditional IRA contribution, and that is next on my list.

15. No Income Limits for Traditional IRAs

There are no income limits to <u>***contribute***</u> ***to a traditional IRA.***

There are income limits on traditional IRA deductibility, but only if you, or you and your spouse are active participants in a company plan, like a 401(k) plan.

However, there are *no income limits* for deducting a traditional IRA contribution for single taxpayers who are not participants in a retirement plan at work and *no income limits* for married couples when neither spouse is an active participant in a retirement plan at work.

You may be eligible to deduct your traditional IRA contribution no matter how high your income for the year is if you or you and your spouse are not active participants in a company plan.

If that is your situation, you may deduct your contribution no matter how high your income for the year is. You may also deduct your full contribution to your IRA even if you are in a plan, if you are under those income limits.

If you over the income limits and in a company plan, you can still make a traditional IRA contribution. It's just won't be deductible.

16. Tax and Penalty Free Roth IRA Distributions

Here's a great tax loophole:

Roth IRA tax-year contributions are immediately accessible both tax and penalty free. You can withdraw your Roth IRA contributions any time and for any reason tax and penalty free. Not earnings though, just your Roth IRA contributions.

There are special ordering rules for Roth IRA distributions. Under these rules, all your Roth IRAs are considered one Roth account. Contributed amounts are distributed first.

This rule is beneficial to you as a taxpayer because these amounts are not taxable or subject to the early distribution penalty, even if the distribution is made before five years or before age 59½.

A distribution from your Roth IRA can never be taxed or subject to penalty until all of your contributions have been recovered. If you need to access your Roth IRA contributions, you can do so without fear of tax or penalty-at any time and for any reason.

In addition, there are breaks for Roth conversions if you are age 59½ or older. Roth IRA conversions are immediately accessible both tax and penalty free if you are over 59½.

Under the ordering rules for Roth IRA distributions, any amounts you converted to your Roth IRA are distributed after all your contributions are distributed. Distributions of converted amounts are not taxable because you already paid taxes on these amounts when you converted the funds.

If you are over age 59½ a distribution of converted funds will also always be penalty-free. There is no waiting period. Once you are age 59½ you can always access your converted funds without tax or penalty.

Amounts that were taxable when converted are subject to the 10% early distribution penalty only if you are under the age of 59½ at the time of the distribution and the conversion was less than five years ago.

17. Saver's Tax Credit for Retirement Contributions

Did you know you might qualify for a tax credit for making an IRA or Roth IRA contribution?

In fact, you might qualify to claim both the saver's credit and a traditional IRA deduction, if your income is below certain levels.

Certain lower income taxpayers are eligible for a nonrefundable income tax credit called the Saver's Credit for IRA or salary deferral contributions. This is a great opportunity for a recent graduate who is just starting out.

To be eligible, you must be 18 or older before the end of the taxable year and you may not be a full time student or claimed as a dependent on another taxpayer's return.

The credit applies to the first $2,000 you contribute and the maximum credit available is $1,000. The rules even allow you to claim the credit for your traditional IRA contribution and also deduct it for a double tax benefit.

18. Inherited Plan Rollovers for Non-Spouse Beneficiaries

Here's a tax benefit for your non-spouse beneficiaries, like your children or grandchildren, who inherit your 401(k) or other company plan you may have.

Non-spouse beneficiaries of company plans can roll over the funds to an inherited traditional IRA or convert them to an inherited Roth IRA.

If you inherit funds in a company plan from someone other than your spouse, you may discover that the payout options offered by the plan are very limited.

There is an alternative. You, as the named beneficiary, can do a direct rollover to a properly titled inherited IRA (the title includes the name of the deceased plan participant) or you can directly convert those funds to an inherited Roth IRA.

You must be a designated beneficiary, meaning you are named on the beneficiary form.

You must do the ***direct rollover*** from the plan by the end of the year following the year of death to avoid the plan's options which could be as little as a 5-year payout.

You must also take the first RMD by the end of the year after death in order to use the stretch options in the inherited IRA (and to avoid the 50% penalty).

This ability to directly roll over to an inherited IRA or convert to an inherited Roth IRA could have a multi-million dollar effect if you are a young non-spouse beneficiary.

You can now stretch those inherited funds in an inherited IRA or inherited Roth IRA over your lifetime.

19. Convert After-Tax IRA Funds to a Roth IRA – Tax-Free

Here's another loophole that can help you to convert after-tax IRA funds tax free to a Roth IRA.

Roll over your taxable traditional IRA funds to a company plan (if you have one, and the plan allows these rollovers in) before converting to a Roth IRA.

When an IRA contains both nondeductible and deductible funds, then each dollar withdrawn from the IRA will contain a percentage of tax-free and taxable funds based on the percentage of after-tax funds to the entire balance in all your IRAs.

That's the pro-rata rule I covered earlier here. You cannot withdraw (or convert) just the nondeductible funds and pay no tax.

The next question we usually get on this is "What if that $30,000 of nondeductible IRA contributions was kept in a separate IRA? Then can you convert only this $30,000 and pay no tax, since it is all after-tax funds?" The answer is still "No." For this pro-rata rule, you must include the balances of all IRAs even if they are in separate accounts, and that includes balances in SEP and SIMPLE plans because they are IRAs as well for this purpose.

But, there is a loophole that allows you to work around this. There's a rule that allows taxable traditional IRA funds to be rolled over to employer retirement plans if the plan permits.

Nondeductible IRA funds are not eligible to go back to a plan. A special exception to the pro-rata rule applies here that says that the first funds to be rolled over to your plan are the taxable funds. The non-taxable funds (the nondeductible contributions) are not eligible to be rolled back to the plan.

You can rollover taxable IRA funds to your employer retirement plan and leave your nondeductible funds behind. Then, convert those nondeductible IRA funds to a Roth IRA, tax-free.

This is another area where you should only do this after consulting with your tax and financial advisors to make sure you properly follow the tax rules.

20. Tax-Free Conversions of After-Tax Plan Funds

Here is yet another way to create a tax-free Roth conversion from plan funds.

Roll over your taxable company plan distribution to a traditional IRA and then convert the after-tax portion to a Roth IRA tax-free.

If you will be receiving a distribution from your company plan that includes both pretax and after-tax money, here is one rule you will want to know about. IRS Notice 2014-54 confirmed that if you have both pre-tax and after-tax employer plan money, you can allocate pre-tax funds to an IRA and after-tax funds to a Roth IRA. Allocating your after-tax funds to a Roth IRA creates a tax-free Roth IRA conversion for you.

Be careful because plan funds are still distributed pro-rata. You cannot simply take out only after-tax funds and pay no tax, while leaving pre-tax funds in your plan.

These rules do not apply to IRA distributions. If you have after-tax funds in your IRA, any IRA distributions will still follow the pro-rata rule, where every IRA withdrawal is a percentage taxable and tax free.

As with many similar tax rules, you should only do this after consulting with competent tax or financial advisors and run this by your company plan administrators to make sure these rollovers and conversions are done correctly under the tax law.

21. Tax-Free Gifts for Roth IRAs

Next on my list is the ability to use tax-free gifts to help children or grandchildren fund their Roth IRAs, pay for their Roth conversions or help them pay for college or medical bills – all tax free to you and them!

Parents or grandparents can make IRA or Roth IRA contributions for children who have earned income, even if the children spent every penny they earned.

You can make the contribution directly to the child's retirement account; ***the contribution does not have to be made by the child***. Money that parents give to their child is potentially subject to gift taxes but you can give up to $14,000 to any person, every year, tax-free.

That not only includes children or grandchildren – these annual tax-free gifts can be made to anyone – up to $14,000 per person, per year.

Consider opening a Roth IRA for an 18-year old earning $5,500 at a summer job and funding it with $5,500.

That will help them start early on their retirement savings. Both the initial $5,500 Roth IRA contribution and all the earnings will grow income tax free in their Roth IRA.

You could go one further and use your gift to pay up to $14,000 of taxes for them if they want to convert their IRA to a Roth IRA. Most children are in lower tax brackets so that $14,000 can go a long way towards helping them get started early building their tax free Roth IRA.

For example, if your child is in a 15% tax bracket, your $14,000 gift could be used to help them pay the tax on converting up to $93,333 of IRA funds to a Roth IRA. The tax at 15% on $93,333 is $14,000.

Note: *If they had that much ($93,333) to convert, their tax bracket would most likely be higher than 15%, but I used the 15% low tax bracket to illustrate the extent of the tax benefit. Also, if they had high deductions or losses or were filing a joint tax return with their spouse, they could still be in a low tax bracket even with a large Roth IRA conversion.*

But most children don't even have that much in their IRAs, so your $14,000 gift should cover all they have.

That's a good move for you and them. At least you know your gift went to help them save for retirement – a worthy plan.

22. Tax-Free Gifts for Tuition and Medical Bills

In addition to the annual $14,000 tax free gifts, the tax law allows you to make UNLIMITED tax-free gifts to anyone if you are paying their tuition or medical bills.

The only catch is that the gift payments cannot go to the person, say your child or children. They must be made **directly** to the school or medical provider, and that is actually a good thing, since you know for sure that your hard earned money is being used responsibly.

This unlimited gift exemption is one of the biggest loopholes in the tax code, so take advantage of it.

But wait there's more…

These tax free gifts do not cut into your lifetime gift or estate tax exemption which gives you the ability to gift or leave $5,450,000 (the 2016 amount) tax free in addition to the annual $14,000 gift exclusions and the unlimited tax free gifts for medical or tuition.

There are some big retirement tax loopholes in this program that are available to most of you so take advantage of all you can, and share this with your family and friends.

And always consult with professional tax, legal and financial advisors before using any of these tax strategies.

Ed Slott's Essential Collection

Fundamental knowledge to build, protect and preserve your retirement savings

(6 DVDs and 2 CDs)

DVDs

10 Questions to Ask Your Financial Advisor

11 Ways to Super-Charge Your Roth IRA

7 Biggest Retirement Mistakes!

Retirement Tax Horrors Your Can Avoid!

Life Insurance for Life and Beyond

Critical Items for Critical Moments

CDs

Life Events

Advisor Check-Up

DVD

10 Questions to Ask Your Financial Advisor

1. I know this area requires specialized knowledge in IRA distribution planning.

Do you have expertise in this area?

How would I know that?

2. What books have you read on the topic?

Look at the books. If they crack when you open them… run. It's the first time that book has been opened.

3. What professional training do you take in IRA distribution planning?

What courses or programs have you taken?

Can you show me the last course manual you received?

4. How do you stay current on key IRA tax rules?

What services or resources do you rely on stay up to date?

Can you show me a sample?

5. What is the latest IRA tax rule you are aware of?

When did that occur?

6. How do you determine the best option for my lump sum distribution?

What are all my choices?

7. How would you keep track of my IRA beneficiary form?

When should I update my beneficiary form? What are the key events that would trigger a need for a review?

8. Can you show me the IRS life expectancy tables?

9. Do you know what will happen to my IRA after I die?

How will you make sure that my beneficiary will get the stretch IRA?

10. Who do *YOU* turn to when you have questions on IRA distribution planning?

No one can know it all.

DVD

11 Ways to Super-Charge Your Roth IRA

Roth IRAs Build Tax-Free Retirement Savings

The goal is to build your retirement savings in a tax-free account. This is what I call moving your retirement savings from accounts that are forever taxed to accounts that are never taxed.

Roth conversions are available to everyone.

Some still think there are restrictions, but those were repealed and now everyone qualifies.

Roth IRAs come in 2 types:

Contributions and Conversions

Roth IRA Contributions

Contributions are the $5,500 ($6,500 if 50 or over) annual contribution amounts for those who have earned income.

2016 Tax Law Update:

2016 Roth IRA Contribution Limits
$5,500 ($6,500 if age 50 or over)

2016 Phase-Out Ranges for Roth IRA Contributions

Married/Joint	Single or Head of Household
184,000 – 194,000	117,000 – 132,000

If filing married-separate, the phase-out range is $0 – $10,000

There are high income restrictions (see chart above) on who can contribute but those are easily by-passed. You can contribute to a nondeductible IRA and then convert it. You have to have earnings though to contribute to an IRA. While you cannot contribute to a traditional IRA after age 70½, you can contribute to a Roth IRA after age 70½.

Roth IRA Conversions

The big money is in Roth conversions and **you can convert unlimited amounts**. Also, there is no income limit on who can convert.

Roth IRAs have no lifetime required minimum distributions (RMDs). You never have to take RMDs for the rest of your life. Your money just grows tax free, and you can pass your Roth IRA to a spouse who also does not have to take RMDs.

RMDs don't begin until a non-spouse beneficiary inherits, like your children or grandchildren.

How to decide if the Roth IRA is right for you

Ask yourself these 3 questions:

When? What? Where?

1. When do you think you will need access to your money?

2. What do you think your future tax rate will be?

3. Where will you get the money from to pay the tax on the Roth conversion?

Not only can everyone convert, the amount you can convert is unlimited. Of course you have to pay taxes when you convert.

But given the historic low tax rates right now, this may be the best money you have ever spent moving your retirement funds to permanent tax-free territory.

11 Ways to Super-Charge Your Roth IRA

1. Contribute the maximum you can

> ### 2016 Tax Law Update:
> **Roth IRA Contribution Limits**
>
> $5,500 ($6,500 if age 50 or over)

You need earnings (from wages or self-employment).

Even alimony qualifies as earnings. Who says you didn't earn it! But child support payments do not count as earnings.

Combat pay counts as earnings, even though it may not be taxable.

Unemployment Insurance does NOT qualify as earnings.

Self-employed income counts too.

You can contribute to a Roth IRA at any age, even after age 70½. With a traditional IRA you can no longer contribute after age 70½. In fact, with a traditional IRA, you have to begin withdrawing and paying tax once you reach age 70½, whether you want to or not!

There is no risk with a Roth IRA contribution. If you need the money, you can withdraw your Roth contributions any time for any reason, tax and penalty free. Not the earnings or converted funds, but the Roth contributions.

If you are age 59½ or older, the converted funds can also be withdrawn tax and penalty free. You don't have to hold that money (the converted funds) for 5 years once you reach age 59½.

2. Capitalize on Low Tax Rates – Do a Roth Conversion

Get 'em while they last! Roth conversions that is – at low bargain basement prices. Taxes are as low as they will ever be. And it seems clear that future taxes will be higher.

Paying the tax now will avoid it later and your retirement money will be tax free for life. You'll actually be saving big money later by taking the tax hit now.

You'll have more tax-free money when you need it the most, in retirement, when you are no longer working and you'll need to keep more of your money protected from future taxes.

3. Roth Conversion Do-Overs can help you convert the optimum amount at the lowest tax rate

Roth IRA conversions come with a built in safety net, so risk can be eliminated.

It's called a Roth recharacterization. It means undoing your Roth conversion like it never happened. Everyone can do it and you don't need a reason. You get to evaluate your conversion decision with more information available to you.

When you first convert, there is uncertainty:

You are unsure of how much tax it will cost you.

You are unsure of your tax bracket for that year.

- you don't know your income for sure until the year ends
- bonuses
- losses
- tax deductions
- other income items

You are unsure of how your investments will perform.

You are unsure if you'll have the money to pay the tax.

You are unsure of any tax law changes that might take place.

But you have until October 15th of the year after the conversion to recharacterize and by that time, these questions will be answered.

You'll have all the information you need to make a better informed decision. You'll have more time to evaluate, and that is a big advantage.

You can convert the maximum, and, if your investments don't do well, you can recharacterize so you are not paying tax on value that no longer exists. It's like getting to bet on a horse after the race is over!

You have until October 15th of the year after the conversion to change your mind, for any reason at all.

So how can this super-charge your Roth conversion?

You can take advantage of lower tax rates. By the time you have to make a decision, you'll know how much the conversion will cost you.

You can make sure that you are paying taxes at the lowest rates by keeping your conversion income in a low bracket, if you wish to. You can recharacterize enough to keep you from getting bumped to a higher tax bracket.

4. Re-Convert

Use the cycle to your advantage

Here's how "the cycle" works:

Conversion – Recharacterization – Re-conversion

Once a Roth recharacterization is done, those same funds can be re-converted, but you must wait until the later of:

> 1. The year after the conversion, or
> 2. More than 30 days after the recharacterization

What's in it for you?

You can maximize your options to lock in Roth IRA tax-free gains and pay tax at the lowest possible rates; also on the lowest possible balance.

Here are some examples of how the cycle works:

Rules on how soon a re-conversion can be done:

You must wait until the later of:

> · The calendar year after the conversion, or
> · More than 30 days after the recharacterization.

Il'll give you a few examples here that span several years:

For a 2014 conversion – no more recharacterizations are available – the deadline was October 15, 2015.

For a 2015 conversion, the recharacterization deadline is October 15, 2016.
For a 2016 conversion, the recharacterization deadline is October 15, 2017.

If a 2015 conversion was recharacterized in 2016, a re-conversion can be done after 30 days.

Example:
2015 conversion done in October 2015
Recharacterized September 20, 2016

It's the 30-day rule:
These funds can be re-converted after October 20, 2016.

Example:
2015 conversion done in April 2015
Recharacterized September 20, 2015

It's the next year rule:
These funds cannot be re-converted until 2016.

Example:
2016 conversion done in April 2016
Recharacterized January 10, 2017

It's the 30-day rule:
These funds can be re-converted after February 10, 2017.

Other IRA or plan funds that still exist (that were not converted) have no conversion timing restrictions.

Hopefully you get the idea of how the cycle works.

Now I'm going to show you how to capitalize on this cycle.

5. Convert to Several New Roth IRAs

Use a **Multiple Account Strategy**. You can cherry-pick winners or losers.

If you convert everything to one Roth, you cannot cherry-pick and only get rid of the losers. You have to add in all the gains and losses.

Better strategy: Consider converting to multiple Roth IRA accounts and keep only the accounts that do best.

Put different types of investments in different Roth IRAs.

For example, let's say you have these different types of investments in different Roth accounts:

> Health care
> Real estate
> Conservative investments
> Aggressive investments
> Utilities

Get rid of losers by recharacterizing those accounts.

Does this mean you have to keep track of 5 or 6 different Roth IRAs?

Yes, but only until the time to recharacterize expires. Keep the separate Roth accounts until the deadline (the Oct. 15th date) to recharacterize expires. Then you can combine all your Roth IRAs into one master account again. This is lots of paperwork but worth it to give you every possible advantage using the tax code to super-charge your Roth IRA.

6. Have grandma convert and have her name her children or grandchildren as beneficiaries

Consider naming grandchildren as beneficiaries since they have a longer life expectancy and it can be worth more to them over time, especially when it is a tax-free Roth IRA.

Benefit to naming children:
-Longer life expectancy and no taxes for life

A 20-year-old has a 63 year life expectancy
$100,000 over 63.0 years at 8% = $2,511,000

A 10-year-old has a 72.8 year life expectancy
$100,000 over 72.8 years at 8% = $4,641,000

A 1-year-old has an 81.6 year life expectancy
$100,000 over 81.6 years at 8% = $8,167,000

All tax free for life! Imagine if someone ever did that for you.

You can gift grandma the money to convert. Make sure she names the right beneficiaries! YOU or your children (her grandchildren).

Benefit to naming you:
Say you are already in a high tax bracket.

Let's say you are an executive or professional in a high tax bracket. The last thing you need is to inherit a taxable IRA from your mom or dad.

But your mom or dad doesn't have the money to convert to a Roth. They need their money and it's not worth converting for them.

You can gift them the money to pay the tax on their Roth IRA conversions. You will inherit these funds as an inherited Roth IRA and will never have to pay tax on those funds.

In effect, you paid tax at your mom or dad's much lower tax rates, instead of what would have been your much higher rates. If you inherited and paid the tax, it would have been at your rates as you withdraw from an inherited traditional IRA.

Also, once grandma has a Roth IRA, she is no longer subject to RMDs, so if she does not need the money, it can keep growing tax free for her beneficiary – YOU!

7. Turn Required Distributions into Roth Conversions

IRAs are subject to required minimum distributions (RMDs) after reaching age 70½. Whether you want to take the money or not, you have to. But most people who are subject to RMDs don't need the money, so they just take the distribution and pay the tax.

Those required amounts _CANNOT_ be converted.

People think they can because they are already paying the tax. It makes sense, but still, the law says you cannot convert required minimum distributions. That's why it might pay to convert before the year you turn age 70½.

Example:
If you will turn age 70½ in 2017, then convert in 2016. If you convert everything, you'll never have to take required minimum distributions, because Roth IRA owners are exempt from lifetime RMDs.

But let's say you are already over age 70½ and subject to RMDs.

As long as you have to withdraw the funds anyway, you may as well use those funds to convert the rest of your traditional IRA funds to Roth IRAs.

8. Consistent Conversions

Contrary to what many people think, a Roth conversion is not an all or nothing choice.

You can do partial conversions.

Consider converting over many years to keep taxes lower.

Take advantage of our graduated tax rates:
$500,000 of income in one year generates more tax than $100,000 each year for 5 years, assuming tax rates stay relatively similar over that time.

9. Helping Your Children Create Roth IRAs

*"Time is the greatest money-making asset
any individual can possess."*   *– Ed Slott*

And young people have it! Take advantage of it and see the exponential growth.

You can make gifts to your children for both types of Roth IRAs

Make gifts to your children so they have money to convert their IRAs to Roth IRAs.

They might not have enough money to convert on their own – and would be wasting a major lifetime tax advantage. They are most likely in a low tax bracket and they likely have a much smaller IRA balance, so now is the time for them to convert. The lifetime growth will be tax free.

Roth IRAs for children:
They need earned income to qualify for a Roth IRA contribution.

See if they can be put on books for legitimate work before the year ends (or get some holiday employment).

If they have earnings, they qualify for a Roth IRA contribution, and that can be made from funds gifted to them by you – their parent or their grandparents.

Make gifts to children to create Roth IRAs or convert their IRAs to Roth IRAs.

What a great start you can give them!

193

10. Estate Tax Benefits

Roth IRA funds will not only pass income tax free to your loved ones, but most likely estate tax free too, depending on the amount of the estate tax exemption.

Your children are better off inheriting a Roth. If they inherit an IRA, they cannot convert that to a Roth IRA.

Inherited plan assets can only be converted by beneficiaries directly from the plan to an inherited Roth IRA.

11. Save the Roth for Last!

Roth IRA money is growing tax free, so let it grow! Leave it alone!

Tax fee money always grows the fastest because it is not eroded by taxes along the way… or ever.

Don't touch this golden tax-free fund.

Save the Roth Money for Last. Use other money first and let the Roth grow tax free. Why use money that's growing tax free when you can use other money?

Extra – Don't mess this up now!

Roth IRA Housekeeping

Now that you are super-charging your Roth IRA, you don't want anything getting in the way or ruining what you've created.

Make sure to name new beneficiaries once you open a new Roth IRA account or convert your IRA to a Roth IRA. You have created a new account and new accounts need new beneficiary forms. The beneficiaries can be the same as the beneficiaries of your traditional IRA, if you wish.

Consider naming grandchildren as beneficiaries since they have a longer life expectancy and it can be worth more to them over time.

Move the money to the Roth the right way:

The best way is via a direct trustee-to-trustee transfer, where you don't touch the money in between.

If you are changing custodians at the same time as converting, most custodians require like-to-like transfers, so you may need to set up a new traditional IRA first and then convert once the money is at the new institution.

You can make a 60-day rollover to a Roth IRA as a conversion, but if you do, don't miss the deadline.

Make sure money went into the correct account – a Roth IRA account.

DVD
7 Biggest Retirement Mistakes
And none of these have anything to do with investing!

It took you a lifetime to build your retirement fund. That's years of working, sacrificing and saving so that this money will be available to you when you need it most – in retirement when you are no longer working and cannot replace these funds.

This is sacred money to you, but it's loaded with complex tax rules when you take it out and that's where the biggest and most costly retirement mistakes are made.

I want to prevent you from making these mistakes that I see almost daily and often right under the nose of a financial advisor who was unaware of the problem.

I bring these to your attention because I don't want them happening to you.

Here is my list of the 7 biggest retirement mistakes

1. Not contributing to your retirement accounts

As some people near retirement, they stop contributing.

That's a mistake.

Often, as you get closer to retirement, other financial obligations, like paying off a mortgage, paying for college or taking care of elderly parents are behind you. Now is the time to, as they say "put the pedal to the metal" and go all in with everything you have. There is often no cost to doing this.

You may be able to simply move money from a taxable pocket to a tax-free pocket.

There is no question that if you keep contributing to whatever retirement plan you have, you'll have more retirement money and it will likely last you longer.

That's a simple fact. The more you contribute, the more you will have.

Even if you are slowing down, making less, still take advantage of every option to keep putting money away in a retirement account. In fact, the tax law encourages you to contribute more as you get closer to retirement. Once you turn age 50, for instance, catch-up contributions allow you to add more to your retirement savings than younger savers.

For example, if you are age 50 or over, and you have earned at least $6,500 for the year, you can contribute that to a Roth IRA (as long as you are under the income limits and those are high) and have that money growing tax free for the rest of your life. It does not sound like much but you can do this every year.

If your income is relatively low, don't contribute to a traditional IRA since the tax deduction won't be worth it, and after age 70½ you can no longer contribute to a traditional IRA anyway.

You are better off contributing to a Roth IRA. There is no age limit to contribute to a Roth IRA. In addition, with a Roth IRA there are no required minimum distributions after age 70½ like you have with traditional IRAs, so if you don't need the money it can keep growing tax free for the rest of your life.

If you are still working for a company that sponsors a 401(k) or some other retirement plan, or even better a Roth 401(k) contribute all you can to that as well.

If you are married and both of you are still working, you should both be contributing all you can, and keep your retirement money building tax free.

Here's another often missed retirement opportunity:

If you are married and only one of you is working, did you know that you can also contribute to the IRA of the spouse who is not working, doubling your annual retirement contributions?

Normally, you have to keep working to contribute to an IRA, but this is a special rule allowing a non-working spouse to make contributions based on the working spouse's income – it's called a spousal IRA – and it is one of the most overlooked retirement opportunities in the tax code.

For example, if you and your spouse are 50 or older, but only one of you is working, as long as whoever works makes at least $13,000 for the year, you can contribute $6,500 (that's the maximum) to each of your IRAs, or better, Roth IRAs.

The only catch is that in order to be able to contribute to a Roth IRA your income must fall under the income limits, but those are very high so most of you will be able to contribute to your Roth IRAs and spousal Roth IRAs.

Tax Law Update for 2016:

For a married couple, as long as your joint income does not exceed $184,000 for 2016, you can contribute the full amount ($6,500 per person if age 50 or over) to a Roth IRA. If you are single, the income limit for 2016 is $117,000

If you file married separate, you generally cannot contribute to a Roth IRA since the income limits are too low for most people.

Spousal IRAs are an opportunity that is now also available to **legally-married same-sex couples** as a result of a 2013 U.S. Supreme Court decision. The Supreme Court ruled that section 3 of the federal Defense of Marriage Act (DOMA) was unconstitutional (*This was the Windsor Case).*

Tax Law Update for 2016:

Obergefell case

In 2015, The U.S. Supreme Court ruled that the 14th Amendment requires that states license same-sex couples to marry and recognize same-sex marriages lawfully performed in other states. This was the *Obergefell* case.

Same-sex couples who are legally married under state law were already recognized as married for federal tax purposes after the *Windsor* case in 2013 and subsequent IRS guidance.

But now, all states must license same-sex couples to marry and recognize same-sex marriages lawfully performed in other states.

Like other married couples, a non-working spouse of a legally-married same-sex couple, can make IRA or Roth IRA contributions to a spousal IRA. In addition, spousal rollovers are now also permitted for legally-married same-sex couples.

Same-sex married couples **MUST** file either married-joint or married-separate returns. They can no longer file as two single individuals.

Spousal IRAs are a double benefit for married couples so take advantage of this.

Never leave an opportunity to build tax-free retirement savings on the table. That's incentive enough to keep working, just to keep salting money away in your Roth IRAs.

And that brings me to another related mistake – retirement mistake number 2:

2. Leaving Your Job and Taking Social Security Too Soon

Retiring too early is often a mistake. If you can, you should keep working. Life may be short, but retirement can be long, especially given today's increased life expectancy. Even if you are retired or retiring from your regular job you can consider working part time – if you are healthy enough and able to.

There are numerous proven benefits to this and not all of them are financial. You feel productive and good about yourself and you are still interacting and keeping your mind active. Not everyone does full retirement well.

You might even find some work in a hobby of yours.

Work doesn't always have to be working for a company or someone else. You can have your own part time business and you might just love it.

The financial benefits are clear. The longer and the more you keep earning, the more retirement money you can continue to sock away in a Roth IRA. Remember that with a Roth IRA there is no age limit for making contributions, so as long as you have earnings from a job or self-employment income you can keep contributing to your Roth IRA and your spouse's – even if your spouse is no longer working.

If you are still earning, you are less likely to need to tap your retirement funds so they can continue to compound tax free. In fact if you are still working for a company that you don't own more than 5% of, you can delay required minimum distributions from your 401(k) at that company – allowing more tax-deferred build up – even tax free with a Roth 401(k).

In addition, if you are still working, you can probably avoid taking Social Security for longer, allowing your future benefit to increase substantially. Taking Social Security benefits too soon is a common mistake for many retirees.

You are generally better off using other money (like earnings, or even retirement money) rather than taking social security before age 70. By delaying social security, your benefits actually build by about 8% a year, and that doesn't even take into consideration any cost-of-living adjustments you'll also likely be entitled to.

The waiting game ends at age 70, though. There's no point in waiting longer because your Social Security benefits won't increase any more. From age 62 to age 70, your monthly check goes up every month you delay. That results in an annual increase of about 8% a year. That's 8% a year, guaranteed by the federal government, with no investment risk. That's a great deal!

But it gets even better. That is not only an 8% increase, it's 8% a year PLUS any cost-of-living increases which could be another 3% depending on the inflation rate.

That's an 11% annual increase for waiting. In some cases, that delay can turn a $30,000 annual social security benefit to a $40,000 annual benefit – not just for one year, but for life!

This is another strong reason to keep working, so you won't have to tap your social security benefits early and you can continue to contribute to your Roth IRA and build that account tax free for your retirement years.

Avoiding one mistake often helps you avoid another.

You can already see how the momentum of not making the first two retirement mistakes can build in your favor.

The combination of keep contributing, keep building your tax-free Roth IRA, keep working and delaying Social Security are a solid 1-2-3 punch to building your long-term financial security during retirement.

3. Required Minimum Distribution Mistakes

With a traditional IRA, even if you keep working, you are required to begin taking your required minimum distributions after age 70½. The actual rule states that you must begin distributions by April 1st of the year after the year you turn age 70½. That is called your required beginning date.

As I said earlier, these rules do not apply to your Roth IRAs because with Roth IRAs there are no distributions required for your lifetime – so if all you have is Roth IRAs this is not an issue for you.

But this a big issue for your traditional IRAs, 401(k)s and other company retirement plans.

I see lots of mistakes in this area and they can be costly, because **the penalty for not taking a required minimum distribution is fifty percent (50%) of the amount you didn't withdraw.**

For example, if your required minimum distribution is $12,000 and you forget to take the withdrawal, that's a $6,000 penalty.50% of the $12,000 you were supposed to withdraw.

If you take the wrong amount, the penalty is on the amount not taken.

For example, if again your required distribution was $12,000 but you only withdrew $8,000, you are short $4,000 and the penalty would be $2,000 which is 50% of the $4,000 you did not withdraw.

The mistakes happen because, as with all tax rules in this area, the rules are confusing, even to advisors.

One common mistake is calculating the wrong amount and not taking your full required amount or even taking too much. Sometimes the bank or financial advisor will make the calculation for you, but even then, that could be wrong and you are the one who is responsible.

The right amount to withdraw – your required minimum distribution is based on your age and your account balance.

For the first year that you are subject to required minimum distributions, this can be overwhelming because you never had to do this before and now you are switching from accumulating and saving to taking distributions – even if you don't want to take them.

Your first required distribution year for your traditional IRA is the year you turn age 70½, so that is your first step.

Maybe have a 70½ party so you know what year it is!

Your first year's required minimum distribution must be taken no later than April 1st of the year after the year you turn age 70½ , but waiting until then could cause a tax problem. Because your second year's required distribution is due by the end of that same year.

For example, if you turned age 70½ in 2016, then your required beginning date is April 1st, 2017. If you take your first required distribution on say, March 30th, 2017, then your second required distribution must be taken by the end of 2017, causing a bunching of income in that year.

It's generally best tax-wise – but of course run this by your tax advisor or CPA first – to take your first distribution in your 70½ year and then your second distribution the following year.

The result is that you are spreading the income from your first two required minimum distributions into two separate tax years and you likely pay less tax overall by doing this – but definitely run this by your accountant first.

You may have lots of tax deductions in the second year and it might pay to bunch the income in that year.

Next is to make sure you are calculating your required distribution on the right IRA balance. You use the IRA balance at the end of the year before your required distribution year. But be careful to use the right December 31st. It's December 31st of the year before the distribution year.

So if you turned age 70½ in 2016, you would use the December 31, 2015 IRA balance, even if you end up taking your first required distribution in 2017.

Next you divide that balance by your distribution period which is essentially your life expectancy according to the tax law – it's based on your age. Your first required minimum distribution is based on the age you turn on your birthday in the year you turn age 70½.

It's only the first year where your age can actually be one of two ages. In the year you turn age 70½, you could be either age 70 or age 71 on your birthday that year.

Don't stress too hard on this one, I have an easy way to know how old you are that first year so you know what age to use.

If your birthday is between January 1 and June 30, you use age 70.

If your birthday is between July 1 and December 31, you use age 71.

For example, if your 70th birthday is April 4th, 2016, then you will turn age 70½ on October 4th, 2016 and you use age 70 to calculate your first required minimum distribution. Your first required minimum distribution year is 2016, because that is the year you turned age 70½. You use age 70 because in that year – 2016 – you will turn age 70 on your birthday.

On the other hand, if your 70th birthday is November 12, 2016, then you won't turn age 70½ until May 12, 2017, so you would use age 71 to calculate your first required minimum distribution.

And your first required minimum distribution year is 2017, because that is the year you turned age 70½. You use age 71 because in that year – 2017 – you will turn age 71 on your birthday.

For each year after your first year, you simply use your age at the end of that year so it's a bit easier after the first year.

That's it, so now you know what age to use for your first required distribution from your traditional IRA.

Once you know what age to use, you go to the IRS table .It's called the Uniform Lifetime Table.

You can find it in IRS Publication 590-B – you can look it up online at www.irs.gov

If you are using age 70 for example, your distribution period is 27.4 years which is your life expectancy for this provision.

There is one exception to this general rule though:

If your spouse is more than 10 years younger than you and is your sole beneficiary for the entire year, then you can use the Joint Life and Last Survivor Expectancy table also found in IRS Publication 590.

This will give you a longer distribution period. Once you know your distribution period factor, you divide the prior year's year-end IRA balance by that factor.

So if you turned age 70½ in 2016, you divide your December 31, 2015 IRA balance by your distribution period – that's either 27.4 years or 26.5 years depending on your age in your first year. And that is your required minimum distribution.

But there are a few more common mistakes that are made here that can be costly to you.

One is not taking all your retirement accounts into account. The Tax law considers all your IRAs as one IRA no matter how many different IRA accounts you have.

You have to account for all your IRAs to arrive at the right required distribution amount for your total IRA balance.

The required minimum distribution calculation I just went through has to be done for each traditional IRA you own and that also includes SEP and SIMPLE IRAs if you have those. You can take the required amount from any one of your IRAs but make sure you know where all your IRAs are and that you don't miss any.

Another mistake I see often is when married couples take their required minimum distributions from their spouse's IRA. You can't do that!

The I in IRA stands for individual.

People do this because it seems logical. They think "Gee, if I take my required amount from my wife's IRA, it's still the right amount coming out and it's all reported on the same tax return, so what's the big deal. That sounds right but it's wrong. You can't use logic when it comes to taxes – you should know that by now.

All you have done is taken too much from your wife's IRA – there's no penalty for that – you just pay more tax for no reason. And you have not taken the required amount out from your IRA and you would be subject to the 50% penalty.

Don't make this expensive error – take your required distributions only from your own IRAs.

Here's another mistake I see.

For those of you who are still working, and have a company plan – like a 401(k), there is a special exception to the required minimum distribution rules that allows you to delay taking your required amounts from that plan until you retire.

This is commonly called the still working exception. This exception only applies if you don't own more than 5% of the company you are working for, so it generally does not apply to you if you have your own business since you probably own 100% – or at least way more than 5% of that business.

The still working exception says that you can wait until April 1st of the year after you retire to begin taking your required withdrawals.

But be careful – here's the big mistake.

This still working exception does not apply to your IRAs or any other retirement account – other than the plan of the company you are still working for.

Some people don't understand that and think the exception applies to all their retirement funds and don't take the required withdrawals from their IRAs for example and cause a 50% penalty.

The 50% penalty can be waived but you need to provide an explanation and a good reason why you made a mistake… that could be illness, bad advice or some other personal situation that caused the oversight. It could also be a math mistake or forgetting to include some IRAs you had.

You can request a waiver – without first paying the penalty by filing tax Form 5329 and providing the explanation.

But it's best not to make the mistake in the first place so you can avoid all the paperwork and worrying whether IRS will waive what could be a very large penalty.

There are also required minimum distributions for inherited IRAs. If you have inherited an IRA, another distribution mistake is taking your required distribution from the IRA you inherited. That too, is a no-no.

Some people who are retired and subject to required minimum distributions also have inherited IRA funds and are confused with the different distribution rules for your own IRAs and inherited IRAs.

Inherited IRAs are subject to their own required distributions based on the amount in the inherited IRA. You also use a different table and life expectancy. Don't do this.

There is an exception for a spousal rollover but technically that is not an inherited IRA in the eyes of the tax law – even though you actually did inherit the IRA.

If you inherit your spouse's IRA and roll it over to your own IRA as a spousal rollover, then that is not technically an inherited IRA. It's your IRA and you include that balance as part of your own IRA.

Also, remember that even though there are no required minimum distributions for Roth IRAs during your lifetime, Roth IRA beneficiaries do have to take required distributions, generally beginning in the year after death. Even though the required distributions on an inherited Roth IRA will generally be tax free, there is still a 50% penalty for not taking them.

Can you imagine paying a 50% tax penalty for a distribution that would have been tax free? Remember to advise your Roth IRA beneficiaries on this.

4. Making the wrong rollover moves when moving retirement funds

As I always say… Your retirement savings are like an eggshell – you break it, it's over. This money has not been taxed yet and the government wants to make sure it gets its cut without anything falling through the cracks.

Moving retirement money the wrong way can end your retirement account by having it all taxed because you made a mistake. Many of these mistakes are not fixable.

Can you imagine spending 30 years or more working and building your retirement account and then one wrong move and you cause a huge tax bill and are left with no retirement account.

When you move IRA or plan funds BEWARE.

The BIG mistake is not using direct rollovers or trustee-to-trustee transfers where the retirement funds move directly from one plan or IRA to another without you touching the money in between.

That's the right way to move retirement funds as opposed to a 60-day rollover where you take possession of the funds and then roll them over to another retirement account.

There are huge tax traps here. But these only happen when you do a rollover – a 60-day rollover – where you take the funds and deposit them in another retirement account. You can do this, but I advise against it because 3 bad things can happen.

3 Big Rollover Problems:

1. 60-day rollover rule –must get deposited in 60 days from receipt

2. Once-per-year IRA rollover rule (from IRA to IRA)
    Exception – Roth conversions
    Exception – rollovers to / from plans don't count

3. 20% withholding tax – for plan distributions only (not for IRAs)

The solution to all 3 of the above rollover mistakes is to do only trustee to trustee – direct transfers.

Another mistake happens when moving your company plan money when you leave the company you have worked for. All the financial companies want you to roll the funds over to an IRA with them. That's the right move a lot of the time, but it's not always the best choice.

The mistake is not knowing your options so you can evaluate them.

There are actually 6 options available to you:

1. IRA Rollover

2. Keep the funds in the plan

3. Roll the funds to your new company's plan if you landed a new job

4. Take a lump sum distribution
   NUA (net unrealized appreciation) – a company stock tax break
   10-year averaging – only for those age 79 or older (age 80 or over for 2015)

5. Convert the funds to your Roth IRA

6. Convert the funds to your company plan Roth 401(k) – an in-plan
   Roth conversion
   – Big drawback – this cannot be recharacterized

Here are even more mistakes moving IRA funds:

These involve combining IRAs.

You cannot combine your traditional IRAs with Roth IRAs.

You cannot combine your own IRA with an Inherited IRA.

   – Exception: Spousal Rollover

You cannot combine your own IRA with a spouse's IRA.

You cannot combine an inherited IRA with an IRA inherited from a different person.

5. Getting Scammed with questionable or risky retirement transactions

We are seeing more IRAs being lost to tax schemes that don't work. There are promoters marketing these schemes to financial advisors and directly to you.

Typical proposals involve exploiting legal tax provisions in ways that were not intended, such as:

   Roth IRAs
   Charity
   Trusts

Watch out for Prohibited transactions!

Prohibited transactions can involve self-dealing with your IRA or retirement account (a direct or indirect benefit to you).

Here are some examples of prohibited transactions:

You cannot loan money to your IRA

You cannot guarantee a loan to your IRA

You cannot borrow funds from your IRA

You cannot use your IRA as security (collateral) for a loan

You cannot buy or sell property between you and your IRA

Watch out for margin loans with IRAs – they can be prohibited transactions if guaranteed by your other non-IRA accounts.

You cannot buy property for your personal use with your IRA funds.

Prohibited IRA Investments:
You can invest in pretty much anything with your IRA funds but you cannot invest your IRA funds in life insurance or collectibles. If you invest your IRA in collectibles, the amount invested is considered distributed in the year invested and you may have to pay a 10% additional tax on early distributions.

Here are some examples of collectibles:
Artwork, Rugs, Antiques, Gems, Stamps, Coins

Metals – but there is an exception for certain U.S. minted gold or silver coins or certain gold, silver, platinum or palladium bullion.

Watch out for promoters showing you how to use your IRA funds to finance your business. This is dangerous.

Here is my guide for not getting caught up in any schemes or scams regarding your retirement savings.

I call it my **five red flags** and here they are:

1 **Multiple Entity rule**	If you need to create multiple entities to mask or disguise the transaction, then it should be avoided.

2 **Long** **Opinion Letter**	The transaction involves a lengthy professional opinion letter. The longer the explanation, the more likely it cannot be understood and the transaction should be avoided. Also, the opinion must be from an independent source, not from someone with a financial interest in the transaction or investment. Where is the authority for this opinion? Do they have an IRS or Court ruling? Show it to me.
3 **Secret** **Formula**	The transaction involves a secret formula (Black Box strategy). The strategy is so good, it is kept secret from everyone. If you have to sign a confidentiality agreement stating that you will not discuss the proposition, even with advisors, then the strategy should be avoided.
4 **Unreasonable** **claims**	The promotional material makes unrealistic claims, for example: claiming that you can withdraw IRA funds tax free. I've actually seen that many times in magazine ads on the plane and shake my head wondering – what's the deal here and it is bogus. Avoid anything with unrealistic claims of guaranteed investment returns that are significantly higher than normal market returns – or claims that the investment never loses money. If it sounds too good to be true, the strategy should be avoided.

5
IRS
Approval

The promotional material claims that IRS has approved or "blessed" the transaction or strategy.

This one is so bad that IRS had to release a publication to warn you about this:

IRS Publication 3125

THE IRS <u>DOES NOT APPROVE</u> IRA INVESTMENTS

June 15, 2010

The IRS Does Not
· REVIEW OR APPROVE investments.
· ENDORSE any investments.
· ADVISE people on how to invest their IRAs.
· ISSUE ANY STATEMENT that an investment in an IRA is protected because a particular trustee or custodian has been approved by the IRS.

Don't use your IRA or other retirement funds for investments you don't understand.

Don't use your IRA to finance your business without understanding the strict rules.

Always check any IRA investments with an independent advisor – like a CPA.

Tell the promoter or salesperson the magic words"
"I'll need to run this by my accountant."

That should scare off the scammers!

6. Not planning for taxes – retirement needs to be tax efficient

Failing to do a Roth conversion may be a mistake, because you are not leveraging the tax code.

Roth IRAs – not using the Roth Recharacterization as a tax planning tool is a mistake. It's not how much you convert; it's how much you recharacterize – or how much of the conversion you keep.

Not taking advantage of low tax brackets to do Roth conversions is a mistake.

Turn your taxable IRA funds into tax-free life insurance.

Life Insurance is a more moldable or pliable investment – it can mold to any situation since it has no required distribution rules and taxes to worry about.

Charity – use your IRA for donations, if you qualify.

Tax Law Update for 2016:

The Qualified Charitable Distribution (QCD) provision is now permanent

The 2015 Tax Law, enacted on December 18, 2015, has extended the QCD provision permanently. It originally expired after 2014, but is now extended retroactively for 2015 and all later years.

For the latest on the IRA tax rules, consult our website at www.irahelp.com

---

QCDs are only for IRA owners and beneficiaries age 70½ or older.

7. Working with the wrong financial advisor

I'm talking about untrained advisors here. You need a specialist!

Most financial advisors are not trained in this area and can do more damage than good, because they don't know that they don't know.

Your advisor may have helped you build your retirement savings and that's great, but once you have to start taking the money out, everything changes.

That's when all of these convoluted tax rules I have be telling you about – and hundreds more I didn't cover – kick in and your advisor has to know them.

And most don't. In fact I can tell you that 99% of advisors do not have the proper education in this area – the taxation of retirement savings.

Ed – are you saying that only 1% of advisors know this stuff?

No… it's less than that. I rounded up – it's pretty bad out there.

Like I said before – most advisors simply don't know that they don't know and that is when your retirement savings are most at risk

That's because most advisors are trained on building wealth – but now you have to protect it from the tax risk and that is an entirely different specialized field that most financial advisors, attorneys or even CPAs are not proficient in.

Just from what I covered in this program, you can see how many ways your retirement savings can be lost to costly tax traps that cannot be corrected.

Remember – many of these mistakes and others are permanent, irrevocable, etched in stone, whatever you want to call it – these mistakes are just not fixable and you are the one who suffers the consequences of not having an advisor that has specialized knowledge in this area.

Let me use a medical analogy that might bring out the point more clearly. You have a general practitioner doctor – your GP – he's a nice guy, but he's not a cardiologist, he's not a neurologist, he's not a specialist.

Sometimes, you need a specialist, and this is one of those times!

Don't leave this to chance since you may only have once chance to get this right. There are too many ways to make a mistake.

In fact, that is why I created a group of advisors who take year round specialized training in this complex area.

The group is *"Ed Slott's Elite IRA Advisor Group"*

To find an advisor who is a member, go to our website www.irahelp.com and go to "Find an Advisor."

They are not the only advisors who have this knowledge, but they have invested lots of their time and money to get educated and stay up to date on these tax rules.

Note: We do not train advisors on investing or financial products. We train them on the tax rules for taking money out of your retirement funds.

When it comes down to it, you need to be educated so you can demand more from your financial advisor. That's why I'm providing this education to you.

So that is my list of the 7 biggest retirement mistakes.

But I must also add one more – a BIG one.

I know I say this in every show, in every seminar in every book and program I do and my staff is sick of hearing me say it, but this is still one of the biggest mistakes of all.

Not Checking Beneficiary Forms!

The beneficiary form determines the ultimate future value of your retirement savings. It not only determines who gets it, but also how much it will be taxed and how soon it will be taxed and if your beneficiaries will be able to take advantage of the tax benefits like a stretch IRA.

Please check these now!

Check your beneficiary forms on both plans and IRAs and Roth IRAs. There are lots of errors on company plans – they are not checking this for you.

Know where all your accounts are and tell your beneficiaries. Check for both primary and contingent beneficiaries. Pay attention to life events that would require your beneficiary forms to be updated.

So there, I've said it again – Check your beneficiary forms for every retirement account you have.

OK, let's review the 7 Biggest retirement Mistakes

    1 - Not contributing to your retirement accounts

    2 - Leaving Your Job and Taking Social Security Too Soon

    3 - Required Minimum Distribution Mistakes

    4 - Making the wrong rollover moves when moving retirement funds

    5 - Getting scammed with questionable or risky retirement transactions

    6 - Not planning for taxes – retirement needs to be tax efficient

    7 - Working with the wrong advisor

Addressing these items now can help you beef up your retirement savings, increase your social security, pay less tax and not lose your retirement savings to costly tax mistakes, bad retirement investments or poor rollover choices – or to the wrong advisor.

I want your retirement to be financially secure and having this information now is a great first step.

DVD

Retirement Tax Horrors You Can Avoid!

These are all actual cases – these things happened to real people.

You know that saying "learn from your mistakes"?

Well that's not too smart… and it's expensive – isn't better to learn from other people's mistakes? So that's what we are going to do in this program.

These are some recent retirement tax horror stories that happened to people who made these expensive and irrevocable mistakes – don't let this happen to you!

This first case once again highlights the importance of the beneficiary form. This is the number one mistake people make.

The beneficiary form for the plan or IRA is essential. It trumps the will. It determines the ultimate future value of the IRA. How much it will be taxed, how soon it will be taxed and it is still it is a big problem. Everyone thinks someone else took care of this.

Check all your IRA and company beneficiary forms and make sure they are up to date – otherwise bad things can happen.

In this case, a man had a $300,000 401(k) plan and his wife was his beneficiary on the plan beneficiary form. But there was no contingent beneficiary listed – that will turn out to be a costly mistake.

His family consisted of his wife and her 2 sons – his step-children. He did not have children of his own, but loved his stepsons as if they were his own. In fact, in his will he left his entire estate to them and referred to them as his "beloved sons".

His wife died, and now, since there was no contingent beneficiary on the company plan beneficiary form, he had no named beneficiary.

This error was never noticed. No one advised him on this and his beneficiary form was never checked. He was still alive so he could have easily updated his beneficiary form to name his 2 stepsons as beneficiaries – but he didn't do that.

He later died without ever updating his beneficiary form.

Who gets the money?

Since there was no named beneficiary, you have to go to the default beneficiaries under the plan – for when someone dies without a named beneficiary.

Now they have to follow the plan rules.

Because he died without a living primary or contingent beneficiary, his plan defaulted to one of five beneficiaries in the following order: (1) his surviving spouse; (2) surviving children; (3) surviving parents; (4) brothers and sisters, or; (5) his estate.

Because his wife was already deceased, the plan's next default beneficiary was his surviving children. He did not have any biological or legally adopted children, but he did have two stepsons. However, under the plan rules, the stepsons *were not his children because they were not his biological children* and were never adopted by him.

Since he also had no surviving parents, the plan distributed the funds to the next category of default beneficiaries – his 6 brothers and sisters.

The stepsons went to court to challenge the distribution, arguing that they were his "children" and should have gotten the money. They cited their close relationship with him and the fact that he left his estate to them, and the fact that he referred to them as his "beloved sons" in his will.

They lost. They were disinherited and lost $300,000 that their stepdad probably wanted to go to them. This could have easily been avoided – in several ways.

He could have added the stepsons as a contingent beneficiary on his beneficiary form. Then after his wife died, they would have moved up and inherited the funds – no questions asked.

Or even after his wife died, he was still alive. He could have named the stepsons as his beneficiary and again, they would have inherited without any problems.

Now they have to go to court …and that took 4 years. Then they lost anyway and lost $300,000 of money that should have gone to them.

One other point this case illustrates is that their stepdad might have thought he had them covered by naming them in his will – but the beneficiary form trumps the will – and *he had no named beneficiary* so the plan default provisions kicked in and trumped the will.

Another point… if he had no siblings which was the last default category on the plan, then it would have gone to his estate and then the stepsons would have inherited under the provisions in his will.

But even if that happened, they would lose the option of stretching the inherited plan funds over their lifetimes, since the funds went to the estate. The estate is not a person so there is no life expectancy and no stretch IRA. So even if it went to the estate, they would have received the funds, but would have to cash them out soon after death.

After major life events, such as the spouse beneficiary's death here, the beneficiary form should have been updated to name the stepsons as the new primary beneficiaries. When that is not done, the retirement plan documents will dictate who gets the money, which may not be what was intended.

You never want your retirement funds to go to the plan's default beneficiary. YOU should dictate who gets your retirement assets, not the plan's default language.

This was a $300,000 mistake – which could have easily been avoided by checking the beneficiary form.

Here is a case where the beneficiary form was not updated after the estate plan was updated.

In this case, the IRA owner named his testamentary trust under the will as his IRA beneficiary. That was fine. However, he later updated his estate plan with a new will and his old will was REVOKED.

But the IRA beneficiary form was never updated before he died. It still listed the trust under his old will as beneficiary – but that will was no longer valid.

It was revoked when he created his new will.

Now there was no beneficiary – after he went to the extent of naming a trust to preserve his IRA for many years after his death. When there is no beneficiary, you go to the IRA custodial agreement default provision and in this case it stated that his estate becomes the beneficiary.

Result: No designated beneficiary.

Now the huge post-death benefits which he wanted to set up to make his IRA last for decades were gone.

When you change your estate plan – as many are doing now with a change in the tax law – make sure it coordinates with your IRA beneficiary form. Don't forget to always update your beneficiary forms to match your plans.

Now here is a group of cases that involve both the beneficiary forms and spousal rights to plan funds.

The general rule is the beneficiary form trumps all.

Also – you should know about spousal rights in plans – for company plans, like 401(k) – not IRAs.

Under plan law – and the law is ERISA – Employee Retirement Income Security Act – the spouse is the beneficiary unless he or she waives that right by signing a spousal waiver.

In this case… The Plan Beneficiary Form was trumped.

You've heard me say many times how important the beneficiary form is and that it trumps the will and everything else. Well now, here is a case where the beneficiary form was trumped…by ERISA rules.

Here's what happened. A man had a 401(k) plan and had his wife named as beneficiary. His wife later died and he updated his beneficiary form to name his 3 children as his beneficiaries – that's good planning.

But then he got remarried and died after only 6 weeks. His children were the named beneficiaries – but in this case the beneficiary form was trumped and the new wife of only 6 weeks inherited his entire retirement savings and his children were disinherited.

How could this happen?

Since this was a company plan (as opposed to an IRA) it is ruled by ERISA (Employee Retirement Income Security Act) and one of things ERISA is very strong on is protecting a spouse.

A spouse is automatically the plan beneficiary, unless he or she waives this right with what's known as a spousal waiver.

In this case, even though the children were the named beneficiaries, the new wife of only 6 weeks never waived her spousal rights. And no one – not him or his advisors ever picked up on this.

When he died, she was automatically the beneficiary. His children went to court to fight this, but they lost and were disinherited. The new wife of only 6 weeks got everything.

The Court determined that under the terms of his plan, a spouse's right to plan assets is immediately vested upon the first day of marriage, and since no spousal waiver had been obtained, the default plan beneficiary was the spouse, even though she was not the named beneficiary.

How can you avoid this horror?

When you have a 401(k) (under ERISA), the spouse is the beneficiary no matter what the beneficiary form says. If this is a second spouse like in this case, and you want to make sure that this spouse does not inherit – two things have to happen.

He or she must execute a spousal waiver and they must not be named on the beneficiary form. In this case, the spouse wasn't named on the beneficiary form but she did not sign a spousal waiver and no one thought to ask about this.

The spouse got the 401(k) after only six weeks of marriage, and the children, who were the intended beneficiaries, were disinherited. The fatal flaw was not obtaining a spousal waiver from her after getting remarried.

One planning point here that also could have saved the day for the children:

If he had rolled the funds over to his IRA *before* getting re-married and named his children as IRA beneficiaries, his children would have inherited, since IRAs are not covered by the plan ERISA rules.

That's exactly what happened in this next case:

Here a divorced man had a company plan, a 401(k). He rolled those funds over to his IRA and named his children as his IRA beneficiaries. He later got re-married and died soon after.

His new wife claimed that since the funds came from his company plan, that she should inherit instead of his children. She claimed spousal rights under the ERISA tax law for company plans.

She went to court and lost. The children inherited. The court ruled that even though the IRA funds came from a company plan, since she was not a spouse when the funds were rolled over to the IRA, she has no spousal rights to that IRA.

Spousal Rights under ERISA do NOT Apply to IRAs. The children inherited. He was also smart to list his children as beneficiaries on his IRA beneficiary form. This way they inherit without question, even after a court challenge by his wife.

Here's another beneficiary form horror story that worked its way up to the United States Supreme Court.

In a court battle that had been ongoing since 2001, a daughter lost a $402,000 inheritance because the beneficiary form did not name her as the beneficiary, even though that is what her father wanted.

Here's what happened:

Her father worked for a company for 34 years and accumulated $402,000 in his 401(k). He was married with a daughter. He named his wife as his beneficiary on the company plan. But he later got divorced. As part of the divorce agreement, his wife waived her rights – she did the spousal waiver as part of the divorce deal.

She waived her rights to any benefits under his retirement plans. He wanted his plan balance of $402,000 to go to his daughter, but he never changed the beneficiary form on this plan. That would prove to be the fatal flaw.

He died after that and now the question was "who gets his $402,000?"

Would it go to his daughter or his ex-wife?

Since the ex-wife was still named on the beneficiary form she claimed the funds, but so did the daughter because of the divorce agreement where the wife – her own mother – signed a spousal waiver releasing her rights to the $402,000 account.

So they went to court – Mother against daughter. This took 8 years and different courts ruled differently so it eventually went to the Supreme Court. The United States Supreme Court *UNANIMOUSLY* (9-0) – ruled that the ex-spouse gets the money because she was named on the beneficiary form –even though she waived her rights to that money in a divorce decree.

Here is quote from the daughter:

> *"My father expressly did not want my mother to have another red cent after their divorce was final. There's no doubt in my mind that he wanted me to have everything he had."*

But that is not how it worked out, because he didn't change his beneficiary form. That would have taken only a few minutes. Who was advising him?

After a divorce it is critical to update the beneficiary form.

Now after 8 years of drudging through the courts and the substantial legal bills, the daughter lost it all. Not only that, can you imagine how awful it must be for a mother and her daughter to be in court battles for years? That cannot be good for any family.

The Supreme Court ruled that a company plan must pay the beneficiary named on the beneficiary form, even in light of contradictory signed agreements – like that spousal waiver.

The Supreme Court ruling is the law of the land and there are no more appeals on this. The beneficiary form controls who inherits the money and all of the Justices agree.

Here's another horror story also involving spousal waivers and a prenuptial agreement – again children were disinherited. Are you starting to see a common theme here?

This case involved two attorneys who married – that sounds like a recipe for a big time court battle for sure!

As a smart attorney, the husband had his wife to be – his fiancé – sign a prenuptial agreement stating that she will waive her rights to his retirement account so it can pass to his children, and not to her. He had children from a prior marriage and he wanted to make sure that they would receive his pension benefits (instead of his new wife) after his death.

She signed the prenuptial and waived her rights to his retirement plan. You might be thinking "that was too easy." Yes, but it turns out that the wife was a smarter attorney than him!

He died and she got the money anyway. She got everything even though she signed a prenuptial agreement waiving her future pension rights as a spouse.

Why? The Rule is:
Prenuptial agreements waiving spousal pension rights *don't work*.

Why?
It's obvious. Only a spouse can waive spousal pension rights on a company plan under ERISA. A prenuptial agreement is not signed by a spouse. It is signed by a fiancé who is not a spouse yet, even if the agreement is signed one second before the wedding.

The tax regulations are clear on this point. This is not new law and has been settled in several previous cases. After his death, his ex-wife and his two children from his prior marriage both went to Court to claim his pension funds.

She won, even though she signed a prenuptial agreement that she would waive her rights to these benefits.

Doesn't this make her a liar? Yes, but she wins anyway because a spouse's rights under ERISA trump any prenuptial agreement since that was not signed by a spouse. She may be a liar, but she keeps the cash and now she is a very rich liar.

What should have been done?

While the prenuptial agreement cannot waive spousal pension rights, it can have a provision stating that as soon as the fiancé becomes a spouse, she will sign a valid spousal waiver or lose other assets in the arrangement.

Then, as soon as they are declared married (I mean right at the wedding ceremony! – it's not romantic – but essential) attorneys should be standing by so that the spouse can sign that waiver in her new capacity as a spouse, and fulfill the promise she made in the prenuptial agreement.

A requirement to execute the spousal waiver after the marriage, including remedies or penalties if this does not occur (if the new spouse won't waive as she agreed to in the prenuptial) should be spelled out in the prenuptial.

One thing that can be looked at is to see if a plan has a provision that if a spouse was married to the plan participant for less than a year, she would not be entitled to any spousal survivorship benefits.

You won't find this provision in many plans but every plan should have it.

If the participant wants to override this, he can still name his new spouse as beneficiary. But if he dies early, this provision would avoid an unintended result if he died within a year of being married without having executed a spousal waiver.

This will help make sure that a promise in a prenuptial agreement to waive benefits upon becoming a spouse will be upheld.

It seems that many of the cases in this area involve an early death, with a new spouse walking off with plan benefits.

How about this case for something interesting…

Man Dies with Two Wives – But Only One Can Be the Surviving Spouse

A man died with two wives (in two states) and a company pension plan. His second wife was the named beneficiary, but the first wife also made a claim, since he never divorced her and she never waived her rights to the plan funds.

Here's what happened:

A man was married back in 1979 in the state of Washington. About 14 years later he traveled by himself – without his wife – to Mississippi to find work. He found work… and he also found another woman and married her in 1995.

He built up a nice pension over his years working and named his second wife as beneficiary on the beneficiary form.

He died in 2007 and now the fun begins…

His second wife claimed the funds under the beneficiary form, but his first wife appeared on the scene to also claim the benefits stating that she was his wife and they never divorced.

This was a company plan so the spouse is deemed the beneficiary unless she signs a spousal waiver. His first – and only true wife – never signed such a waiver and claimed all the spousal benefits.

They went to court and the first wife was awarded the pension funds if she could prove she was never divorced and that she never waived her spousal pension rights.

The new spouse as it turns out – was never a spouse.

The court case had to determine who the true spouse was. The first spouse won the case.

Under the plan rules – under ERISA, only the legal surviving spouse can be the beneficiary, unless that spouse waives the benefit. There can only be one surviving spouse. In this case it was the first spouse.

Even though the second spouse was named on the beneficiary form, she lost because the first spouse was actually still married to the man and did not waive her benefit.

What's the lesson here?

When doing planning you should always take into account any prior marriages and divorces to determine if there might be anyone coming out of the woodwork that would affect the planning being done.

This may be an odd case – and it is, but strange things can happen.

You have to cover all bases when doing planning. Here's what I do when planning with clients.

While we are doing the planning for a married couple, I look at both of them and ask them:

"Are there any former spouses?"

"Are there any children from former spouses?"

"Is there anyone else that we need to know about?"

"Are there any surprises I should know about?"

"Is there anyone who could come out of the woodwork that would affect your current planning or who could trump your beneficiaries' rights?"

I then tell them, you don't' have to tell me now, in front of each other… but if there is something I should know, call me tomorrow.

Sometimes… I get a call.

Inherited IRA Horror Stories

Now a few cases on inherited IRA mistakes:

These are classic and costly errors. Why? These cases illustrate what **_not_** to do with an inherited IRA. It's sad because these usually involve large amounts and represents a lifetime of working, sacrificing and saving.

Then, after death that entire lifetime of savings is gone because a mistake was made. Often, these mistakes are made by advisors who did not know the special inherited IRA tax rules. That's why you need to work with an advisor that has been trained on these very complex tax rules.

It's good for you to learn this now so your loved ones can inherit your IRA correctly and it can last them for the rest of their lives …if they don't make these mistakes.

This is an error that sadly, is too common and it wipes out the entire estate plan – we see this one frequently. It happens when a trust is named as the IRA beneficiary. That is not the problem; the problem is not knowing what to do after death.

Many advisors and even estate attorneys blow this. Once the IRA owner dies, they distribute the IRA funds to the trust – because the trust is the beneficiary. That sounds like it makes sense – but this is a fatal error!

Once you do this, you can kiss that entire inherited IRA goodbye. The entire distribution is taxable – and in some cases it is taxable at much higher trust tax rates, and the IRA ceases to exist as a tax-deferred account.

All the tax is owed in the year of the distribution.

Once an IRA owner dies, the account should **not** be distributed.

The only distributions that should come out of the inherited IRA are the annual required minimum distributions that are paid to the trust. There may also be trust provisions that allow additional distributions. But other than that – nothing should come out of that inherited IRA.

Once the funds come out of the inherited IRA they are taxable and this mistake cannot be corrected. The funds cannot be rolled back to the IRA.

That's because only a spouse beneficiary can do a post-death rollover. A non-spouse beneficiary can never do a rollover – and a trust is a non-spouse beneficiary.

Once this mistake is made, it's over. All of the funds are taxable.

Here is one of the many cases on this error:

An attorney advised a terminally ill IRA owner to change the IRA beneficiary from his wife to a newly created IRA trust. That's fine. When the IRA owner died, the attorney advised the bank to distribute the entire $608,000 IRA to this IRA trust.

Result: Over $240,000 in unnecessary taxes and the tax deferral on the inherited IRA was lost forever.

The mistake could not be corrected, because once the funds came out of the inherited IRA, they are taxable and cannot go back into the IRA to undo the mistaken distribution.

The only amount that should have been paid to the trust was the annual required distribution (only about $24,000 in this case), NOT the entire IRA account balance!

So much for this estate plan… all that expense and planning – down the drain and the IRA is gone…much of it to unnecessary taxes. That is not the legacy you want to leave your family.

What should have been done?

Once the IRA owner dies, the IRA is retitled as an inherited IRA, but no funds come out, other than annual required minimum distributions. Any funds withdrawn from a traditional inherited IRA are taxable and cannot go back to the inherited IRA.

Be careful here.

If you named a trust as your IRA beneficiary – make sure you have advisors that know these rules and know what to do after death. One wrong move and it's over.

You should really grill your advisors on this and alert your family to these rules.

That's the reason you set up the trust – so the funds can last 30, 40, 50 years or more. Not to be taxed at excessive tax rates right after death.

Here's another classic and expensive inherited IRA error in the same vein:

In this case, a daughter inherited her mother's IRA – very common.

She did not know that it had to be retitled as a properly-titled inherited IRA. The same as if a trust was the IRA beneficiary – as in the case I just covered.

A properly-titled inherited IRA means that the name of the deceased IRA owner must remain in the title of the account, and the account should be designated as a beneficiary IRA account, so as not to confuse this account with the inheritor's own IRA funds.

The daughter made the mistake that lots of new IRA beneficiaries make. She took the funds out of the inherited IRA – and that was it. Once the funds come out they cannot be rolled into even a properly titled inherited IRA.

Her entire distribution was taxable and instead of stretching her inherited IRA over 40 years, it was all taxed in one year – and a big tax too!

When she found out what she did wrong she went to tax court to fight this.

She lost her case because a non-spouse beneficiary cannot do a rollover. This mistake cannot be corrected. The funds cannot go back to an inherited IRA.

The only way for a non-spouse beneficiary to move inherited IRA funds to a different custodian is via a direct transfer (a trustee-to-trustee transfer) without the beneficiary ever gaining control or use of the funds. In this case, she received a check made payable to herself, meaning she did have control and use of the funds.

She argued in court that she really did intend to do the transfer correctly as a direct transfer. The Court responded by saying that a taxpayer's intention does not determine the tax consequences of her transaction; what actually <u>was done</u> determines the tax treatment.

Unfortunately this is just one of a long line of cases with the same facts – and the same mistake.

If you are naming a non-spouse (a child, grandchild, or a trust) as your IRA beneficiary make sure they know what to do – actually – what NOT to do after death.

I always tell beneficiaries "two words" "*touch nothing*" after you inherit.

Make sure advisors know these rules too – many don't! It's sad, but true.

You worked probably for decades to build your IRA. It would be a shame if the entire account is taxed right after you die because of this terrible and fatal mistake.

Let's switch to another topic – a mistake made by a spouse who inherited an IRA:

Here's a $100,000 rollover mistake – actually $97,789 penalty!

In this case a young wife (under 59½) inherited a $2.6 million IRA from her husband. She rolled it over to her own IRA – a spousal rollover. No problem there… except in this case. But then she withdrew almost a million dollars from it – actually she withdrew $977,888 as a taxable distribution. But because she was under age 59½, she was subject to a 10% penalty for an early withdrawal from her IRA. 10% of a $977,888 distribution is a penalty of almost $100,000 – which could have easily been avoided.

She went to Tax Court to fight it but this was a battle she could not win. The tax law was clearly against her. She lost her case and had to pay the enormous $100,000 penalty.

She argued that she is a beneficiary and the death exception to the 10% penalty applies. It's true that an IRA beneficiary is never subject to the 10% early withdrawal penalty. In her mind she was a beneficiary because this was not her IRA. It belonged to her deceased husband.

But once she rolled the funds over to her own IRA, the funds were hers, as if she put all the money in herself. She was no longer a beneficiary and an early withdrawal would be subject to the 10% penalty unless some other exception applied.

IRS assessed a $97,789 early withdrawal penalty and the court agreed that the penalty applied since she rolled the funds over to her own IRA and withdrew the funds from there.

If she had remained a beneficiary and withdrew from an inherited IRA instead, there would have been no penalty since the early withdrawal penalty never applies to a beneficiary, but it does apply to a spousal rollover account since those funds are treated as the spouse's own and she is an IRA owner of those funds.

What should she have done? As a spouse, she has the option of doing the spousal rollover or remaining a beneficiary. By remaining a beneficiary she can take penalty free distributions from her inherited IRA. But not so once she does a spousal rollover.

The Expensive lesson:
If a young spouse (under age 59 ½) inherits an IRA, it's best to remain a beneficiary in case funds are needed. This way the funds can be withdrawn penalty free.

Choosing to be a beneficiary – with an inherited IRA – does not mean that she cannot roll the funds over later when she reaches age 59½. There is no deadline for a spousal rollover.

The best advice is generally not to do the rollover until you reach age 59½. At that point you can do the rollover and any distributions from your IRA will be penalty free.

Whether you remain a beneficiary or do a spousal rollover, always name beneficiaries on your inherited IRA or spousal rollover IRA.

This was an expensive – $100,000 lesson – I hope you can learn from this.

IRA Trust Horror Stories

Now let's switch to IRA trust horror stories:

An 83-year old woman went to an estate planning seminar and put her $850,000 IRA into her revocable living trust.

This was her life savings she inherited from her husband… who worked over 40 years to accumulate these funds.

This is the exact text of an email I received from her:
"My estate lawyer is having me put all my IRAs into my new Revocable Living Trust. Is this appropriate in view of my wish to leave my IRAs to my sons?

The problem was that she had already done this! The entire $850,000 was taxable!

The transfer was a total distribution and the end of her IRA. Can you imagine the tax on $850,000 in one shot? It would be over $250,000 counting state taxes.

And this was all in an effort to be careful with her money. The attorney here advised her to name her trust as her IRA beneficiary – that's fine.

This is a common and extremely costly mistake.

The IRAs can be left to the trust upon death, but if you put them in the trust during your life, that is a fully taxable IRA distribution and the IRA ceases to exist.

This story ended ok though – she was able to get a ruling from IRS allowing her to put the funds back into her IRA and remove the tax liability. But that was years ago when IRS was more lenient on these mistaken transfers.

Here's another IRA trust horror story:

The IRA owner had a very large – multi-million dollar IRA and wanted to leave it to an IRA trust to preserve it for many years after death for his beneficiaries. However, after he set up the trust, no one ever followed up to check that he named the trust as the beneficiary of his IRA.

How would his IRA get to the trust after his death? Only by being named as the IRA beneficiary on the IRA beneficiary form.

He paid over $20,000 in planning fees to many advisors and not one of them thought of updating the beneficiary form to name the trust as the IRA beneficiary.

All this incredibly expensive planning to keep the IRA growing for years after his death, and it turns out that after he died – there was no beneficiary named. His IRA funds never got to the trust and the IRA had no designated beneficiary.

By default, his estate became the IRA beneficiary – the worst possible option. So instead of the funds being carefully looked after through the trust – they will be taxed quickly and extensively after his death – completely opposite of the tax planning he paid for.

Now, all those millions will be taxed much more quickly and the inherited IRA will end well before it's time. The amount of the taxes on this size IRA were never planned for. A good chunk of the IRA was consumed to pay the taxes.

Not only that, his estate had different beneficiaries than the trust he set up – so his trust beneficiaries were disinherited from millions!!!

Can you imagine the lawsuits coming from this one!

It's fine to name a trust as your IRA beneficiary especially for post-death control reasons, but **you still have to actually name the trust as the beneficiary on the IRA beneficiary form.**

If you have a trust set up to inherit your IRA, better check right now that it is named on the IRA beneficiary form – otherwise you don't have the plan you thought you had. And that's too bad.

So how do these things happen?

1. Advisor error – an uninformed / uneducated advisor
2. Your own error – not knowing the rules and not seeking proper advice
3. Financial institution error – so called "retirement specialists" often don't know what they are doing
4. Company plan administrator errors
5. CPA mistakes – giving incorrect advice – very common!
6. Attorney mistakes – especially with IRA trusts

That's why it is so important to make sure you are working with an advisor that has specialized knowledge in this complex area of the tax law.

In several of the gifts you received with this program, I show you how to find advisors all over the country that have this specialized training.

They are members of Ed Slott's Elite IRA Advisor group.

You can find them at **www.irahelp.com**

I hope you can learn from these retirement tax horror stories so they don't happen to you. I want you to have happy stories, not horror stories!

These are all Retirement Tax Horrors you *absolutely* can avoid!

Good luck to you!

DVD
Life Insurance for Life and Beyond

Why I am talking about life insurance?

Because life insurance may be the most underused strategy to protect large retirement balances from being decimated by the highest levels of taxation.

Who's most at risk?

Those who have the largest IRAs or other tax-deferred savings accounts.

Just so you know…

I don't sell life insurance, so why should I care?

I don't sell stocks, bonds, funds, insurance or annuities.

I am a tax advisor, but it's about the taxes.

I also believe most people don't understand how life insurance works as an effective planning tool.

I don't sell it and I am no expert in exactly how the various life insurance contracts work. That's why there are life insurance professionals that you need to work with for all the details.

But I do know how life insurance can fix lots of money and retirement problems, and even create wealth, tax-free wealth!

And you know… I love tax free!

I only care about the end result – the benefits. I want you to know how powerful the end result is. I want to give you enough here so that you'll understand what life insurance tax planning can do for you and your family; both during your lifetime and after your death.

So why don't most people take advantage of life insurance?

Because every time you hear life insurance you tune out, or put it off. Most times when you hear about life insurance you are hearing about it from someone who sells it, so you feel like you are being sold rather than being advised.

They're just trying to sell me something… you think. So you avoid the meeting or the discussion. And you may be right. Maybe you feel that you are just being sold, so you don't see a benefit to you. But you could be wrong!

I want you to understand what's in it for you from an objective, unbiased tax benefit point of view.

Well now you're meeting with me, so let me tell you why I believe life insurance is the missing piece in most people's retirement and estate plans.

"The tax exemption for life insurance is the single biggest benefit in the tax code." – Ed Slott

I don't even think life insurance professionals use it or appreciate enough. That's why they don't sell enough of this product.

I put this brief guide together for you in the hope that you will see how tax planning with life insurance provides powerful benefits. Then, hopefully you'll continue this conversation with your life insurance agent who can fill in the details.

But now when you meet with him or her, you'll have a better understanding of the benefits and what questions to ask. You'll definitely be more involved in the discussion, especially when it comes to your retirement.

First let's see what the problem is? And what the solutions are?

The good news is that **taxes are generally money problems and life insurance puts tax-free money in your pocket,** so most tax problems can easily be avoided with planning.

Here are both the problems and the solutions:

On two levels:

The problems that affect you – **during your lifetime**

AND

The problems that affect your beneficiaries – your family – **after your death**

Why would you care about a solution if you didn't think you had a problem? If you have retirement savings, you have a problem!

If you have taxable savings, you have a problem and so do your beneficiaries.

Risk

Most people think of investment risk, as in the stock market. But when it comes to your retirement savings – especially taxable IRAs and 401(k)s – an even bigger risk is **tax risk.**

Many people think that simply having retirement savings is enough. It's not. **It's what you keep that counts, AFTER taxes.**

There's a mortgage on your tax-deferred retirement savings. Most of that is owed back to the government.

Future taxes could be 50% or 60% or more by the time you reach in for yours. That's not real money. The only real money is tax-free money: spendable money – where you keep it all.

Plus with IRAs and 401(k)s, you have to take required minimum distributions (RMDs) on that money after you reach age 70½ years old and you are forced to pay taxes on the government's schedule , not yours. That's the government plan.

That's **not REAL money,** since it is all subject to tax.

Are you wondering what future taxes will do to your retirement security?

You should be. You have actually caused the problem. Especially if you have done everything right. You saved, sacrificed and built a healthy retirement account – a 401(k) or IRA.

So… What's the problem with IRAs?

They are tax-deferred, not tax free. With an IRA, SEP IRA, SIMPLE IRA, 401(k), 403(b) or any other type of tax-deferred retirement plan, you received your tax deduction upfront. Your retirement funds have grown tax-deferred all these years.

So far, so good. You have done well. But there will be a day of reckoning. You'll owe income tax when you begin to withdraw, just when you need the money the most. How much tax? We don't know? That's the problem.

You won't know that until you need the money the most – in retirement – or after you die when your family inherits. This uncertainty keeps people up at night.

So that is the tax risk.

But there is another risk – market risk.

Your retirement savings and other investments, if invested in the stock market are also at risk of being lost to more Wall Street fraud and manipulation, or a market crash at the wrong time for you.

Let's review up to this point:

Typical tax-deferred retirement savings like IRAs and 401(k)s are subject to 2 major risks:

> Investment risk and tax risk.

> Life insurance can be used to remove both of these risks.

Investment risk:

> With life insurance you get certainty – a guarantee.

> You cannot get a guarantee in the stock market.

Tax risk:

> You'll never pay income tax on this money.

You need to create a plan to move your money from accounts that are forever taxed to accounts that are never taxed. Life insurance is the best provision in the tax code to do that.

Wouldn't you sleep better at night if you knew your retirement savings were no longer subject to these risks?

But still, the benefits are misunderstood and not used enough in planning.

So what are the benefits and exactly how would you use life insurance in your planning?

First, when I talk about life insurance I'm referring to permanent insurance. Even with permanent life insurance there are several options, so you need to speak with an insurance professional for those details.

I'm not talking about term insurance here, which is more for younger families looking to get the maximum death benefit for their money.

I am talking about permanent insurance – for those looking for retirement security and tax and estate protection.

As I've already told you, you have a tax problem especially if you have significant funds in taxable and tax-deferred accounts. Your family also will have a problem after you die if no planning is done and they inherit mostly taxable funds. They will be dealing with the tax issues too.

They may also be dealing with estate taxes, depending on the tax law when you die. That changes all the time so you need to plan for the worst case scenario, and hope for the best.

Your family will most likely have a liquidity problem if retirement funds and other assets have to be cashed in quickly to raise money after death for taxes and other post-death expenses.

Money is often needed after death to resolve all kinds of issues besides taxes: family squabbles or family members wanting money quickly.

The last thing you want is for them to have a fire sale, especially if there is a family business or other valuable property in your estate. You don't want your family wasting or cashing out retirement accounts or other valuable property prematurely because cash is needed quickly.

Do a liquidity analysis

You need to do a liquidity test right now, so you can see if your family will have a cash problem after death. To gauge the problem I take clients through my own type of **liquidity analysis**, because most people are not liquid enough to avoid having their family start selling off investments, cashing in retirement accounts and triggering unnecessary taxes.

What does my Liquidity Analysis do?

It shows you how much of your estate can be turned into cash quickly without triggering taxes or losing property value.

Cash is often needed after death. There could be state estate taxes, even if there are no federal estate taxes. There are always expenses and the IRA is the last account you would want to have to tap to pay those bills and taxes. IRAs are subject to both income and estate taxes, which could eat up lots of cash quickly.

You can work on this with your advisor or accountant/ CPA

Here's what I do for my clients:

Make a list off all the assets you own, less liabilities, mortgages, loans, debts, etc. to get to your net worth.

Code all your property as liquid or non-liquid.

By liquid I mean assets that can most easily and quickly be turned into cash, without triggering a tax or without some cost. When you have to pay any type of toll to get to your assets, those assets are NOT liquid. Liquid assets are basically cash.

Here's how to find out how liquid you are:

Do a fraction:

Numerator

The numerator is liquid assets: basically cash
Cash, bank accounts etc.

Do not include IRAs or 401(k)s here. Sure they can be cashed in, but that will trigger a tax, so they are NOT liquid.

Include only assets that could be sold quickly without triggering a tax or other expenses, or without losing significant value – like a fire sale.

Denominator

The ENTIRE value of your entire estate, including cash.
Include all your assets – business interests, real estate.
Include all property owned in addition to the IRAs.

Now look at that percentage. For most people it's about 5% if that much. In other words most estates are 95% illiquid.

That's the problem, unless you actually do have a ton of cash available, which most people don't. Most people realize at this moment that they have a huge liquidity problem.

Now you know you have tax exposure, stock market risk and a liquidity problem.

How can life insurance help?

Two ways:

> During your lifetime
>
> And... After your death

Lifetime Benefits for You!

During your lifetime, you have the ability to reduce both stock market risk and tax risk, by moving your money from accounts that are forever taxed to accounts that are never taxed.

You can actually do that two ways:

Roth IRAs and Life Insurance

Both cost money now, but with life insurance, you'll be creating a bigger pot of tax-free money later on, when it's most needed.

It would be great if you could do both (Roth IRAs and life insurance) and turn your entire estate into a tax-free windfall both during your life and after death.

But the more powerful way is with life insurance. Again, I'm talking about permanent life insurance that has cash value. You can contribute more with life insurance than you can to a Roth.

With a Roth though, it's easier to access your money if you need it.

Roth IRAs are income tax free too, but they are part of your estate and are subject to estate taxes.

But Roth IRAs provide no additional death benefit as life insurance does. Life insurance comes with a guaranteed death benefit and that benefit, unlike a Roth IRA, can be set up to be estate tax free.

So what can you do to remove both the stock market risk and the tax risk?

You can leverage your retirement savings. You can leverage your IRA.

If you have a large IRA, it may pay to draw it down now and pay tax on the distributions. Then use those distributions to invest in a permanent life insurance policy.

Tax rates are still at all-time lows right now, so now would be the time to strike. Even if it cost you tax money, it still pays because you are lowering your tax exposure on your IRA.

After age 70½, mandatory withdrawals from the IRA must begin. Since the money will eventually have to be withdrawn anyway, it may as well be leveraged by using the money to pay the life insurance premiums. You are basically paying off the mortgage on your IRA early. This way, you never have to worry about tax risk. And the funds invested in your permanent life insurance policy are now growing tax and risk free.

You can have lifetime access to the cash value tax free if you need it for retirement. During your lifetime you can in effect turn your taxable IRA and other taxable savings into a tax-free savings vehicle.

It's really just like changing pockets from taxable accounts to tax-free accounts, except that now you also have a built in guaranteed death benefit for your family. It's generally judgment-proof too.

If you have other taxable funds you might want to keep those protected from future taxes too.

Many people who are looking for places to shelter money from taxes, stock market risk and lawsuits are stuffing taxable money into permanent life insurance as a lifetime personal protected savings account. All the growth is tax free for life, and beyond.

Post-Death Benefits for Your Family

If you don't need to tap into the funds during your lifetime, your beneficiaries are guaranteed a death benefit. The stock market has no such guarantee. Your family will now have guaranteed access to a ton of tax-free cash. Tax free means they keep every cent – no tax erosion here.

They will have tax-free cash to pay estate taxes if needed. To pay expenses, debts, and mortgages, all without triggering taxes or having to sell a family business or other valuable real estate or other property that could trigger taxes.

If they had to use your IRA to pay these bills, they would first have to pay income taxes and maybe estate taxes too, leaving very little to pay bills, or for them.

So don't sit there and admire your IRA like most people do.

Leverage it now.

Use it. Leverage it, or lose it to possible higher future taxes!

Never underestimate the value of leveraging IRA money by using it to pay life insurance premiums.

The larger the estate, the higher the estate tax. Having enough insurance money available to cover the estimated estate tax will avoid having to invade the IRA to pay the tax.

Some people might say:

But the current estate tax exemption is now so much higher that there will probably be no estate tax.

That is not an option you can plan with. The estate tax exemption has been changing up and down and you cannot take that risk.

Anyway, what's the downside? If there is no estate tax, the beneficiaries will inherit more money and it will all be tax-free! That's the down side.

But what if there is no estate tax?

There are plenty of uses for life insurance even if there is no estate tax.

Use life insurance to replace stock market losses.

Life insurance can also be used to provide tax-free money for beneficiaries so that they do not have to withdraw amounts in excess of their required distributions on inherited IRAs.

This will keep their income taxes lower, since the excess IRA distributions would have been taxable. The money they use from life insurance is tax free. This allows them to stick with the stretch IRA schedule instead of depleting the IRA before its time.

This is even more powerful for a Roth IRA, since the Roth IRA is growing tax free. This allows inherited Roth IRAs to last longer and continue to grow tax free for beneficiaries.

Life insurance can also be used simply to create wealth.

Your family can easily end up with millions more than you ever had – all tax free!

That's why when I talk to clients I give them this scenario. First we find their net worth, like I said earlier; the entire value of your estate.

Then I ask:

If I could create a plan so that after you die, your family will end up with your entire net worth, or much more, would that be a good plan?

Yeah…where do I sign up for that? Who wouldn't want that?

Does that mean there were no taxes or other expenses that depleted the estate?

No, but we planned for that. And those items can be paid from the additional tax-free life insurance money, with plenty more left for your family.

That is how any family's assets can be leveraged with life insurance, to eliminate the effect of taxes and turn what was a taxable estate into a much larger tax-free estate.

Here are some other uses for life insurance planning:

If you have no retirement account, you can actually create one with life insurance and have death benefit protection too – all guaranteed, by moving other taxable money into your permanent life insurance policy. This provides a lifetime benefit for you.

Life insurance can be a pension alternative, providing beneficiaries a tax-free stream of cash for the rest of their lives, similar to the stretch IRA, except that the insurance is better than a stretch IRA because it's tax free.

Another benefit: Money solves a lot of problems, but not all problems are money problems:

It can help in situations where families don't get along. And it's not usually your children; it's the ones they marry!

We had a case where one of the daughters would not even talk to the other 3 children. But mom had come to see me and decided to take out $500,000 of life insurance,

239

naming the 4 children as equal beneficiaries. When mom died, it didn't matter that one of the daughters wasn't talking to the others. They all got their money quickly with no arguments, no fuss, no courts, no probate and no dealing with other family members.

Life insurance does not pass through a will. It is not subject to probate or income tax.

To review:

This is the basic strategy. Turning taxable money into tax-free money using the tax exemption for life insurance.

Moving your money from accounts that are forever taxed to accounts that are n ever taxed.

As tax rates increase, tax free becomes more valuable.

Life insurance like Roth IRAs removes the uncertainty of what future tax hikes could do to your retirement savings.

But is it all good?

What's the Downside?

You might not qualify. You might be too ill.

You can get annuities for that. Annuities also give you a guarantee of income for life.

You must commit to funding the policy. You need to have funds available to invest. But that is where your IRA and other taxable funds come in.

Life insurance is not for everyone.

Don't go broke. If you don't have enough assets, you probably also don't have a tax problem and then it might not be for you.

Maybe you only need enough to protect a young family in case of an early death.

The bottom line is that life insurance provides tax-free cash – **tax-free cash is always the best source of money and also solves lots of non-tax problems.**

This is all good but people make mistakes when it comes to life insurance planning and understanding life insurance.

Here are the 5 most common life insurance mistakes:

(Again, I am referring only to permanent insurance – with cash value.)

1. Thinking that life insurance is a cost and not looking at it as an investment

A bank account is a good example. The more you invest, the more you'll have. Putting money in a bank account is not a cost, it's yours. It's an investment.

Think of permanent life insurance the same way. It's an investment.

2. Trying to pay the lowest amount for life insurance

Sounds good right?

Do you want to pay $1,000 or $10,000?

With permanent life insurance, the more you invest, the more you have protected from taxes.

3. Not understanding the benefits

For example:

Life insurance provides a tax-free payout after death.

It's generally judgment proof.

Lifetime access to cash value – tax free.

It won't cause Social Security to be taxed and you won't lose tax benefits, such as exemptions, deductions and credits.

Life insurance can be exempt from estate tax.

With life insurance you get a guarantee. This removes stock market risk.

The government has restrictions on how much you can invest, but you generally want to put in the maximum you can.

4. Improper Ownership

Don't own it in your own name. Why would you?

Keep it out of your estate.

For estate tax purposes, you should not own your own policy. It should be owned by someone else or a trust.

One caveat though: If you don't own the policy (which is good for estate tax purposes), you may only have limited lifetime access to the cash value.

The life insurance premiums should be paid by the beneficiaries or by the trustee of an irrevocable life insurance trust so that the life insurance proceeds will be estate tax free.

5. Not knowing it's tax free

I don't know if this is a mistake or a misconception.

Still, people don't know that life insurance is tax free.

Let's review:

Risk is a silent retirement killer.

Life insurance can eliminate both stock market and tax risk.

It can be used during life to create a tax-free retirement fund.

Life insurance is not only income tax free; it can be estate tax free too.

You can contribute almost unlimited sums to a permanent life insurance policy and have tax-free access to your cash value during life, without increasing your income.

And don't forget about the most basic life insurance benefit. Aside from the estate and retirement planning advantages, life insurance protects families when there is an early death.

It's hard enough to deal with the loss of a parent, but at least life insurance can provide the needed cash so that life can go on, without having to make any severe changes due to lost income.

Life insurance provides money for the family – tax-free money.

I never met anyone who didn't wish they had more life insurance, especially a widow.

"Life insurance takes care of families without first going through the government." – *Ed Slott*

You need to review all of these points with your life insurance professional who can fill in the details, but now you are much better informed and ready for the conversation. You'll actually enjoy your conversation with your life insurance agent! Can you believe it?

Life insurance is not only the single biggest benefit in the tax code, but it is also the most cost effective way to protect a large IRA.

You need to have a discussion with a competent educated advisor that in addition to being a life insurance professional, has the specialized knowledge in retirement tax planning.

The coordination is essential, especially if you have built up significant balances in your taxable IRAs or 401(k)s.

As tax rates increase, <u>life insurance becomes more valuable than ever before.</u>

Taxes will be increasing – especially "stealth taxes." You can plan for that now. And if it doesn't happen, what's the downside? You and your family have sheltered that much more money, since it won't have to be used to pay taxes.

Here are the most frequent questions I get about life insurance?

If the tax exemption for life insurance is so good – won't government take it away?

No. Why?

It's a social reason. Why do you think our government encourages us to give money to charity? If you give to charity, you get a tax deduction. Why does the government want us to give so much money to charities?

So they don't have to; to remove the burden from them.

It's the same with life insurance. Our government wants us to take care of our families so they don't have to. They want us to take care of our families with our own money and private insurance company money, so that the government does not have to.

What if I don't qualify for life insurance?

More people qualify than you think.

I've had very ill clients who qualified, so you never know until you try, so don't assume you won't qualify. Leave this to your life insurance professional to check for you.

How can insurance companies do this?

People constantly ask me this because the benefit seems too good to be true. How can insurance companies stay in business paying out these huge sums of money, when you pay them so much less?

They have actuaries. Don't worry about them. We won't hold any benefits! It's in the numbers and a large pool of people.

Insurance companies are among the most solid financial institutions.

Why doesn't everyone do this?

I don't know.

I also think that insurance is not sold properly so you look at it as a cost rather than an investment. Many people think they are buying something and don't see how it fits into a plan.

A good financial advisor or insurance professional can explain the planning aspects.

Which is better – saving in an IRA or an insurance policy?

Life insurance, hands down.

Let's compare life insurance to tax-deferred retirement plans like IRAs and 401(k)s:

If you compare life insurance to tax-deferred plans, life insurance has several advantages:

244   Life insurance provides a tax-free death benefit.

Life insurance cash value can be accessed tax and penalty free.

With an IRA, withdrawals can be heavily taxed, and you could incur penalties too.

With a traditional IRA, you are forced to withdraw and pay taxes after age 70½.

Life insurance provides an income tax-free death benefit. Estate tax free too, if owned properly.

With life insurance there is NO risk of future tax rates increasing.
– The Roth IRA provides this benefit too.

But…

Here's what you **DON'T** get with life insurance that you do get with an IRA or 401(k). You don't get a tax deduction. But a tax deduction these days is a trap because you'll pay much more later!

Come on Ed – Are you working for the insurance companies?

No. I am here for you!

I'm telling you how to create and build tax-free wealth using the single biggest benefit in the tax code.

"Life insurance is the only legal way to print money."
– Ed Slott

So there you have it: The problems and the benefits – both to you **during your lifetime**, and for your family **after your death**.

Bottom Line:

Don't just sit there and admire your IRA or 401(k).

If you have a large IRA, you have a tax problem. It's tax-deferred. It's a sitting duck just waiting to be taxed.

Use it, Leverage it, or LOSE it to future taxes.

Do something now while the best options still exist.

Move your money from accounts that are ***forever taxed*** to accounts that are ***never taxed.***

DVD

Critical Items for Critical Moments

This is a list of essential items you and your family need to be aware of.

Where can they find these items when they need them?

Personal and Business Information	It's often we see clients who cannot find anything. They just have files of papers, scraps totally disorganized.
	You don't want your family scurrying around looking for items under pressure when an illness hits or after death (when you can no longer help them). I've received calls from the hospital. That may be too late.
Wired Stuff	We're in a wired world now and much of the critical information is online somewhere or even in "the cloud."
Passwords	1. Social network site passwords: Facebook, AOL, Twitter, etc.
	Do you want family members to have access to your personal email after you die? Now is the time to let them know.
	2. Online bank passwords
	3. Brokerage account passwords
	4. Email passwords
	5. Online Credit Card Passwords
	6. Other online account passwords (e.g. PayPal, EBay)

7. PIN Numbers

8. Telephone passwords:
   There's so much information in our advanced telephones. Smart phones have lots of banking and investment info on them too. That's why people go crazy when they lose them.

9. Location where other valuables are stored, including who may access, any passwords or codes needed to enter.

Banking and Investment Information

1. Bank Name, Phone # and Location of Safe Deposit Box

2. List of all bank, brokerage and other investment accounts

   Bank statements and cancelled checks – online access

   Account Numbers: Many people have several linked accounts

   Who are the contact people there?

   Anyone at the bank in particular that is your contact person?

   What's their name and phone number?

   Investment advisor, CPA, Broker, Insurance professional?

   What's their contact info? Phone numbers, email, etc.

3. Retirement Accounts

   IRAs and Company plans
   Roth IRAs, SEP, SIMPLE IRAs
   401(k)s, 403(b), Roth 401(k)s, Roth 403(b)s, 457 plans, Roth 457 Plans, Thrift savings plans, Keogh Plans etc.
   Inherited Retirement Accounts, inherited Roth IRAs

4. Annuities – who are they payable to?

5. Municipal Bonds

6. Treasury Bonds and Notes: some people have these in drawers from family events; from births, graduations and weddings – and family may not know about them.

7. Stock options

Beneficiary Forms – Where are these kept?

1. IRA beneficiary forms

2. Plan beneficiary forms

3. Annuity beneficiary forms

4. Transfer on Death or Payable on Death beneficiary forms

5. Life insurance beneficiary forms

6. IRA custodial agreements

7. Plan documents – Summary Plan Description

Essential Documents

These might not all apply to you, but some of these will apply to everyone. For example: a birth certificate. Everyone was born, I think?

1. Birth Certificate

2. Adoption Papers

3. Marriage Certificates

4. Death Certificates: Obviously you are alive, but you should have these from people you inherited assets from, so you know when you inherited and what the basis of the assets were. You'll need this info when you sell these assets.

5. Immigration and Naturalization Documents

6. Passports

7. Visas

Estate Planning Documents and Medical Directives

1. Wills

2. Trusts – including separate irrevocable life insurance trusts, other irrevocable trusts, IRA trusts, living trusts

3. Powers of Attorney

4. Health care proxies

5. HIPAA releases – Health Insurance Portability and Accountability Act of 1996 – to authorize the disclosure of your medical information

6. Other medical directives

7. Living wills

Other Benefits

1. Social Security Benefits

2. Veteran's Benefits

3. Military Information

4. Club membership benefits

5. Inheritances or funds in trusts

Tax Returns

1. Personal tax returns

2. Business tax returns

3. Business and Personal Financial Statements

4. Gift Tax Returns – there are lifetime exemptions that have to be kept track of, including basis information

5. Estate Tax Returns from people you have inherited from

Basis information – tax information that can provide valuable tax deduction information

Agreements

1. Business or partnership agreements

2. Business and personal contracts in force – are there provisions that have to be fulfilled; money owed or money due?

3. Copyrights or patents – some famous estates became worth much more after death because of copyrights

4. Accounts receivable – money owed to you, loans you've made, even family loans. I know of a client who included money loaned to her daughter in her will so it gets paid back after death, from her share of any inheritance.

5. Installment sales – You want your family knowing who owes you money; otherwise, it may never be collected.

6. Accounts payable – money you owe. You don't have to worry as much here. Anyone you owe money to, will find your family, but it's good to know anyway.

7. Credit card info: People have lots of credit cards. How much is owed?

Property Information

1. Deeds to real estate – homes, second homes, co-ops, condos

2. Mortgages

3. Lines of credit – balances on those

4. Vehicle titles, loan documents and location of vehicles – Autos, Boats, Planes

5. Household furnishings

6. Family heirlooms – to avoid fights and squabbles later on

7. Collectibles, Antiques, Jewelry – again, to avoid any post-death problems, and so people can find these items

8. Foreign property

9. Leases on property – How much might be owed?

Post-Death Instructions

1. Funeral instructions – prepaid funeral arrangements
2. Cremation or burial wishes
3. Cemetery plots
4. Beneficiary instructions

Insurance

1. Life insurance policies
2. Health insurance policies
3. Long-term care policies

Marital Agreements

1. Divorce or separation agreements
2. Prenuptial agreements
3. Postnuptial agreements
4. Spousal waivers of plan assets; this does not apply to IRAs
5. Civil Unions – same-sex marital agreements (like a prenuptial agreement)

Family Members

Your family tree – so you know who all the players are. This would be very helpful to anyone planning your estate.

Spouse

Children

Parents

Grandparents

Grandchildren

Great Grandchildren

Partners (unmarried partners you want to provide for)

Friends

Other relatives

Special needs individuals you want to provide for

Prior Marriages – this list may be long for some!

Children of prior marriages

Advisor Information

Names and contact info, email, phone numbers, addresses

1. CPA

2. Financial Advisor

3. Insurance Agent

4. Attorney

5. Letter to beneficiaries detailing wishes/suggestions

6. Trustees of trusts

7. Executor or Administrator

Names of other professionals and friends who might be helpful

Names and contact info, email, phone numbers, addresses

Doctors

Clergy

Charities you care about

CD
Life Events

Life events mean that something in your life has changed. It might be big or small, but it should be evaluated to see what else changes as a result.

What kind of changes am I talking about?

Both personal and financial.

For example, you had a birth, a death, a marriage, a divorce, an illness. These would be examples of changes in your personal life.

A tax law change, stock market decline, business or employment changes are examples of financial items that may require changes in your plans.

One thing is for sure, it is unlikely that a year would go by for most people without some change in their lives – personal or financial – and that means your plans need to be updated.

How will these life events affect any of your existing legal or retirement documents, like your will or beneficiary forms?

Too often we see people who have not updated their wills, beneficiary forms or other legal documents in years, even though some of the people that are in these documents may have died years ago. This is a common occurrence. This can give rise to costly legal and tax problems. Taxes and retirement issues could be affected.

Will there be tax benefits to take advantage of?

Will there be tax provisions you now have to comply with and should know about?

How will these changes affect your investing?

Your financial and tax advisors may need to be notified, as well as anyone involved in planning your estate.

The point of this program is to alert you to assess the effect of any of these life events on your current plan.

Reacting to life events:

Evaluate what must be done.

Notify the proper people, advisors or financial institutions.

Then make any changes that are needed.

Make sure that your tax and retirement plans take these life events into account.

In addition to life events, you need to be aware of tax law changes that affect your planning.

Here are the more common life events that would probably call for changes in your planning, updating key documents and notifying advisors and family members.

Birth or Adoption

New child, new grandchild

That usually means that beneficiary forms need to be updated – your advisors or financial institutions should be notified.

Setting up stretch IRAs to include the new child

Wills need to be updated – notify your attorney or CPAs

New dependents on your tax returns! – tell your CPA

Look into life insurance – to provide for the child in case of your early death – notify your insurance professional

Updating trusts if you have them – to include the new addition to your family. Some trusts already take this into account, but it's good to check anyway.

Maybe set up gifts to minor accounts – something to talk with your advisor about

Taking advantage of gift tax exemptions – putting money away for school

Maybe setting up education accounts

Death

Again… beneficiary forms need to be updated to remove the deceased if he or she was a beneficiary.

This has been a problem – leaving deceased individuals on the IRA beneficiary form. The estate might end up the beneficiary. That would cause the loss of the stretch IRA benefit for children or other beneficiaries.

Contingent beneficiaries can become the beneficiary, if the beneficiary form was not updated after the death of the primary beneficiary. Your IRA, plan or life insurance money could go to an unintended beneficiary.

Wills need to be updated

Property records need updating

Estate tax returns may need to be filed

Keep track of date of death values – for step-up in basis if beneficiaries sell property

Life insurance proceeds need to be paid out.

Inherited IRAs need to be properly set up so that beneficiaries can take advantage of the stretch IRA.

Your beneficiaries should know about this and about the required minimum distribution rules so they take the right amounts each year and don't incur any penalties.

If the IRA or plan beneficiary is a spouse, there will probably be a spousal rollover that has to be done. This should be done as soon as possible. I have had more than a few cases where the second spouse died before the rollover was completed and it was a mess… and costly too. Tax benefits, like the stretch IRA were lost for the children.

Marriage

This changes everything! As you probably already know.

Beneficiary forms and wills – for sure:
Notify your attorney and your financial advisor.
You probably want to name each other as beneficiaries – or not, depending on your situation.

There also might be a prenuptial agreement involved.

Taxes for sure – you will now probably file jointly

Property ownership will change as you might change some property to joint ownership and acquire property that you will own jointly.

Life insurance – that may be something you would want to have now that you have a spouse that you want to provide for.

Non-traditional Marriage – same-sex marriage

> ### Same-Sex Marriage Update
> ### Supreme Court Ruling Grants Rights to Same-Sex Marriage
>
> This was the 2015 *Obergefell* case.
>
> Same-sex couples who are legally married under state law were already recognized as married for federal tax purposes after the *Windsor* case in 2013 and subsequent IRS guidance. But now, **all states must license same-sex couples to marry and recognize same-sex marriages lawfully performed in other states.**
>
> It's important to remember the *Obergefell* decision relates to married couples and married couples only.

Divorce

- Getting divorced
  Make sure IRA and plan accounts are separated properly.

These days the retirement accounts are more valuable than some homes, especially homes with large mortgages or mortgages that exceed the current value. The home is not the bargaining chip it used to be when it comes to divorce. Now, it's the IRAs and other retirement accounts.

Beneficiary forms need updating

Property ownership needs to be revised

Wills need updating

- Already divorced
  Check beneficiary forms

- There have been too many cases where the retirement account went to the ex-spouse because the beneficiary form was not updated.

Remarriage

Children from prior marriages that must be considered

Updating beneficiary forms

Prenuptial agreements

Losing a Job, Retiring or Getting a Job (or changing to a new job)

6 Options for rollovers
You need to be advised on all your key Rollover Decisions

Six Options:
1. IRA rollover
2. Lump-sum distribution
3. Leave it in the company plan
4. Roll it to a new company plan
5. Roth conversion
6. In-plan Roth conversion

For example:
Will you need income from your retirement savings?

Use the age 55 exemption from the 10% penalty – but to do that, you cannot do an IRA rollover, because this exception only applies to distributions from company plans, like your 401(k) plan, not from IRAs. You'll need to leave the money in your plan. To qualify for the age 55 exception, you need to have been separated from service in the year you turned age 55 or a later year. This exception only applies to distributions from plans, not from IRAs, so in this case, an IRA rollover would cause the loss of this benefit.

Selling a House

Changing to a state that has different taxes – like NY to FLA, for example

Health Issues

- Getting sick

- Someone in your family getting sick

Being Healthy

That's the time to look into life insurance; while you are still healthy.

Years ago I advised a client of mine with a large taxable IRA to get life insurance and create tax-free money for his family. But he wouldn't do it. He said he hated life insurance, but his wife who was healthy took the insurance. Turned out she died first and the children received $500,000 each, tax free. He then came back to me and said that NOW he wanted the life insurance but by this time he was too ill and no longer qualified.

He died soon after and the children ended up using most of Mom's tax-free life insurance money to pay taxes on his estate which could have easily been avoided.

Remember that the planning you do now benefits YOU first, and your loved ones later.

As you can see, most of these life events mean changing your plans and documents.

But to make it all work for your family, they have to know where everything is, before it's too late and your family ends up wasting thousands to figure it all out; not to mention unnecessary taxes. This is money that you worked for going down the drain.

Right now, could you find your IRA or 401(k) beneficiary form?

This is NOT covered in your will, as many people think.

Do you know where all your accounts are? How they are owned?

Do you know all of the items to look for?

Does your family know where to find the most important documents?

There is still time to answer these questions by taking action now.

Life events also include reaching certain ages

Reaching Key Ages

18 or 21 – Children are no longer minors when they reach age 18 or 21 (depending on state law). They will now have access to funds in accounts that you might have set up for them.

50 – Catch-up contributions can now be made to IRA, Roth IRA and company plans

55 – The age 55 exception for penalty-free distributions from company plans

59½ –The age where the 10% early withdrawal penalty no longer applies to IRA and plan distributions

Key ages for Social Security Benefits:

62, 65, 70

70½ – Required Minimum Distributions must begin

Let's review:

When you have changes or events in your life that change, take the following actions:

Assess the effect of any of these life events on your current plan

Evaluate what must be done

Notify the proper people, advisors or financial institutions

Then make any changes that are needed

Your plan should always be based on the most current information available – both personal information and financial information.

CD

Advisor Checkup

First things first: Do you have a financial advisor?

Do you have the ***right*** financial advisor for you?

Are you working with the right financial institution (your bank, broker or fund company)?

How would you know?

That's what we are going to find out right now.

When it comes to rescuing your retirement, you'll need the help of a financial advisor – the right advisor for you… or several advisors. They might specialize in different areas.

What can a financial advisor do for you?

They can guide you through the process of protecting your retirement savings from needless and excessive taxation. That's going to be a big deal when taxes increase as I believe they will, especially the taxes on your retirement savings.

An advisor can help you protect your retirement savings from risk and uncertainty, and help you keep more of the money you make. They can help you make sure it lasts as long as you do, and beyond.

Your retirement savings are loaded with taxes and you'll need guidance at some point, to avoid costly errors.

You might ask "Why do I need an advisor?" I already know where to invest. It's not how much you make, it's how much you keep, ***after*** taxes that counts.

In this program, I am not talking about making money. I am focusing on keeping it protected from taxes, especially future taxes, just when you need the money the most… in retirement.

You also might say… "Why do I need an advisor? I've got you!"

Yes, you do and you have all this great information.

"Ed – with all your books, DVDs, CDs, website and other items, you have provided me with a boatload of info – so I think I can take it from here and get this all done without an advisor."

No, you can't! This is too important, and most mistakes in this area cannot be fixed. They can cost you and your loved ones a fortune.

Yes, you have a ton of great, reliable, unbiased information from me, including this program. That is great, because the first thing you must do is educate yourself, so you can make the right choices, be better prepared, ask better questions and demand more from your financial advisor.

But you still need to find a competent, educated financial advisor to help you implement your plan, so you don't end up with the government plan.

I want you to use and benefit from this information, but with professional guidance.

I am providing this program:

1. To educate you

2. To help you get the most from your professional advisors and the financial institutions (banks, brokers, fund companies) that have your money. They need to measure up too. Having a big name financial company does not mean that you are working with someone who has been educated in this area.

This information is critical to you, so you can better evaluate the financial professionals you work with.

Medical analogy:

Let's say you have a medical problem. So you do all your research and learn all you can so you can make better evaluations, understand the problem better and make better decisions; but you still need a doctor to do what's needed.

This is one of the most complex areas of the tax code and you have to know how to both comply and take advantage of the opportunities. That is where you need a professional or several of them, but they must have specialized knowledge.

There are lots of moving parts here. One mistake can be fatal to your retirement savings. When it comes to your retirement savings, you rarely, if ever, get a second chance to get it done right.

What if you already have an advisor or several advisors?

Then you should be using the education I am giving you here to make sure that they know what you need them to know to help you, and not hurt you.

Advisor mistakes are rampant.

I see this almost every day and it is heartbreaking, especially since most of these costly advisor mistakes could have been avoided if the advisor was better educated – and the consumer had more knowledge as well.

That's why you need to be educated with unbiased, objective, independent, untainted and accurate information like I am giving you here.

I don't sell stocks, bonds, funds, insurance, annuities, etc. I am a tax advisor and educator. That is why I brought my message to Public Television, where it's all about life-long learning.

You have to be educated, so you can trust yourself and your own judgment when you receive advice.

No one will ever care about your money as much as you do.

I am sickened over the horror stories I hear way too often. By horror stories, I mean when tax mistakes consume a retirement account. Or when poor planning means you and your family miss out on huge tax benefits in the tax code. These are costly and preventable mistakes. I am providing you with as much education as I can in this area so these things don't happen to you or your loved ones. You also need to be sure that your advisor is up to the task and does not make fatal errors when it comes to your retirement savings.

Your current advisors may be good at investing but they might not have the tax knowledge you need them to have to protect your retirement savings. This is a critical component.

Now that you have all of the information I have provided, you are ready to do an advisor checkup, of either your current advisors or new advisors that you are looking at.

Both current and prospective advisors need to go through this checkup. No one is exempt, even if they have been your advisor for years. They still need to be up to the task and now you have all the information you need to put them to the test.

No one gets a free pass... your retirement savings are at stake!!!

No free passes!

You should demand more:

Here's a list of 5 demands for your financial advisor.

As I go through each of these, think about how your advisor stacks up:

This is your advisor checkup!

1. **Education – specialized knowledge**

2. **Loyalty – to YOU!**

3. **Proactive planner – addressing items before mistakes happen**

4. **Back-up plan – who does he or she rely on?**

5. **Follow-up – especially AFTER the sale**

1. Education, education, education

Education for your advisor or your financial institution is critical to you.

Think about this:

You are considering a major purchase. Think about what steps you would take to prepare yourself for a major purchase, such as a car, a major appliance or something that costs a lot of money for you – a major expense. You would probably take some time. You would get all the information you could (getting educated on the topic), look at comparative prices and options and other features.

Now you have all your research and information and you walk into the store, and within the first 10 seconds of talking with the salesman, you realize that you know more than him!

Has that ever happened to you? I can almost see you nodding in agreement.

It's happened to me. How does that make you feel? You're spending a lot of money. You want to work with someone who knows MORE than you, not less than you.

Well, wouldn't you agree that your retirement savings are a major purchase? This represents your life savings. This is money that you have worked for most of your life and you have one chance to get this right.

That's why you need an advisor that is educated in this area, and now you are raising the bar and demanding more from them when your level of knowledge is higher. The better educated you are, the better educated and more competent your advisor has to be to impress you.

You'll know in 10 seconds if your advisor has the required level of specialized knowledge. They better know their stuff to earn your business!

I am here for you – not them – so I am being tough on advisors for **_your_** benefit. And, because frankly, most advisors out there do not deserve your business!

I know because I train more advisors in this area than anyone in the country, and less than 1% of advisors take this training. Does yours?

That means that more than 99% of advisors might not have the knowledge you need them to have and you should not be working with them.

What kind of education should they have?

They should have specialized knowledge in tax and estate planning for your retirement savings. **_NOT_** sales training, but real specialized education in retirement account taxation. Remember that your retirement savings are loaded with taxes and taxes will be the single biggest factor that will separate you from your retirement savings.

Do they have the training?

Not sales training or persuasive technique training – using the right words or phrases to bait you and get you to buy what they are selling, even if it's not right for you. These are gimmicks used to disguise their lack of knowledge in this highly complex and specialized area.

Also, don't get sucked in by sales ads and gimmicks touting free advice. That cannot be good.

The biggest financial companies are running TV ads that say they have retirement specialists standing by to help you… for free!

Anybody who knows what you need them to know is not "standing by" waiting to give you free advice!

What happens when the free advisor gives you the wrong answer but you don't know it until it is too late? Who do you speak to then?

Low cost does not mean no cost.

It could cost you a fortune later in unnecessary and excessive taxes that probably could have been avoided, not to mention lost opportunities that could have turned your retirement savings into a tax-free windfall, for you and your family.

The better educated you are on these issues, the better questions you will ask and the better prepared you will be to rescue your retirement.

You'll make better choices and know if you're working with the right advisor for you. You'll know if the institution that has your money knows what they are doing. Most don't.

The biggest problem with many financial advisors is that they don't know that they don't know, and you and your family will pay the price.

Sorry to say, most people who call themselves financial advisors are really just salesmen and do not have the knowledge you need them to have to help you manage the taxes.

You need a specialist. This is a specialized area and one of the most complex areas of the tax code. Your current advisor might be able to make you money, but it's what you keep at the end of the game that counts *AFTER* taxes!

But here's the problem, and it's a BIG problem.

When you ask, everyone says that they know everything. Everyone says they are a specialist. I have never seen a time where the word "specialist" has been so overplayed, so much so that it has become meaningless.

The term is overused as much as the word "sale" in a store window. Have you ever noticed that in some stores they have a "sale" sign in the window – all the time? In fact, it's in the window so long, that the sign is faded. If everything is on sale all the time, what does it mean? Nothing.

It's the same with the word "specialist".

You see it in every ad – big full page ads from the biggest financial institutions say they have specialists all over the country, at every branch. How is that even possible???

Do you have any idea of the years of training it takes to be a specialist in this complex area of taxes and retirement planning?

I do!

I've been studying, advising and teaching in this area for over 25 years and there is still plenty to learn and the rules are constantly changing.

It's not simple and one size doesn't fit all.

What about credentials? Or what I call "alphabet soup."

It may look good, but these designations are getting out of control.

The Wall Street Journal recently ran a series of articles about these designations citing over 200 of them. Many of these are meaningless and more gimmicks than anything.

That's why we do not provide any credentials to advisors who train with us. They get education, not alphabet soup.

Here is an excerpt from one of those stories in The Wall Street Journal:

THE WALL STREET JOURNAL
October 16, 2010

Is Your Adviser Pumping Up His Credentials?

Those Fancy Initials After Your Financial Adviser's Name Might Not Be As Impressive as They Seem

By JASON ZWEIG and MARY PILON

"Just when Americans seem more desperate than ever for trustworthy investment advice, financial advisers are brandishing a baffling array of new credentials – some of which can be earned with minimal or no study and a few hundred dollars."

"Increasingly, say regulators, financial advisers are using these dubious designations as marketing tools to win the trust of older, wealthier clients, in hopes of selling high-fee investments that aren't appropriate for them."

There are some solid designations of course which they did mention such as a CFA (Chartered Financial Analyst), CPA (Certified Public Accountant), and CFP (Certified Financial Planner).

Also:

CLUs – Chartered Life Underwriter

ChFC – Chartered Financial Consultant

These are professional designations in the insurance industry.

The Journal called most other designations "less rigorous" to put it nicely.

A serious designation is the first good sign, because it means they have something valuable to lose – like a professional license – and certain standards need to be met and maintained. But even these advisors need to be educated in this complex specialized area.

And...
Steer clear of know-it-alls!

If they tell you they know everything about IRAs and 401(k)s , they've just told you that they know nothing.

When it comes to the taxes on your retirement savings – your single biggest lifetime expense, a specialist in this area should know that they don't know it all. Only a true specialist would know this. It shows they have a depth of knowledge so vast that they know they cannot ever know it all.

So what's the solution?

You should only work with competent, educated financial advisors who work for you and have the specialized knowledge required to advise you on each of these retirement and tax issues.

Check every advisor who wants to work with you. See if they have taken any real training in this area.

Your first loyalty is to you and your loved ones, not your brother-in-law or some other advisor who happens to be a nice guy.

A specialist in retirement tax planning should be taking extensive advanced education. They should be continually updating that education on a regular basis, since laws change so often.

For example:

Here is our training format for advisors:

In our basic foundation course – like basic training, we put advisors through two solid days of training. Additionally, they take many more days of advanced training throughout the year, if they choose to continue.

Advisors who train with us sit for several days, several times a year with us. We provide detailed course manuals that are up to 400 pages filled with updated technical material.

This is the most intensive and rigorous training available anywhere in the country in this area. Nothing even comes close.

Has your advisor ever sat through this kind of training?

Ask them to show you a recent course manual or book they read on the topic.

Tax laws are constantly changing. That's why advisors that we train are constantly returning to our programs throughout the year.

But most advisors do not take this kind of training and that is why I am warning you about this now.

Make sure your advisor is investing in this specialized education.

Demand more – this is your life savings!

My rule:
If an advisor doesn't want to invest in his or her education, then you should not invest your retirement funds with them.

They have to earn your business!

Most advisors will not like what I have just said… but that's ok.

I'm here for you… not them.

2. Loyalty – to YOU!

Whose side are they on? It better be yours.

You'll know by who pays them. That is who they are loyal to. You should be paying your advisor, so you know they work for you.

If they are working for free, you are still paying somewhere.

You need to know that your advisor is doing what's best for you 100% of the time.

You'll need someone to guide you through all of this, who works only for you.

How can you tell?

What do they sell?

If they only have one or two products or strategies, that's probably what you'll get. That may not be a problem if that fits your needs.

A good advisor will always try to find the right product or strategy for you. He or she should not try to fit you into the one product he offers, if that is not what's best for you.

Advisors at some of the biggest financial institutions (banks, brokers and fund companies) are told to sell you products that earn the biggest fees for the companies. That is not good for you.

For example:

Fund company phone operators advise you to do IRA rollovers.

That is usually a good option, but it may not be the best option for you.

You need to know that there are five other options to consider, six options in all. But you won't get that from them, because they are paid to bring in IRA rollovers.

You need to be advised on all your key Rollover Decisions

Six Options:

1. IRA rollover
2. Lump-sum distribution
3. Leave it in the company plan
4. Roll it to a new company plan
5. Roth conversion
6. In-plan Roth conversion

If you are not paying them, they are not working for you! This means their loyalty is to their company, NOT YOU!

The result is often costly mistakes.

For example:
A person I met at a recent Public Television seminar in St. Paul, Minnesota, told me that he saw one of the ads from the big financial institutions about rolling his retirement plan over to an IRA. Normally that is good advice, but the specialist on the 800# did not ask him two critical questions. (See below for the two questions).

They never do because they don't know, AND, they want you to roll your money over whether it is good for you or not.

He told me this after it was too late to fix this dreadful, costly mistake. Yes, he did a tax-free rollover, but when that money eventually gets withdrawn, when he needs it most, in retirement, he'll pay top dollar in taxes at the highest tax rates. He'll pay at ordinary income tax rates, and probably on a larger balance. The IRS is going to love this guy!

What if I told you he had the opportunity to pay less than half that amount at capital gains rates by not doing the IRA rollover?

He had that option but did not know it at the time. He realized it later after seeing one of my Public Television programs and getting the gifts offered on that program.

He told me that he probably could have saved over $200,000 in taxes if he got the right advice. This is horrendous. I felt terrible for him, but I could not fix the error.

Just so all of you know: The two questions that should have been asked were:

1. Do you have company stock in your 401(k) plan?

2. If yes, then what is the appreciation on that stock from the time it was purchased in your plan?

Only an advisor that is both educated and is providing advice based on your best interests would know to ask these key questions.

There is a huge tax benefit for what is called "Net Unrealized Appreciation" (NUA) in company stock in your 401(k) plan – stock of the company you are working for. By meeting certain technical tax rules, including taking a lump-sum distribution (as opposed to the IRA rollover), the appreciation on that stock can be taxed at long-term capital gain rates instead of much higher ordinary income tax rates.

But if these two questions are not asked, you would never know if you are eligible for the tax benefit, or how much the tax savings might be. The NUA tax benefit is forever lost however once the 401(k) funds are rolled over to an IRA. That is what happened to the person above, because he was not asked the right questions or given all the options.

When you are leaving a retirement plan, an IRA rollover is generally a good option, but you should know about the other five options as well. Each one must be considered and evaluated with a knowledgeable advisor… BEFORE you move your life savings!!!

This is serious business and you do need a specialist. Not someone given a title to make them appear to know more than they do.

Actually, at some companies, they actually do believe their people can be overnight specialists, because they don't know how much there is to know. Your biggest risk is that they don't know that they don't know.

The rollover option was best for the fund company but it is not best for every person. They weren't loyal. They were not giving their client the right options enabling him to tell which one was best for him.

Look at the financial crisis. Look at how much garbage was sold to the banks' own customers – worthless mortgage securities. Their customers lost a fortune. And at the same time, these big Wall Street institutions bet against them and made a fortune while selling their own customers down the river.

You need to know that your advisor, even if he or she is working for a big financial bank or firm, is loyal to you and only providing advice and products that are in your best interest – 100% of the time… NO EXCEPTIONS!!! –- and of course – is educated as I talked about earlier – not in selling you stocks and other investments, but in tax planning for your retirement savings.

Ask tough questions and use your sixth sense to get an idea if you believe what they are saying. If your gut says no, then move on to an advisor that you are certain is working for you.

And this applies to family members who happen to be your advisors. They need to be checked too! Your first loyalty is to you and your loved ones, and your advisor should be loyal to you, even if his or her firm says otherwise.

3. Proactive Planner

Let me ask you something:

Would you rather have a problem solver or a problem finder?

You want a problem finder – someone who finds the problem and can fix it before it becomes a tax disaster you cannot fix.

That is how I train all of the financial advisors who attend our programs. I continually advise them to be proactive advisors and check things "before it hits the fan".

Your plan needs to include flexibility too, since tax laws are changing so rapidly.

To earn your business, your advisors should be advising you on a proactive basis. They should be contacting you when tax laws and planning options change and advising you when new opportunities are created.

When was the last time your advisor called you with this kind of proactive planning information? I'm talking about a call that was all about you, without trying to sell you something.

When was the last time your advisor checked your beneficiary forms? That is critical and is one of the most common and costly mistakes when it comes to your retirement savings.

For example:
Has your advisor been proactive in helping you plan out what happens after you die – setting plans in place now to guarantee a stretch IRA for your beneficiaries?

You need proactive planning from your advisor, but only an advisor who has the education and loyalty to you can provide this planning.

Now you are seeing how each of these advisor checkup points build on each other.

We have now covered 3 of my list of advisor demands – 3 advisor checkup points.

4. Back-up plan

Who does your advisor turn to for retirement tax questions?

If they say they know it all, as I said earlier here, that means they have no clue of the depth of knowledge required in this critical area of protecting your retirement savings.

Your advisor should have no problem referring you to other advisors if he or she does not have the required knowledge in this area. That shows you that YOU come first and they have your best interests in mind.

Often other CPAs call me when they have specific IRA or retirement-related tax questions. They want to make sure that their clients get the right answers, even if they have to get them from outside experts.

Who does your advisor turn to for questions and back-up advice in this area? What if he or she is sick or is not available to answer questions? You need to know what the back-up plan is.

I used to get that question all the time from clients. "What happens if something happens to you? Who do I call?" It is important that you feel confident that your affairs will be handled if your advisor either is unavailable or does not have the expertise in the particular area.

What did I do?
I built networks of colleagues and other professionals including attorneys, other CPAs, financial advisors and other specialized advisors, so that my clients had back-up beyond me.

I was never worried about losing business to other advisors because my main concern was that my clients get the best advice, especially when that was not in my area of expertise. Your advisor should be able to do the same, even if they are a sole practitioner or have a smaller firm, like I did.

Not knowing everything is ok, as long as they have relationships with others that do.

They also have to be confident and secure enough to build a network of advisors and colleagues to work with that have expertise in all types of specialized areas, whether it is divorce, real estate, estate planning, trusts, charitable planning, special needs planning or other areas.

5. Follow-up AFTER the sale

You just made what might be one of the largest purchases of your life. You handed over your life savings – your retirement savings – to someone.

Follow-up after the sale is a critical point. This is the time when you need reassurance that you made the right decision when hiring this financial advisor.

See how your advisor follows up and keeps in touch with you... *after* **the sale.**

Where is he or she now? Has he moved, changed locations?

That's ok. Did he notify you?

I worked with an attorney years ago and he moved to another state and did not tell his clients. He did estate planning, and when clients died, their family called me to find out where he was. No one should have to do that.

Just because you have hired an advisor, that does not mean you cannot fire him or her later. They have to continually earn your trust and be available even after the sale – in fact, especially after the sale.

Think about how great you feel after you bought something and the company calls you back after the sale. You want to be reassured that you made the right decision.

This is the time a good advisor will build their relationship with you.

Does your advisor know your family?

It's not only the knowledge, but relationships too. You want a relationship and a succession plan for your loved ones. You want someone to help pass the torch later.

We see advisors either go out of business or pick up and leave town, change locations or change companies. That's ok, but they need to follow-up with you. You need stability in your advisor.

We have been in the same location for over 30 years. We make an effort to meet the next generation so they are familiar with us, in order to have a smooth transition. Your advisor should do the same.

So there you have it.

This is your advisor checkup!

Your 5 demands – let's review them:

1. **Education – specialized knowledge**

2. **Loyalty – to YOU!**

3. **Proactive planner – addressing items before mistakes happen**

4. **Back-up plan – who does he or she rely on?**

5. **Follow-up – especially AFTER the sale**

This is your money. You worked for it. You need to DEMAND more from your financial advisor. He or she has to work for it too!

I've seen too many family horror stories and I am on a mission to match consumers with competent financial advisors.

Your job is not to rescue your advisor; it's your advisor's job to rescue you!

Good luck – and do your advisor checkup!

For your reference:

Here is how to find advisors that have gone through our highest level of training. These advisors are members of **Ed Slott's Elite IRA Advisor Group,** an advanced education program focusing on tax and estate planning for retirement savings. You can find these advisors on our website at: www.irahelp.com.

They are not the only advisors to consider, but they have been exposed to my training and have access to our team of IRA experts when they have questions.

By Ed Slott, CPA
www.irahelp.com
Copyright © 2016